The Materiality of Stone

The Materiality of Stone

Explorations in Landscape Phenomenology: 1

Christopher Tilley
with the assistance of Wayne Bennett

Oxford • New York

First published in 2004 by
Berg
Editorial offices:
1st Floor, Angel Court, 81 St Clements Street, Oxford OX4 1AW, UK
175 Fifth Avenue, New York, NY 10010, USA

Berg is the imprint of Oxford International Publishers Ltd.

Library of Congress Cataloging-in-Publication Data
Tilley, Christopher Y.
    The materiality of stone : explorations in landscape phenomenology / Christopher
Tilley with the assistance of Wayne Bennett.
        p. cm.
    Includes bibliographical references and index.
    ISBN 1-85973-892-3 (cloth) — ISBN 1-85973-897-4 (pbk.)
    1. Megalithic monuments. 2. Architecture, Prehistoric. 3. Landscape settlement
patterns, Prehistoric I. Bennett, Wayne. 1954– II. Title.
    GN790.T55 2004
    930.1′4—dc22

                                                                                    2004006645

British Library Cataloguing-in-Publication Data
A catalogue record for this book is available from the British Library.

ISBN 1 85973 892 3 (Cloth)
         1 85973 897 4 (Paper)

Typeset by JS Typesetting Ltd, Wellingborough, Northants.
Printed in the United Kingdom by Biddles Ltd, King's Lynn.

www.bergpublishers.com

Contents

List of Figures

List of Tables

Preface

This book is the first in a projected series of three volumes concerned with landscape phenomenology and prehistory. It follows on from themes introduced in two previous works, *A Phenomenology of Landscape* (Tilley 1994) and *Metaphor and Material Culture* (Tilley 1999a). All the studies presented here are concerned with the significance of 'natural' and 'cultural' stones in various landscapes of prehistoric Europe from the Neolithic to the Iron Age. Chapter 1 discusses the phenomenological perspective of Merleau-Ponty in relation to bodies, places and landscapes. It provides the theoretical and conceptual basis for Chapters 2–4, which are detailed case studies designed to show the manner in which a phenomenological approach works out in the practice of doing research and interpreting archaeological materials.

Chapter 2 is concerned with one generic class of Neolithic monuments, menhirs in the landscapes of Finistère, western Brittany, and is a large-scale regional analysis. Chapters 3 and 4 consider small-scale landscapes, roughly equivalent in size. Chapter 3 discusses the internal spaces and landscape settings of Neolithic temples in the Maltese islands and interprets them in relation to artefacts and substances and related places of burial. Chapter 4 is concerned with Bronze Age rock carvings in the far south-east of Sweden and their relationship to barrows and cairns and places where artefacts were deposited. In the Conclusions, issues of research methodology and interpretation are considered.

The book attempts to demonstrate the manner in which a phenomenological perspective, in which the past is understood and interpreted from a sensuous human scale, as opposed to an abstracted analytical gaze, can provide a radically different way of thinking through the past in the present, and shed new light on old monuments.

Acknowledgements

I am indebted to Wayne Bennett, who has acted as my research assistant and collaborator throughout the extended periods of fieldwork on which this book is based. Many of the ideas discussed here resulted directly from our constant dialogues while working in the field and in discussions in the evenings when we would often try together to write down the implications of what we had experienced during the day. A substantial amount of the text was written in a preliminary way while sitting on, moving between and encountering the stones in the landscape. I dictated various descriptions which Wayne wrote down – and modified or disputed – as we went along. We filled in various recording forms that had been devised to help us understand the sites together. We worked together to check visual fields and modes of encounter with the sites. We visited and studied artefacts in museums. All the fieldwork was very intensive and very much a joint enterprise of observation and encounter. We also kept each other going during the hard times, which was equally important. When I wanted to give up looking for a particular menhir, rock carving or cairn, Wayne would insist that we should continue to do so, or vice versa, and as a result we almost always found them. He has also drawn the line diagrams, contributed photographs and provided critical comments on draft versions of the individual chapters. Were it not for his help, and enthusiasm for the project, this work would be much the poorer.

I am grateful to Mark Anthony Mifsud, director of the Maltese Museums Department, for permission granting free access to the temple interiors.

Christopher Tilley, London

From Body to Place to Landscape

A Phenomenological Perspective

[Phenomenology] is a philosophy for which the world is always 'already there' before reflection begins – as an inalienable presence; and all its efforts are concentrated upon re-achieving a direct and primitive contact with the world, and endowing that contact with a philosophical status . . . It also offers an account of space, time and the world as we 'live' them.

Merleau-Ponty, *Phenomenology of Perception*, 1962: vii

Introduction

Epoché is the Greek word meaning 'suspension of belief', a bracketing of experience, which provides a starting point for all phenomenological analysis. The beliefs to be called into question are those dogmas arising in that which is ordinarily termed common sense or the 'natural attitude'. Phenomenology involves the attempt to describe the objects of consciousness in the manner in which they are presented to consciousness. It attempts to reveal the world as it is actually experienced directly by a subject as opposed to how we might theoretically assume it to be. The aim is not to explain the world (in terms, say, of physical causality or historical events or psychological dispositions) but to describe that world as precisely as possible in the manner in which human beings experience it. Such description, if it succeeds, is necessarily a re-description and thus may lead to fresh insights and new knowledges of what there is in the world and how it impacts on human consciousness, and vice versa. Phenomenology is a style or manner of thought rather than a set of doctrines, rules or procedures that may be followed, a way of Being in the world and a way of thinking in it. It stands directly opposed to the empiricist or positivist (scientific) 'natural attitude' when applied to the study of people or society. Such thought may tell us something of value about physical objects, but it is incapable of coping with that attribute which is most distinctively human: subjectivity.

Phenomenology, like other living and developing philosophical positions, involves thinkers adopting often very divergent and contradictory views (see Hammond et al. 1991), from the initial transcendental position of Husserl, to

Heidegger's later mediations on time and Being, to the more existentialist view-points of Sartre and Merleau-Ponty. In this chapter I discuss the work of Merleau-Ponty, and some inspired interpreters, whose emphasis on experience always being experience *of* something, from a bodily point of view, seems to be of most direct relevance for conceptualizing the complex lived experience of place and landscape in the past and in the present.

The Bodily Basis of Experience

> We get into place, move and stay there *with our bodies*. But the fact is neither innocent or trivial; it is momentous in its consequences. It is also massively obvious, despite being massively overlooked in previous treatments of space and place.
>
> Casey, *The Fate of Place*, 1997: 239

The distinctive feature of Merleau-Ponty's exposition of a phenomenological perspective is that it is grounded in the physicality and material existence of the human body in the world. From this basic fact all our experience, understanding and knowledge of the world flow. In this sense he exposes a materialist position running counter to any form of idealism or intellectualism that would try to situate and understand the world from the perspective of a disembodied mind somehow outside of the body. Precisely because people are physical objects we are able to perceive the world, but there is no purely objective 'outside' vantage point for doing so: for example, a disembodied mind outside a particular setting and a flux of temporal events. We experience and perceive the world because we live in that world and are intertwined within it. We are part of it, and it is part of us. Our bodily Being-in-the-world provides the fundamental ground, or starting point, for our description of it. Analysis starts from the standpoint of the body-subject, which, however, does not encounter or understand itself mechanistically as an object amongst a world of other objects or as a transcendental ego, a pure consciousness without a body. The body-subject is a mind physically embodied, a body and a mind which always encounters the world from a particular point of view in a particular context at a particular time and in a particular place, a physical subject in space-time. An epochal consciousness of this world is dependent on self-consciousness of this embodied situation which in turn makes our own experience possible.

For Merleau-Ponty, the problem of meaning, or rationality, is explicable in terms of the perception of the body-subject. Perception constitutes the bond, or contact, between consciousness and the world from which meanings arise. It is necessary to raise the questions: who is it and what is it that perceives? In raising and answering this question, Merleau-Ponty provides a radically different kind of answer than that given in empiricist and intellectualist (idealist) philosophies. For empiricists, a body-object registers passively sensations imposed on it externally. For idealists, the object is actively registered by the internal operation of an intellectual *Cogito* or mind. Both positions separate mind from body and both consider the body as an object among other objects in the world. Breaking with both positions, Merleau-Ponty sets out to transcend a mind/body dualism and an objectivism that would reduce the body to a mechanical object. For Merleau-Ponty, the lived body is both object and subject. From the point of view of a subject, the body is not an object outside of consciousness but the only way of being present in the world and being conscious of it. In other words consciousness is corporeal. The lived body is a way of viewing and feeling the world and the way a subject comes to know and express this viewing and feeling. Perceptual consciousness cannot be an absolute interiority, a pure presence to itself. It is rather a bodily presence in the world and a bodily awareness of it. The relationship of a subject and his or her body is an inner one: I have a body and that is my consciousness. Such a perspective creates a significant break with a mechanistic approach to the body in which it is a mere thing which belongs to no-one, only being individual-ized by the mind. The lived body, the body with a mind, is for every person a particular way of inhabiting the world, of being present in it, sensing it. The lived body combines *being-in-itself* (an object form) and *being-for-itself* (a subject form), but is reducible to neither. The lived body allows us to know what space, place and landscape are because it is the author of them all. From the body we learn what is near, what is far, that which is above, that which is below, etc., the horizon line: the limits of our vision.

Consciousness is 'being towards-the-thing through the intermediary of my body . . . we must therefore avoid saying that our body is *in* space, or *in* time. It *inhabits* space and time, (Merleau-Ponty 1962: 138–9). So consciousness is not a matter, in the first place, of 'I *think* that' but of 'I *can*' (*ibid.*: 137). Perceptual consciousness arises from a body-subject, a knowing body. In this manner a phenomenological approach transcends traditional distinctions between subject and object. The lived body is neither, but a dynamic combination of the two, and in this manner it is possible to claim that subjectivity arises from objectivity, and vice versa, and it is therefore not possible to be 'purely' objective or 'purely' subjective. Our experience and knowledge of the world is a combination of both. The experience of the body is intrinsically ambiguous precisely because this experience transcends subject/object dualisms. The body is not an object, nor is my consciousness of the body a thought. I can only know my body through living it. The body is me myself but I can also know it 'from the outside'. When I touch my left hand with my right hand my body is both touching and touched, subject and object, a union of the two. So the human body is a presence in the world always marking a point between being a 'thing in itself' (a pure thing) and a 'being for itself' (a pure consciousness), a third kind of thing (Low 2000: 12), *being* that body and sensing that being.

So this body is my presence in the world and only this body allows me to sense myself and others and things. The immaterial mind, somehow divorced from the body, is a philosophical mirage or phantom. At the basis of all, even the most abstract, knowledge is the sensuous, sensing and sensed body in which all experience is embodied: subjectivity is physical.

We are always in and of our bodies and cannot leave them. We can turn away from a physical object, or walk away from a person, but we can never escape our own bodies. Since I cannot move my body away from me, it can never be an object in the sense of a table or any other physical entity. Similarly, I may move around and experience different aspects of a thing but I always experience them through my body in the same way. I cannot alter the manner in which I sensuously experience the world. I can choose the side which a physical object presents itself to me. This freedom is not possible in the perception of my own body (Merleau-Ponty 1962: 90). We necessarily see the world in profiles, or from certain angles, but cannot experience ourselves in the same way. While I may observe the world according to the situation I take up in it, I can never observe myself in the same way. I can never, for example, perceive of my body being over there. To do so would require a second body (*ibid.*: 91). In the mirror I appear as an object, but this is a reversal of the phenomenological facts because as a subject I am what I can only see of myself by using it: I both am there and am invisible to myself (Merleau-Ponty 1968: 249; Priest 1998: 79). We do not and cannot experience our body as just another thing, yet the physicality of our bodies structures the manner in which we experience things, places and landscapes.

Bodily Dyads: Elementary Structures of Embodied Experience

The body, in relation to the experience of place and landscape, has six basic and concrete dimensions: above/below or up/down; in front/behind and to the right/to the left. It is around and in terms of a living moving body that these terms have somatic relevance and relate to each other and come into specific sets of relationships. These dimensions relate both to the body itself, which may be thought of in terms of up/down (head/feet) and of having a front side to which the head faces and a back side, and in relation to basic bilateral symmetry (a left and right hand, arm, foot, etc.). But such terms extend beyond the body itself and connect the body with the world: there are things to the front and right of me and things to the back and left of me, and so on. So bodily dimensions are not internal to the body but link the body to the world, and are always changing and relational. In addition to these six basic dimensions, there are other bodily terms fundamental to human experience:

here/there: where my body is as opposed to where it is not, or might be; and near/far. In relation to the body the latter opposition may refer to things that are in reach (near) and those out of reach (far) or things in close proximity to myself as opposed to those far away: the land on which I stand and the line of the horizon that lies beyond me. But none of these oppositions can be unambiguously defined, and all are constantly changing in relation to the body in motion where things that were to the left of me may now be to the right, things that were far away become near, and what was near (here) becomes distanced through motion. The proper locus for all these dimensions is *between* my body and the world. Bodily motion takes place in terms of the six basic dimensions which always exist in relation to a particular person and a particular place. From an embodied perspective we relate to place and landscape through these relational coordinates of our body. The body embeds and apprehends itself in terms of what is above or below it ('height'), to the right or left ('breadth') and to the front or back ('depth'), and in all known human languages there appear to be lexical items naming these asymmetrical axes of spatial orientation (Casey 1993: 76).

The up/down, above/below or vertical distinction thus comes to have fundamental metaphorical significance in expressions in which 'up' is equated with 'happy' and 'sad' with being 'down', in which drooping posture typically goes along with sadness and depression, erect posture with a positive emotional state (Lakoff and Johnson 1980: 15). Similarly, consciousness tends to be equated with up and unconsciousness with down (we sleep lying down). Additionally, in Anglo-American culture the following associations are usually made (*ibid.*: 16-18)

Health and life	Sickness and death
Power	Absence of power
More	Less
High status	Low status
Good	Bad
Virtue	Depravity
UP	DOWN

and all the associated metaphors (e.g. he has a lofty position; things are looking up) are rooted not only in common cultural connotations but also in the physical bodily experience of the body and its various states of waking and sleeping, sense or otherwise of well-being, etc., and it is virtually impossible to disentangle the two. The up/down distinction is rooted not only in the upright standing and moving posture of the human body as it stands or walks on the earth, but also in relation to the world that envelops it: things that are above and below you, that you must move up to or down to in order to reach. The horizon line is an epitome of the limits of our horizontal vision of the earth but it also serves to separate above from below, the visible and the visible, the present and the future, that which lies beyond. We may move ahead or behind, forward or backward, higher or lower. Standing on a horizontal plane, things in front of us tend to be up (a map will usually be orientated so that what is ahead of us is up) and those behind us tend to be down. Through movement the former may usually correspond to the future, the latter to the past. And we refer to what comes before and that which comes after.

Aristotle comments that '"above" is not anything you like, but where fire, and what is light, move. Likewise "below" is not anything you like, but where heavy and earth things move' (*Physics* Book 4). This fundamental distinction between the lightness of the sky associated with spirit powers and the heaviness of the land, the domain of humans, is one made over and over again in world religions and countless ethnographies. Uprightness is manifested both in the body and in the world. This is the source of medieval and Renaissance views on the *concordia mundi*, whereby the head and the sky as well as the genitals and the sublunar region correspond to each other (Casey 1993: 80). And this corresponds to a distinction between the noble orifices of the head compared with the genitals, excrement and defilement (Douglas 1970). Places such as sacred mountains associated with light and air that lie up and above always tend to be priviledged culturally and emotionally while places situated down below tend to be associated with darkness and death. Up and down are thus become terms to which are attached essential moral purpose and the values of superior and inferior. Natural and cultural things of significant height (mountains, cliffs, waterfalls, church spires, buildings, stones, ceramic vessels, monuments) most usually impress and we find them awe inspiring as they relate to the physicality of our bodies.

The vertical axis of up/down appears to be more important in matters of our bodily spatial orientation than either front/behind or left/right distinctions, which organize things in terms of a horizontal axis. And the left/right distinction is itself dependent on a prior front/back distinction. It is only in terms of a distinction between front and back that left and right can be distinguished in any systematic way. The body is always between front and back, left and right. A sense of encirclement by what is to the front of us and what is to the back is fundamentally different from the manner in which a distinction between up and down constitutes an independent dimension of which the body is always a part as part of an earth/ heavens cosmic axis. What lies ahead or behind me is always delimited by sensory visual, tactile, auditory and olfactory fields. That which is above or behind, to the left or the right, is intimately connected to the body in place, sensing place. In terms of front and back there is a fundamental asymmetry. We look forward, move and do things, act in the world, primarily in terms of that which is in front of us. Thus the front/back axis separates the world that can be seen and manipulated from the world that cannot easily be seen or manipulated. While our back side is relatively undifferentiated, our face, feet, hands, limbs, point forward to engage with and grasp the world. Because the back field is out of sight and difficult to touch, it has a relative property of hiddenness. Yet, of course, we hear things all around us and our ears are positioned between our front and back zones. Despite this, 'ahead of' is usually metaphorically positively evaluated, while we talk of bad things being done 'behind our backs'. However, the back can also be an intensely familiar zone. We speak of going back home, 'home' metaphorically referring to the familiar, the intimate (sitting on a favourite chair) and the safe, while to move forward may entail uncertainty (Casey 1993: 86). Like persons, many things may be said to have a proper front and back side (cars, houses, gardens, fridges, computers, books), and it is the front side that is positively evaluated and on show. Front and back equally relate to differential use of places and landscapes and appropriate social relations, e.g. types of behaviour, relative degrees of formality, informality, etc. For example, the Samoan landscape is a world structured by the presence of village and bush, mountain and sea. Modern villages are strung out along the coast with a road, or path, separating the seaward half from the inland half (Shore 1996: 269). Villages have front and back regions. The front of the village is the sea side, the back, the land side, and according to Shore this resolves itself in terms of a typical set of oppositions in which geographic features are used for mapping social, kinaesthetic and moral attributes. The sides of a landscape have social and moral implications and the back is generally associated with low rank and with impulsive rather than socially correct behaviour:

Seaward	Inland
Light	Darkness
Civil life	Uncivilized
Social control of behaviour	Bad speaking
Formality	Intimacy
Women's work	Men's work
FRONT	BACK

Shore interestingly contrasts this dualist model of village space with another concentric or 'graded' model, less frequently articulated by Samoans. The reference points in village orientation are not the sea and bush but the central village green and the outskirts. The 'front' of the village is interior and the outskirts are exterior: a centre/periphery distinction. The periphery may mean either 'toward the shore' or 'toward the bush'. The centre is the residential core of the village with sacred political meeting grounds and chiefly residences. From the centre outwards there is a decrease of dignity and power. This is clearly a sociocentric model of place and landscape but it also relates to the relative positioning of the body in place.

Shore makes the claim that the dualist model is based on a digital logic, is impersonal and easy to explain to outsiders, whereas the concentric model is based on an analogic logic and grounded in egocentric bodily experience. But both front and back and notions of centre and periphery are equally grounded in the body. One is not more intimate than the other. They instead relate to two alternative modes of bodily experience. In one mode the logic is of categorical oppositions working through the axis of the body. In the other they work outwards from the body. These are, then, two complementary and alternative ways in which place and landscape are bodily experienced, and we cannot assert that either is somehow primary in relation to the other. Place and landscape may be conceived both in terms of bodily based left/right, back/front dualisms and in terms of being graded outwards from an embodied centre. Concentric and diametric dualism thus provide alternative ways to think about the manner in which place and landscape become embodied.

Right and left, as opposed to up/down and back/front, is the most unstable and mutable of the bodily dualisms affecting the way in which we experience the world. What is to our right, or to our left, is dependent on the direction in which we face, but we are far more likely to confuse what is left and what is right compared with up/down or back/front. Nevertheless the basic bilateral symmetry of the body together with being right- or left-handed suggests that this dimensional distinction is of crucial importance. Right- and left-handedness are grounded in a non-trivial body asymmetry discussed long ago by Hertz. Our hands, feet, etc., are counterparts of each other yet different in shape (Hertz 1960). They cannot occupy the same place. A right shoe will not fit a left foot. With the exception of only a few ethnographically documented societies, a positive valorization of right in terms of left is pervasive. For example, among the Amboyna of Indonesia the following oppositions arise (Van Der Kroef 1954):

Male	Female
Land/mountain side	Coast or sea side
Above	Below
Heaven/sky	Earth
Worldly	Spiritual
Upwards	Downwards
Interior	Exterior
In front	Behind
East	West
Old	New
RIGHT	LEFT

Here a distinction between right and left is linked with the cardinal directions east and west, a distinction between land and sea, above/below and front/behind. In other words it grounds the body in the landscape and in relation to the heavens, the passage of the sun across the sky from left to right and east to west. When the Amboyna posit a link between right and mountain side, sky and interior, and left and sea side, earth and exterior, this entails that actions and movements of the body involving the right hand or right side are linked with going upward and inward whereas the left side is linked with going outward and down into the sea.

The association of right with upwards and in front represents an association with an already established asymmetrical bodily dualism. The association of right with east, life and the rising sun, the domain of the sacred, and left with west, death and the setting sun, the domain of the profane, right with good and left with evil, is commonplace and has been linked to dual symmetrical organizations (Hertz 1960; Needham 1973; Faron 1962).

We order places and their significance through our bodies, through the articulation of basic distinctions between up/down, front/back and left/right. The experience of places is thus in part grounded in human bilaterality. Casey comments:

> A given side of my body, whether right or left, is predelineative of place and region by virtue of possessing not just one element such as the hand but a series of connected articulatory factors, including arms, fingers, legs, toes, etc. My right hand *belongs* to my right arm, which in turn belongs to a movable shoulder, and this in turn to a mobile neck, etc. All of these closely coordinated body parts, acting together as an articulatory arc, reach out to circumambient places and regions in continual outbursts of corporeal intentionality. (Casey 1993: 96)

So we can suggest that experiencing the world in terms of dualisms is not so much a product of the invariant operation of a human mind, as Lévi-Strauss claims, but is instead grounded in our bodies. Up and down, back and front, left and right, are all sensible from the point of view of the embodied person, logical and biological dispositions deriving from the manner in which the world is perceived through our bodies, making sense out of the world because of sensation, a practical taxonomy for action in Bourdieu's (1977) sense.

We can also note here that artefacts, places and landscapes may become parts of bodies: the hand and arm which bear an artefact become fully animate and continuous with the arm that grasps it; houses and canoes may be metaphorically conceived as bodies engendering social relationships in space-time; and, like persons, things may have biographies (Munn 1986; Gell 1998; Hoskins 1998; Tilley 1999a). In a similar way places belong to our bodies and our bodies belong to these places. We learn how to orientate and reorientate ourselves in relation to them and form internalized representations of them (cognitive maps) which play a powerful role in how we perceive them, and which in turn become articulated through a somatic nexus. So what is in front of me, and behind me, above and below me, to the right and to the left, extends through my lived body. It is through this body that I find my way into and out of places and landscapes, experience and understand them. Here and there, near and far, up and down, back and front, left and right, constitute the most intimate link between my body and the world. The body thus brings with it a spatial framework organized in terms of these five dyads, the first two of which remain absolute (I cannot be both here and there, things are either near to me, in grasp, or far away), the last three relational.

Perception

A theory of the lived body provides the basis for understanding the manner in which we experience, or perceive, the world in an embodied, rather than abstracted, understanding of that process. The world that exists is a world that exists for the subject and is continually defined and redefined in relation to the subject: 'our own body is in the world as the heart is in the organism: it keeps the visible spectacle constantly alive, it breathes life into it and sustains it inwardly, and with it forms a system' (Merleau-Ponty 1962: 203). 'We see the things themselves, the world is what we see' (Merleau-Ponty 1968: 3): as humans we live in the world and necessarily must have perceptual faith in the world that we perceive to be there, an 'animal' faith in the perceptual world as the basis for all our knowledge, prior to any abstract intellectual thought. Consequently, the perceived world and the body form a dialectical relation in the body in which each is mutually adjusted to the other. Sensation is a communion, or coexistence, between body and thing. Because perception is mediated through the body there is a fundamental corporeal element to experience. This is neither a matter of the thing imposing itself externally on the body or the mind imposing itself internally on the thing. The body is continually improvising its relationship with things precisely because it is not a closed mechanical system but constantly opening out itself to the world as it moves in it. The manner in which we sense the world remains forever incomplete and ambiguous because we always experience things from a particular point of view or relationship. The body is both open to the world yet things are always hidden from it. Therefore perception always involves a relationship between the visible and the invisible, the title of Merleau-Ponty's last, and unfinished, book (Merleau-Ponty 1968). I can never see all the sides, faces or surfaces of a stone at the same time. I can, of course, experience them in sequence, one by one, in a particular structure of encounter, but as one face appears in view, another disappears. I cannot see inside the stone, and if I break it in order to do so, I have destroyed that which I set out to discover and simultaneously created something new. Thus the manner in which I experience an artefact, or a place, very much depends on the structure of my encounter with it. From different directions and different sequences of directions I encounter different things that do not have the quality of self-sameness.

The size and shape of objects in a landscape appear to alter as we change our relationship to them. A large stone will appear to be small when seen from far away. As we look at the stone from different angles, its shape will change; so what is its true size and shape? And what size and shape of the stone are illusory? Merleau-Ponty's answer to this problem is to relate the stone to the body: the true size and shape of an object is when it is in reach (and can be measured). Knowledge of a thing is grounded in our bodily relationship with it. The experience of things, each with its own definite size and shape, is given in our bodies. There is thus an optimum distance for perceiving things. When a thing is too far away, it cannot be seen in detail, or touched. When it is too close, it becomes blurred to our vision. At an optimum distance we can see a landscape feature, such as a mountain ridge, as being both rugged and large. Seen too far away it will seem large, but may not appear as rugged, and so on. The same is true looking at a picture: we adjust our bodies in order to see it in relation to its size. Human beings are thus, according to this account, attuned to experience the world in a certain way. This experience is not innate but acquired through the passage of time. The child learns as it interacts with things what the properties of size and shape are. In a landscape and a place a person acquires habitual knowledge of things and their relationships. It is only in a new landscape, or an unfamiliar place, that one has to consciously think about relationships and learn where things are.

From an empiricist point of view, objects may be said to possess certain primary characteristics, those that can be measured, and certain secondary characteristics, such as colour or how a thing feels, which cannot. We can obtain objective knowledge of the former, but only subjective and therefore imprecise knowledge of the latter. From a phenomenological point of view, such a perspective has to be rejected. Just because we can measure the size of a stone does not imply that size is more important than texture or colour. The qualities of a thing, in fact, may tell us far more about it than any number of measurements of its geometrical properties that we might like to take.

Our knowledge of an object is limited insofar as it is always impossible to give a complete description of it, listing every attribute. Such attributes anyway change according to how we perceive it and in what context: for example, the character of the light and from where it shines may fundamentally alter the qualities of a stone. Descriptive accounts are fundamentally open-ended and objects, as we experience them, are fundamentally ambiguous. This is because (a) it is often impossible to decide whether a thing has a determinate property or not. One will often be unable to choose between alternatives (e.g. whether a stone has been carved or not); and (b) things may have two or more conflicting or contradictory properties according to how one sees them and how one interprets them. An empiricist would claim that a landscape truly appears to us in a particular manner, so a landscape seen on a misty day is somehow less real than that landscape seen on a clear day. But to claim this is to abstract that landscape from the person who perceives it. We cannot so simplistically distinguish appearance from reality. Rather we have multiple and alternative descriptions of landscape and place. By approaching landscape and place by describing them from alternative and different points of view, we may hope to understand them better.

For an empiricist, the properties of an object are external to and independent of each other, their size, shape, colour, texture, etc. From a phenomenological perspective, these properties are internally related. So, for example, the yellow colour of a stone and its surface texture make that stone what it is and cannot be clearly distinguished from each other. Rather than regarding properties such as the colour of a thing, or the texture of a thing, as being abstracted characters, we could rather say that things have their own properties. In discussing Maori perception of colour, Merleau-Ponty comments: 'The Maoris have 3,000 names of colours, not because they perceive a great many, but, on the contrary, because they fail to identify them when they belong to objects structurally different from each other' (Merleau-Ponty 1962: 305). Such a perspective is clearly an embodied, human, rather than abstract knowledge. The latter would abstract 'red' as a category and lump all red things in terms this category irrespective of context and association. But what does such an abstracted knowledge really tell us about the things we are to investigate by this technique? Instead we can regard the perception of colour as part of the thing perceived, part of its existence and significance for the perceiver. Colours are perceived differently in different circumstances. Whether the red thing is smooth, rough, shiny, large or small matters (*ibid.*: 313). The unity and the reality of a thing can only be fully appreciated when all the senses with which we relate to the thing are acting together.

Things and places, like persons, are temporal beings. Time is in, or part of, a person, as it is in a thing and in a place. Thus things, persons and places are never static entities but constantly changing and altering their nature. Time is the fourth 'hidden' dimension of being or existence, always part of places, landscapes and things. Our bodily existence and perception of the world always involves a stretching out of the present towards the past, which thus remains in contact with it and in relation to the future. Thus experience is temporally coloured and constituted. Memories of previous places we have experienced colour present perceptions and how we react to the future and the new. Past experiences are carried forward through the activity of the incarnate subject and provide structures through which that subject is able to interpret the world or fit it into a pattern. The body carries time into the experience of place and landscape. Any moment of lived experience is thus orientated by and toward the past, a fusion of the two. Past and present fold in upon each other. The past influences the present and the present rearticulates the past.

Gestalt Theory and Experience

For gestalt theory, the most basic unit of visual experience is that of a figure on a background. It is elementary in perception. An isolated datum of experience (the manner in which empiricists view the world) is inconceivable. Merleau-Ponty comments: 'a figure on a ground is the simplest sensible given that we can obtain . . . The perceptual "something" is always in the "milieu" of something else, it always forms part of a field. A really homogeneous area offering nothing to perception, cannot be given to any perception (Merleau-Ponty 1962: 4). The main findings of Rubin ([1915] 1958), who did the basic work on figure–ground relationships, were as follows:

1. When two fields have a common border, it is the figure which seems to have the shape while the ground does not.
2. The ground seems to extend behind the figure.
3. The figure appears to be object-like (even though it has an abstract shape) while the ground does not.
4. The colour of the figure seems more substantial and solid than that of the ground.
5. The ground tends to be perceived as farther away and the figure nearer the observer even though both are at the same distance.
6. The figure is more dominant and impressive and tends to be remembered more easily.
7. The common border between figure and ground is called a contour, and the contour appears to be a property of figures. (Dillon 1998: 66)

When we shift from visual images to include all the senses working together, instead of the terms 'figure' and 'ground' more general terms are required to describe the relationship: 'theme' and 'horizon' and the essential unity of a theme, or a gestalt, is a function of the relationships between its parts that make up a whole. Merleau-Ponty's reworking of the position characteristic of early gestalt theory takes it in another direction. He notes that form and perception are intimately related such that perception is always pregnant with a notion of form. This recognizes that gestalts are dynamic and emergent rather than static entities. Furthermore, 'themes' or 'figures' are always inherently ambiguous because their meaning is codetermined by the unity provided by the parts of a theme and the relation between the theme and the horizon that provides its context. Hence the same grey figure appears dark against a light background and light against a dark background. It follows from this general principle that a theme is polysemous and can take on a wide variety of meanings. This is to stress the fluidity of the phenomenal field. The partiality of perception is an attribute of phenomena observed within a lived real world which is always changing in its spatiotemporal characteristics. In our temporal experience of this world, our way of perceiving, figure or theme can always turn into ground or horizon and vice versa. The elements of any gestalt field cannot be precisely calculated because horizon or background participates with foreground or theme in a way meaningful to the perceiver which cannot be quantified. Perceived objects, sounds or smells, etc., always compete for an observer's attention. When one wins out, the others slip into a ground for that experience that still helps to articulate it as part of a constantly shifting field of figure–ground or theme–horizon reversal. Experience is thus mediated by experiential gestalts meaningfully structured and constrained through the materiality of the body in a way that is not arbitrary.

Synaesthesia: The Fusion of the Senses

In relation to the body in a place, and in a landscape, we might note in general terms that taste involves an interior relation: the substance to be tasted must be imbibed by the body. Touch involves an extended relation of limited extent, that which can be encountered, primarily through the feet and hands, in contact with the body. Smell, hearing and sight do not require bodily contact, and of these three sensory modalities vision is most extended in relation to the body. But the corollary does not necessarily follow that a distant view is always already an abstracted (analytical) gaze whereas taste and touch are far more intimate. I can have an intimate relationship with the mystery of the moon while my hand touches the table, for which I feel nothing.

In analytic thought the different modes of sensory perception – sight, touch, smell, hearing and taste – are usually treated separately. From a phenomenological perspective this is misplaced. Perception involves the simultaneous use of the senses. In considering landscape and place, we participate in the world in such a manner that we do not distinguish between the visual, audible, olfactory, etc. They impinge on us and contribute to our experience all at once. We may only artificially separate out such sense impressions after the event and thus sever the manner in which our bodies participate in the sensuous terrain. Synaesthesia, the overlapping or blending of the senses (seeing sounds, hearing colours), is usually regarded as a peculiar, romantic or even pathological experience of certain individuals which needs special analysis, but instead it can be regarded as our primordial preconceptual experience of the world (see Dann 1998). We *typically* speak of cool or warm colours, hard or soft sounds, thus transposing qualities from one sensory domain to another. When we read silently we may simultaneously hear the sonorous sounds of the words in our heads as we do so. Tasting with the tongue relies simultaneously on a sense of touch, and taste discriminations such as sweet or bitter frequently involve smell. Eating a meal combines sensing the tastes, textures, appearances, smells of the food, and the sounds involved in imbibing and masticating, not to mention the colours, degrees of heat, the clink of cutlery, voices surrounding us – a total sensory experience in which the whole is more than the parts.

The senses are all modalities of the body's existence in the world. If the body participates in the world, an overlapping of the senses is part and parcel of this participatory relationship. Merleau-Ponty argues that 'synaesthetic perception is the rule, and we are unaware of it only because scientific knowledge shifts the centre of gravity of experience, so that we have unlearned how to see, hear, and, generally speaking, feel, in order to deduce, from our bodily organization and the world as the physicist conceives it, what we are to see, hear and feel' (Merleau-Ponty 1962: 229). Sensory experience is a totality, and if we describe the operations of the senses, one after another, we can only convey a very impoverished account of reality. To truly know is to feel and perceive through all the senses. As Leach has put it, 'the cult [in the social sciences] of the fact has converted subject into object; it has alienated the individual from his feelings (Leach 1979: 91).

Many have commented on the dominance of the visual in Western culture, in which the other senses have been relegated to being of lesser importance. This has been attributed to the advent of the written word and the rise to dominance of print media (McLuhan 1962). Some historians and anthropologists have contrasted the supposed dominance of vision in modernity with other cultures, past and present, where other senses, particularly sound and smell, are held to have been far more dominant (Ong 1982; Stoller 1989; Classen 1983; Howes 1991). In all these accounts a culture dominated by vision is regarded with suspicion and compared unfavourably compared with, for example, an 'aural' culture. Ingold describes well the kinds of contrast drawn:

> sound penetrates whereas sight isolates . . . what we hear are sounds that fill the space around us whereas what we see are things abstracted or 'cut out' from the space before us, that the body responds to sound like a resonant cavity and to light like a reflecting screen, that the auditory world is dynamic and the visual world static, that to hear is to participate whereas to see is to observe at a distance, that hearing is social whereas vision is asocial or individual, that hearing is morally virtuous whereas vision is intrinsically untrustworthy, and finally that hearing is sympathetic whereas vision is indifferent or even treacherous. (Ingold 2000: 251–2)

From a phenomenological perspective, there is something peculiar about these contrasts being sharply drawn between supposedly aural or visual or olfactory cultures insofar as the senses of the body continually overlap or intermingle and inform each other in how we experience the world. As Ingold points out, such perspectives may reflect more upon the preconceptions of anthropological analyses than anything else (*ibid.*: 252). If the 'West' is a visual culture, anthropologists might naturally be expected to find a non-visual counterpart elsewhere in the world. To compare different cultures or peoples according to whether they give priority to one sense over another in their encounters with the world is a project of dubious value, however. Nor do we have to argue for some kind of natural hierarchy of the senses in each culture, as Gell (1995) and Feld (1996) appear to do. Ingold highlights a more pertinent point about vision:

> it is through its co-option in the service of a peculiarly modern product of objectification that vision has been reduced to a faculty of pure, disinterested relection . . . Having installed vision as the chief instrument of objective knowledge, leaving hearing to float in the primordial realms of emotion and feeling, we know what it means to hear sound but have effectively lost touch with the experience of *light*. (*ibid.*: 253)

In the *actual* practice, as opposed to the representation, of a person's encounters with landscape and place, the senses are always involved in a dynamic intertwining. It is to an understanding of this multisensorial dimension of landscape and place as encountered in the life paths of individuals that our analyses need to be directed. Exactly which of the senses may or may not be most important at any particular moment depends on the activity or task being undertaken and the context and cannot be specified in advance. But the most important point is that to see is not to be simply exposed to sensory data; it involves embodied interaction with the world. We see with the whole body just as we think with our body rather than part of it.

Encountering the World: The Reversibility Thesis

The ontological thesis providing the basis for Merleau-Ponty's exposition of phenomenology, as for Husserl, Heidegger and Sartre, is that of the ontological primacy of phenomena. He advocates this in conjunction with the epistemological thesis of the primacy of perception providing the foundation for rationality, value and existence. The real world is the perceived world is the phenomenal world. Perceptual faith is a belief in the veracity of perception, that our vision 'goes to the things themselves' (Merleau-Ponty 1968: 28) through the process of inhabiting the world through our lived bodies. Such a perspective entails doing away with subject–object dualisms, and the manner in which Merleau-Ponty attacks this traditional epistemological problem is manifested most clearly in his thesis of reversibility. My right hand touches my left hand. Is my left hand, then, like a passive object being touched in exactly the same way as I might touch a stone or a book? Merleau-Ponty denies that any clear separation can be made between the hand which is touching and that which is touched. The acts of touching, and being touched, are both simultaneous and coincident but they are not the same thing. One hand touching another is a simultaneous act encompassing touching and being touched, which occurs at the same time and therefore cannot be conceived in terms of an external relation of linear causality, i.e. touching/being touched. The general thesis here is one of identity through difference. In the case of the hand touching and the hand being touched, there is an overlapping or encroachment because my body is involved in the sensing. But the acts are not the same, so there is a dehiscence that opens my body into two (*ibid.*: 123).

This is at the heart of all acts of perception. To perceive anything, including my hand, a relation of distance must be established from my own body, yet, even in the case of looking at something, I am 'touched' by that which I look at. It has an effect on me, and my perception of it. Merleau-Ponty's argument is that there is a fundamental relation of unity between the perceiver and the perceived in all acts of perception which transcend a distinction between subject and object. The act of perceiving the world binds the subject with the world of which he or she is already a part. The act of one hand touching another hand provides, for Merleau-Ponty, a paradigmatic model for all processes of perception. The process of perception at a fundamental level involves ambiguity precisely because it is not amenable to a clear-cut subject–object dualism. Distinctions between 'properly' being a subject and 'properly' being an object thus break down.

In the process of touching an object, the same thesis of the reversibility of sensation/perception can be posited to be at work. I touch the stone and the stone touches me. To feel the stone is to feel its touch on my hands. There is a reflexive relationship between the two. I and the stone are in contact with each other through my body but this process is not exactly the same as my touching my own body because the stone is external to my body and not part of it. Touching the stone is possible because both my body and the stone are part of the same world. There is in this sense a relation of identity and continuity between the two. Yet there is also asymmetry and difference. The stone is not sentient, and even though I am touched by the stone, through touching it, there is not the same relation of reversibility as in the case of my left hand touching my right hand, an action that could be reversed with my right hand touching my left hand. However, we can make the general claim, as Gell (1998) does, that things, like persons, possess agency because they bodily affect us, help to structure our consciousness. It is not strictly necessary to always anthropomorphize things in order to 'validate' such a thought, to suggest that things have active effects on persons, although such animistic thinking is a prevalent conceptual strategy for doing so (see below).

In the case of vision, the act of seeing entails a body capable of being seen just as touching requires a body capable of being touched. Merleau-Ponty, in his famous essay 'Eye and Mind', writes of a reversal of roles between the painter and the painted. He cites the painter as saying: 'In a forest, I have felt many times over that it was not I who looked at the forest. Some days I felt that the trees were looking at me' (Merleau-Ponty 1964a: 167). There comes a point, Merleau-Ponty comments, in which who sees and what is being seen, who paints and what is being painted, is thoroughly ambiguous. And this is because painting is not just an act of pure vision; it establishes bodily contact between the painter, who paints with his or her body, and the painted. Painting is a bodily process linking the two. The painter sees the tree and the trees see the painter, not because the trees have eyes, but because the trees affect, move the painter, become part of the painting that would be impossible without their presence. In this sense the trees have agency and are not merely passive objects. Dillon comments:

> The trees 'see' the painter in a manner comparable to that in which the mirror 'sees' the painter: that is, the trees, like the mirror, let him become visible; they define a point of view on him which renders visible for him something that otherwise would remain invisible – his outside, his physiognomy, his carnal presence . . . The trees and mirror function as Other. (Dillon 1988: 161–2)

Perception thus involves reciprocity between the body and the world and a continuous interchange between the two:

> In so far as my hand knows hardness and softness, and my gaze knows the moon's light, it is as a certain way of linking up with the phenomenon and communicating with it. Hardness and softness, roughness and smoothness, moonlight and sunlight, present themselves in our recollection not preeminently as sensory contents but as certain kinds of symbioses, certain ways the outside has of invading us and certain ways we have of meeting this invasion, and memory here merely frees the framework of the perception from the place where it originates. (Merleau-Ponty 1962: 317)

Thus perception links the carnal subject with the world in which the body is immersed like a fish in water. The sensible world, from such a perspective, is animate, alive, active, an intercourse between my body and the things that surround it. To define a thing as an inanimate object is misplaced because such a perspective cannot understand the manner in which the object world provokes our senses.

Carnal being, for Merleau-Ponty, is the 'prototype of Being' (Merleau-Ponty 1968: 136). He goes further to claim that the relation of the body to the world is that of flesh to flesh, but this takes place at a primordial level prior to the emergence of conscious personal reflection in which the I comes to the fore. This takes us away from notions of an individual ego, or body-subject, relating independently to an object in the world, to a pre-reflective level of consciousness, to an anonymous perceptual unfolding, a dehiscence, a splitting open of the body putting it into contact with the world which may be shared and compared by different persons:

I look at a landscape . . . I speak of it with someone. Then, through the concordant operation of his body and my own, what I see passes into him, this individual green of the meadow under my eyes invades his vision without quitting my own, I recognize in my green his green . . . There is no problem of the *alter ego* because it is not *I* who sees, not *he* who sees, because an anonymous visibility inhabits both of us, a vision in general, in virtue of that primordial property that belongs to the flesh, being here and now, of radiating everywhere and forever, being an individual, of being also a dimension and a universal (Merleau-Ponty 1968: 142)

The commonality between other persons or other things and me is that we all fleshily exist or have our carnal being in the world and participate in it together. There is both dehiscence, fission, in this relation and an intertwining, but not an identity of me and the Other. The human body is that kind of flesh of the world that allows the flesh of the world (things, places, landscapes) to double back on themselves and be seen. Such things as trees are sensible without being sentient. Dillon beautifully explains this point:

flesh is, then, elementary. Perception is the relation of flesh to itself that Merleau-Ponty describes with the images of reversibility. How does perception reach its object? Perception is the flesh touching-seeing-feeling itself. There is no representation at the level of perception: there is only flesh in touch with itself. We have to learn to think of perception as we live it in perceptual faith, that is, as a relation between sensibles in which the flesh of the perceiver necessarily admits of being perceived. That is the essence of the reversibility relation; not that the tree I see sees me, but that I am visible from the standpoint of the tree as it is from mine because we are both made of the same stuff: the flesh of the world. Thus conceived perception is a worldly event and not a private occurrence that takes place within an invisible sphere of immanence. (Dillon 1998: 170)

Consciousness from this point of view is not a private awareness of the interior of one's mind but an active relation to the world.

Participation: Animism and Anthropomorphism

Merleau-Ponty's work suggests that participation is a fundamental process of perception, an active interplay between the body and that which it perceives. In our sensorial engagement with the world we engage with it, flesh to flesh. Participation was also the term used by Lévy-Bruhl ([1910] 1926) to refer to animistic and anthropomorphic systems of thought, which have always preoccupied anthropologists, in which 'inanimate' natural objects, such as trees, stones or mountains, or artefacts, buildings and monuments, are regarded as being alive or having a soul, and akin to a person; a thought system in which people and animals and things reciprocally participate in each other's existence: for example, the prey may give itself to the hunter. A participatory relationship to the world is an emotional and sensuous one initiated by fellow feeling and bodily activity. Interestingly Lévy-Bruhl argued that it was only with the advent of an 'individual consciousness' that such sensuous concepts took on an abstracted ideological quality. He put central emphasis in his account on the concept of participation to explain the workings of the primitive mind: participation is a mode of 'primitive' logic which creates correspondences and promotes resemblances. It links together culture and nature, the human and non-human world, subject and object, in a seamless web of connections. This is a system of knowledge of the world embedded in embodied sensory experience. By contrast, logical or so-called 'modern' thought is derived from an abstracted mental realm of disembodied ideas based on setting up categorical distinctions and oppositions between things and persons, culture and nature, mind and body.

A participatory relationship between culture and nature remains at the heart of Lévi-Strauss' (1966) discussion of the 'savage' mind, and in particular the act of bricolage in which concrete reference points such as differences between birds, plants and animals and their behavioural characteristics are used to construct models of the social world. The major difference is that while for Lévy-Bruhl mythic thought was considered to be participatory because it was an emotional and pre-logical response, for Lévi-Strauss it was a particular kind of concrete logic not based on the conceptual abstraction characteristic of modernity: 'the exceptional feature of this mind which we call savage and which Comte described as spontaneous relates principally to the extensive nature of the ends it assigns itself. It claims at once to analyze and synthesize, to go to the furthest limits in both directions, while at the same time mediating between the two poles' (*ibid.*: 219). As Shore has more recently pointed out, what Lévi-Strauss identifies here as 'synthesis' is that which Lévy-Bruhl earlier characterized as a participatory relation between persons and the world (Shore 1996: 31). Totemic and animistic systems of thought represent different modes by which people conceive of their manner of participating in the non-human world. Totemic classifications model social relationships primarily in terms of discontinuities between species (birds, animals, plants), while animism endows natural species and things with human attributes. As Descola has noted, they are symmetrical inversions of each other as animistic thinking does not exploit differences between species to confer a conceptual order on society but uses elementary categories structuring social life to organize relations between human beings, species and things. In totemic systems non-humans are treated as signs; in animistic systems they are conceived as relations (Descola 1996: 88). Such modes of thought do not necessarily exist in opposition or isolation but may be combined. Both systems of thought arise, and have their basis, in the ordinary everyday bodily understanding that human beings are part of a world, an environment, a landscape, rather than radically separated from it in which it becomes an autonomous domain.

Totemism and animism are particular modes of thought, not only characteristic of the 'primitive' or 'savage' mind but present within all of us, a concrete and sensuous rather than abstract logic of the human mind by means of which we relate to the world. The essence of such participation is that it requires not the binary categorical and digital logic in terms of which Lévi-Strauss characterized the human mind, but an analogic logic whose principal forms are the metaphorical and metonymic connections between things (Tilley 1999a). Bird-David has rightly referred to such a mode of thought as being a 'relation epistemology', i.e. one that is not dependent on prior subject–object and nature–culture dualisms:

> it involves dividuating the environment rather than dichotomizing it and turning attention to 'we-ness', which absorbs differences, rather than to 'otherness', which highlights differences and eclipses commonalities. Against 'I think, therefore I am' stand 'I relate, therefore I am' and 'I know as I relate'. Against materialistic framing of the environment as discrete things stands relationally framing the environment as nested relatednesses. (Bird-David 1999: 78)

An analogic logic is not a 'primitive' logic but a form of human reasoning pervasive in all human cultures and for which we can suggest ontological primacy in human thought. In this sense, totemism, anthropomorphism and animism are a fundamental part of our own modernity, and our continued, but generally un-acknowledged, bodily relations to things and the world. All that has happened in modernity is that the focus of this thought has progressively shifted from 'nature' to 'culture' and is now embodied in our relationship with mass-produced things, a 'technototemism' (Shore 1996; see also Gell 1998). We no longer primarily speak to, and identify ourselves with, a relationship to a non-human world of stones and artefacts we ourselves have made. In a culture of mass production and mass consumption we primarily speak instead with an intrinsically alienated artefact world of computers and cars and trainers and lawnmowers, which, through a love and labour of consumption, we relate to and animistically make our own. Things, places and landscapes influence us, alter our consciousness, constitute us beyond ourselves. In this sense they are not radically divorced from us.

In all indigenous world views the person is not individuated in the manner in which Western analytical philosophy might have us believe but diffused with other persons and things in a unitary sociomythic domain in which the most mundane of activities can be imbued with cosmic significance. For Lévy-Bruhl, participation was a perceived pre-logical relation between diverse phenomena. For Lévi-Strauss, it is a particular kind of concrete logic characteristic of a 'savage' mind. For Merleau-Ponty, the same general notion becomes extended as a defining attribute of all perception involving a dynamic interplay between the perceiving body and that which it perceives. In this sense we are all primitive animists. Merleau-Ponty's philosophy is effectively a modern Western exposition of animistic and totemic thought in which the essences of persons and things are intertwined through an embodied mind in which perception is a worldly event governed by participation rather than a disembodied mental image.

Metaphor and Metonymy

Merleau-Ponty can be described as being not only *the* philosopher of animism, but *the* philosopher of metaphor. His philosophy is written through metaphor, which resides at the core. Striking metaphoric images such as 'flesh', a connective fabric or tissue binding us to the world, provide the very medium for an ontology linking physical embodiment to the incarnational quality of linguistic meaning through the essential metaphorical qualities of speech and writing (see Gill 1991).

An embodied mind is a corporeal, bodily mind, part of culture and part of the world rather than something separate from it. Such a mind establishes connections between things through the practical work of metaphor establishing resemblances. A metaphor does not tell us that one thing is like another (simile) but that it *is* another. Metaphors and metonymy (part–whole relations) allow us to see similarity in difference, permitting us to connect the world together. They thus can be said to constitute the flesh of our language and the flesh of things. Linguistic metaphor and the solid metaphors of material forms (see Tilley 1999a) doubly constitute our meaning and experience, providing a meeting ground between languages and discourses of representation and feeling, emotion and embodiment, experiential modes of engagement with the world.

Metaphor is a primary way in which persons and cultures make sense of the world. This position, which may be labelled a poetics of mind (Gibbs 1994), emphasizes that thought arises from our embodied experience. Hence many metaphors are grounded in the body and in mental images of the world based on bodily experience. Such experiences and images are mediated through social experience and thus are culturally variable. To cite just one example, the Dogon of Mali conceive the world as a gigantic human organism. The village is a person lying north–south, smithy at its head, shrines at its feet. The Dogon house is an anthropomorphic representation of a man lying on his side and procreating. There is an entire geology of the body. Different minerals correspond to different bodily organs. Rocks are bones, red ochre is blood. Words are likened to grain, speech to germination, divination to winnowing. Body parts have analogues in grain, the nose being likened to the germ (Griaule 1965). This is a corporeal and sensuous (animistic and anthropomorphic) way of relating self and culture to the world. Metaphor and metonymy are situated in the practical activity of the Dogon in engaging with the land and the growing of grain, a participatory logic of practice.

Metaphors are creative and infinitely generative in their allusions and the manner in which they permit the creation of meanings. They are not an embellishment or an elaboration of an originary and primary literal language (the traditional theory of metaphor going back to Aristotle) but constitute its very essence as a mode of communication. 'Dead' bodily metaphors are so ubiquitous and embedded in our own thought that we rarely realize that we are even using them when we speak (e.g. expressions such as the leg of a table, the face of a clock, I *see* [i.e. understand] what you mean). To be human is to think through metaphors and express these thoughts through linguistic utterances and objectify them in material forms. The essence of metaphor is to work from the known to the unknown, to make connections between things so as to understand them. A metaphorical logic is an analogic logic serving to map one domain in terms of another. This is precisely what we do in all interpretative work in the social sciences. Metaphors are thus the medium and outcome of any phenomenological analysis.

Nature and Culture

The world can only be 'nature' to a being that does not belong there.

Ingold, 'Hunting and Gathering as Ways of
Perceiving the Environment', 1996: 117

In traditional philosophical approaches, there are two radically distinct ways in which nature is conceived in relation to culture. In empiricist accounts, nature becomes the sum of unaltered elements of the environment external to humanity. In idealist accounts, it becomes what is perceived to be out there, again in opposition to humanity, that which is transformed through history and practical activity. What is natural gets defined by culture and tradition, a product of reflective consciousness. Nature becomes either eternal external object or an internalized representation, an infinite blank slate on which culture is written. From a phenomenological perspective, nature is neither a thing outside us nor something which we produce inside a cultural consciousness, but an embodied relation to a preexisting world external and in that sense 'natural' to the body. Merleau-Ponty puts this thesis in the following way: 'the distinction between the two planes (natural and cultural) is abstract: everything is cultural in us (our *Lebenswelt* is "subjective") (our perception is cultural-historical) and everything is natural in us (even the cultural rests on the polymorphism of wild Being), (Merleau-Ponty 1968: 253). The relation of the subject to the world can be characterized as an *ek-stance*, a stretching out of itself towards a horizon that runs beyond it and yet remains in contact (Low 2000: 81). Meaning is created neither by an external nature mechanically impacting on a passive subject nor by that subject's active intellectual construction but by the presence of an incarnate sensuous activity of being in the world. The world does not exist independently of us, nor do we create it. Our interaction with the world brings it and us into being. As such it is mistaken to drawn distinctions between natural and cultural landscapes and places or the material and the mental. They are intertwined in social Being.

Places and landscapes provide a series of 'affordances', to use Gibson's (1986) useful term. They provide or furnish possibilities, either for good or ill. An affordance is neither an objective nor a subjective property but both: 'equally a fact of the environment and a fact of behaviour. It is both physical and psychical, yet neither. An affordance points both ways, to the environment and the observer' (*ibid.*: 129). From such a perspective, meaning is neither imposed on things, nor pre-given in consciousness, but discovered in the course of practical activity. People pick up information by attending to the environment in which they live. Knowing is developing skills of attending to the environment, educated through practice and aids to perceiving such as models and stories of things, words and pictures which facilitate knowing (*ibid.*: 258). Perception is a mode of action in relation to life activities, providing knowledges of what the environment affords, and such knowledge is potentially inexhaustible because of the possibilities for sensitizing the perceptual system and attuning it to phenomenal diversity of the environment: its textures, colours, surfaces, smells, sounds, tastes and sights.

Landscape to Place and Back Again

Landscape – the term in Western thought has both an abysmal history and contemporary resonance implying separation and disinterested analytical observation, a particular way of seeing exemplified in the linear techniques of perspective developed in landscape painting since the Renaissance to create a 'realistic' image (Cosgrove 1984). Use of it would appear to be antithetical to a phenomenological perspective because our entire cultural baggage encourages us to regard landscapes as objects of aesthetic contemplation rather than being bound up with power and domination, labour, love and life. Why bother to continue to write about landscapes? The short answer is that to do so should entail revitalizing the concept and attempting to rescue it from the structures of objectivist and subjectivist thought in which it has become historically enmeshed in a manner that can link landscapes with structures of human feeling, emotion and activity, movement and the place world.

Experience of the world always extends from the body and expands beyond the particularities of place. A more holistic perspective is required, one that links bodies, movement and places together into a whole, and this is why the term 'landscape' has utility and remains preferable to a 'neutral' analytic term, such as region. Landscapes have massive ontological import from the moment we conceptualize them as being lived through, mediated, worked on and altered, replete with meaning and symbolism and not just something looked at or thought about, objects for contemplation, depiction, representation and aestheticization (Tilley 1994: 26). From such a perspective landscapes can be most parsimoniously defined as perceived and embodied sets of relationships between places, a structure of human feeling, emotion, dwelling, movement and practical activity within a geographical region which may or may not possess precise topographic boundaries or limits. As such, landscapes form potent mediums for socialization and knowledge for to know a landscape is to know who you are, how to go on and where you belong. Personal and social identities are played out in the context of landscapes and the multitude of places that constitute them. To be human is to be place-bound in a fundamental way. Places are elemental existential facts, and the social construction of place, in terms of others, is a universal experiential medium. When people think about social or cultural, or their individual, identity, they inevitably place it, put it in a setting, imagine it and feel it in a place. Ideas and feelings about identity are inevitably located in the specificities of familiar places together creating landscapes and how it feels to be there. Places nest in landscapes, and their borders cannot usually be strictly defined. Like landscapes, they are *kinds* of things rather than *sorts* of things that might be strictly defined. There is an essential ambiguity therefore to what a place or landscape is, where it begins, what makes it up and where it ends. Our bodily experience of both flows from a structure of sensuous feeling, a kinaesthetically felt situation (Casey 1997: 232). Clearly there can be no non-contextual definition of landscape or place. One place may contain within itself another place: a tree within a square within a village within a river valley. What kinds of places and landscapes we are interested in affects both the scales of our analyses and the comparisons we may legitimately make.

Places and landscapes produce spaces and times in relation to the bodies that inhabit, move around and use them, rather than the other way round. As Casey states, 'we come into the world – we come into it and keep returning to it – as already placed there. Places are not added to sensations any more than they are imposed on spaces. Both sensations and spaces are themselves emplaced from the very first moment' (Casey 1996: 18). Lived bodies belong to places and help to constitute them so much so that the person can become the place (Gaffin 1996). The body is the medium through which we know place. Places constitute bodies, and vice versa, and bodies and places constitute landscapes. Places gather together persons, memories, structures, histories, myths and symbols. Mental and material, symbolic and practical, wild and domestic, they constitute landscapes, collections of place-bound structures and meanings. Landscapes are thus structured in terms of the relatedness and relative depths of places within them. Their experience includes the body as it is animated and moves, what spreads into the distance, a region where some things are sensible and other things hide themselves at one moment to reveal themselves to the ambient body at another. Places and landscapes are created and experienced through mobility as much as stasis, through the manner and sequence in which they are explored and sensed, approached and left. In a fundamental way that which a place *is* bound up in its relations with other places that I encounter. In many cultures there is an art to movement in the landscape and the manner in which places should be encountered from the 'right' or socially prescribed direction. Furthermore, as Gibson (1986) has emphasized, human (and animal) perception is a fundamentally ambient activity, a flow of eventful sensuous activity opening out the body to the world. When we undertake a journey, we move from place to place, each with its own setting, its unique heterogeneous character or placiality. The starting and ending place may be the same (home) or of an entirely different character, as on a pilgrimage or a sacred rite. Movement between places involves their sequential experience, in their description the production of a narrative, linking the body to place and events in place. The existence and nature of time, like place, depend upon the existence and nature of a perceiving subject, and there is no perception of place and landscape without memory. Past experiences become selectively conjoined with present perceptions and serve to colour them. Temporality is carried by the movements of the body into, out of, around and between places. We carry times to places through our movements and prior experiences, and direct contact with these places acts as a mnemonic trigger for stories and the construction of personal biographies.

Writing Experience: Text and the World

From a phenomenological perspective, language flows from the body rather than the mind, or, rather, from a mind that is embodied, bound up with the sensorial world. It cannot be an entirely autonomous arbitrary realm separated from the world of bodily experience. Although Merleau-Ponty accepts many of Saussure's structural theses on language, he stresses its meaningful character. Language has meaning to a speaker produced through word structure. Like art, it does not transparently represent the world. Instead it makes parts of it visible. We understand the meanings of words through their place in contexts of action and through our socialization (Merleau-Ponty 1962: 179). In this sense, language does not primordially arise from 'I think' but from 'I can', i.e. situated practical contexts in which part of learning to speak involves our bodily being in the world and interaction with the things around us (Merleau-Ponty 1964b: 88). Language exists ontologically as part of life, part of our being. As Abram puts it:

if we are not, in truth, immaterial minds merely housed in earthly bodies, but are from the first material, corporeal beings, then it is the sensuous, gestural significance of spoken sounds – their direct bodily resonance – that makes verbal communication possible at all. It is this expressive potency – the soundful influence of spoken words upon the sensing body – that supports all the more abstract and conventional meanings that we assign to those words. (Abram 1996: 79–80)

When I speak a foreign language, however technically competent I might be, the words, their sequences, their nuances, their sounds, simply do not have emotional and bodily resonance for me as those in the language I acquired as a child. I do not *feel* for them in the same way; they do not arise from the innermost core of my emotional being but instead take on the character of a gloss: words that possess meaning but do not have depth. This is not a matter of phonological iconism, which Gell (1995) refers to – words in a language somehow echoing the sounds of a landscape in which they arise: the sounds of birds, the flow of water, the rustle of kinds of leaves – but of emotional depth.

In virtually all the academic literature it is quite striking how disembodied written landscapes become. This is because virtually everything written about landscape is not only written on paper; it is principally derived from paper. Landscape is not bodily experienced; it becomes a variable historical or social discourse principally derived from maps, paintings, archives and texts. Being 'out there', bodily sensing place and relationships between places has hardly been that much on the agenda. Bodies remain at the desk rather than in the field (with the exception of the occasional afternoon site visit). What we are left with is paper landscapes, paper perspectives, and Merleau-Ponty's own philosophical work is no exception. The closest he gets to landscape is a discussion of the paintings of Cézanne (Merleau-Ponty 1964a), who, he interestingly claims, attempted to represent landscapes as he actually saw and felt them rather than adopting the abstracted rules of linear perspective.

It might be claimed that most academics cannot understand landscapes, except in an abstract objectified manner, because most of them have not been there or experienced them except in a vicarious way, and temporal experience is lacking, which is precisely why most reduce landscape to a matter of visual representation as opposed to bodily experience. Thus a geography of landscape becomes, peculiarly, a geography of paintings (Cosgrove and Daniels 1988), an anthropology or history of landscape similarly a study of a series of pictorial representations (e.g. Pinney 1995; Ingold 2000: Chapter 11; Schama 1996), an archaeology of 'natural' places a series of sites whose contours and specificities are barely described (Bradley 2000), Stonehenge a place through which one does not need to walk in order to talk (Bender 1998), Wayland's Smithy or Hambledon Hill somehow representative of the meanings of a Neolithic landscape elsewhere in England

(Edmonds 1999). I do not single out these publications because they are 'bad' but precisely because they are particularly sophisticated and insightful recent discussions. However, what they all have in common is the lack of any embodied perspective: they can only provide us with abstract models for thinking landscapes rather than models *of* landscapes as they are sensuously lived. Anthropology, with its long-standing emphasis on participant observation, is perhaps where we might expect such a study to be developed, but the work has been very limited (see Bender 1993; Tilley 1994; Hirsch and O'Hanlon 1995; Feld and Basso 1996; Lovell 1998; Gooch 1998; Ingold 2000) and all too often appears to be an afterthought or appendage to other studies principally concerned with language or a consideration of sociopolitical relations rather than landscapes as synaesthetically experienced through the body.

It is, of course, far easier for us to attempt to describe or represent the sensual visual qualities of such an experience than any other of our senses, where our words remain peculiarly impoverished. To discuss what a landscape, or a place, looks like is easier than to write or talk about how it feels to touch a wall or to describe a smellscape or a soundscape in words. But we may hope to do so better by taking on board the phenomenological implications of synaesthesia: that sensing the world involves a continual interwining of the various ways in which we perceive it. Anyway, in a purely visual description of a landscape, or in a photograph of it, we do not arrive back at that which we experienced. The relationship between an act of thinking and its object cannot capture the richness of our lived encounter with the world. It is necessarily reductive and transformative. In a text all we can hope to do is to evoke the sensuous qualities of place and landscape in a multisensorial way through our choice and use of words and the types of narrative structures employed, and this is the task of a richly textured carnal phenomenological 'thick' description in which we truly attempt to reflect on the character of our experience, as opposed to a thin and sensorily impoverished 'analytical' account. Such an account must, of necessity, exploit the tropic or metaphoric nature of language, avoiding a deadened and deadening literalism, to make writing a voice for the stones, the places and the landscapes in which we are bodily immersed. This is to exploit the carnal dimensions of language, rooted in sensorial experiences of other persons and the world, to make communicative meaning affective. Perceptual experience can thus be only described by expressive use of language, an attempt to exploit the sensuous evocative dimension of writing and speaking as opposed to the denotative and structural aspects of communication emphasized in contemporary linguistic theory, the expressive and poetic as opposed to the abstract and conceptual potency of words. The language in which we write must attempt to capture our bodily perceptual participation in a sensorial world, always paradoxical, always ambiguous; an 'operation through which using words of a given sense, and already available meanings, we try to join up with an intention which necessarily outstrips, modifies, and in itself, in the last analysis, determines the meanings of the words which translate it' (Merleau-Ponty 1962: 114). Language is invocation, a meditative translation of our contact with the world.

Conclusions

A phenomenological perspective provides an ontological ground for the study of things, places and landscapes, a means of approach and a way of thinking through the body in its participatory relation with the world. I summarize some fundamental principles.

1. A phenomenological approach to landscape and place, as discussed here, using the framework of Merleau-Ponty's thought and interpretations of this thought by others, is not a philosophical approach emphasizing the personal and the subjective. It is an approach emphasizing the intertwining of subject and object, things and persons, mind and body, places and Being in the world. The rejection of any possibility of an objective approach does not mean that we pass into a realm of personal subjectivity, because meaning is grounded in the sensuous embodied relation between persons and the world, an invariant ontological ground for all feeling and all knowing taking place through persons with similar bodies.

2. Any study begins with lived experience, being there, in the world. It must necessarily be embodied, centred in a body opening out itself to the world, a carnal relationship. The exploitation of basic bodily dyads provides one entry point into the study of place and landscape. A concentric graded sense of place and landscape provides another basic way in which meaning may be explored. Both originate in the body and extend outwards.

3. Perceptual meanings of place and landscape are constituted as gestalts, themes against horizons, to which the human body and the external world both contribute, a lived structure of experience formed through engagement and interaction in which the body-subject and the world flow into each other and form part of each other. The body is concretely engaged in the world from a particular point of view that is always unfolding and changing in space-time. The mobile interaction of the body in the world creates a framework for experience which is produced in this lived interaction. What is experienced is an articulated sensuous theme, against a horizon, in which perception is a meaningful bodily organization of the perceptual field. There is a dialectical exchange between the embodied structures of the engaged perceiver and the structures of that which is perceived.

4. This involves a dehiscence, an opening of my body to things, a reversible relationship between touching and being touched, myself and other, the effect of myself on things and those things on me.

5. In an experiential relationship with things there is always a chiasm, an intertwining between 'outside' and 'inside', which mediate each other but never totally fuse. So my body is in contact with the world but still separate from it. My body experiences from the inside but opens itself to the outside. Since, as an embodied observer, I perceive the world through a set of frameworks which are habitual and grounded in the body, to a certain extent anonymous, these frameworks cease to be mine alone and are not therefore 'personal'. They are, however, both objective and subjective insofar as they simultaneously stem from my own body. First-person experiences can be used to gain access to the experiences of other persons because of the incarnate and sensuous opening out of the 'primal' embodied subject to the world.

6. Our primordial experience is inherently animistic, disclosing a field of phenomena that are all potentially animate and expressive because our perception involves the reversibility born out of our participation in the world.

7. Direct prereflective perception is inherently synaesthetic, disclosing the things and elements that surround us not as inert objects but as expressive subjects of experience, born out of our multidimensional sensorial participation in the world.

8. There is a fundamental temporal dimension to the body, place and landscape carried through movement and sedimented into what places and landscapes are and how we experience them.

9. Persons do not passively receive information and knowledge about the world but always act in accordance with practical projects, values, needs, desires and interests. What information and knowledge is indeed received can only be understood in the context of these needs, desires, etc. It is in the context of a needful body reaching out to the world that meaning and significance are found. The manner in which we experience place and landscape is, however, forever unfinished, uncertain and therefore ambiguous. The ambiguity inherent to both that which we investigate (place, landscape) and how we perceive is not a problem for analysis. Instead it provides an inexhaustible field of affordances for us.

10. The aim of a phenomenological analysis is to produce a fresh understanding of place and landscape through an evocative thick linguistic redescription stemming from our carnal experience. This involves attempting to exploit to the full the tropic nature of our language in such a way as to seek the invisible in the visible, the intangible in the tangible. The mode of expression must resonate with that which it seeks to express.

Endnote: What Places and Landscapes Do and What They Mean

What a philosophical consideration of phenomenology clearly cannot tell us about is anything with regard to particular bodies, particular places and particular landscapes, particular histories and meanings, particular cultures and social relationships. The embodied carnal sensuous body-subject that has been almost exclusively referred to in this chapter is both ahistorical and lacking a culture. What is being referred to here is what places and landscapes *do* to the body, what effects they have, prior to the specificities of cultural meaning. What is at issue here is the notion of a prereflective embodied consciousness that is necessarily anonymous and which all humans share prior to and irrespective of the distinctive cultural and linguistic worlds in which they are enmeshed. Clearly bodies carry specific knowledges and traditions, meanings and symbols (culture) into places and articulate them there. To be encultured is to be embodied is to be emplaced. So the body provides the framework for perceptual processes ending in objectification, an existential ground for understanding culture and the self (Csordas 1994). Cultural meaning is as intrinsic to embodiment as Merleau-Ponty's notion of 'wild Being'. Basic to a thickly textured sensuous local knowledge is the body in place, and it is through cultural embodiment that places take on their specific cultural, as opposed to 'wild', character, that which Bourdieu (1977) refers to as the habitus: shared bodily dispositions and deportment, classificatory categories and generative schemes. What I have been suggesting is that rather than regarding things, places or landscapes primarily as systems of signs, or as texts or discourses which encode meaning and reflect social identities in various ways, we can regard them as *agents* which actively produce that identity. In other words we need to think about places and landscapes animistically, in an analogous manner to the way in which we like to think about persons, as entities who can and do make a difference. The move is from considering things as representing the world to us to things as producing that world for us. It is a move from the cognitive sign value of things to the embodiment of things, from the code of the world to the flesh of the world, from symbol to action. Producing human meaning in the world is all about establishing connections between ourselves and the disparate material phenomena with which and through which we live, the plants and animals, landscapes and artefacts that surround us, and this is the work of tropic language, of metaphor and metonymy.

The concern in this chapter has necessarily been abstract: with embodied participatory relationships in general but not how these are played out in relation to determinate cultural and social circumstances: persons entangled in relationships with each other, traditions and the past. Here we have to leave the domain of a general philosophical analysis and turn instead towards a consideration of specific contexts of action, meaning and structure, the subject of the following chapters in this book; to the intertwining of a 'wild' embodied primal perception with 'domesticated' cultural meanings.

–2–

Shooting Rhizomes and Giant Axes
Experiencing Breton Menhirs

Menhirs, which began to be erected in Brittany around 5000 BC, are almost certainly the earliest of the megalithic monuments. These standing stones, erected singly, and less frequently in pairs or groups of three, continued to be put up and used throughout the Neolithic and into the early Bronze age – a time span of some 2,500 years or more. Nineteenth-century statistics record around 1,200 isolated menhirs in Brittany (Giot 1988: 320), of which less than half have survived as upright monuments today.

We can suggest that these stones were the first culturally fixed and enduring points in the landscape and are closely associated with its post-Mesolithic transformation. Some standing stones may have replaced or been raised in conjunction with timber posts. Even so, their character was fundamentally different in terms of materials, mass, permanence and meaning. Menhirs were almost certainly intended as permanent markers of place which would fix in the soil a part of the identity of those who erected them. Even today the power and significance of the stones live on in a rich body of folklore. In recent centuries many have been appropriated by Christian communities who have added crosses and carvings and incorporated the stones into the precincts of churches and their graveyards. There can be little doubt that menhirs have always possessed a powerful and potent role in the social geography of the past, as they continue to do in the present. But why was there a need to erect such stones in the first place? And why erect so many of them? Why were huge ancient trees, wooden posts, rock outcrops or the large stones that would have served as physical markers of place and identity during the Mesolithic deemed no longer sufficient?

There have been a varied set of interpretations: menhirs have been suggested to be landmarks or territorial or boundary markers set up in association with the gradual post-Mesolithic clearance of the land for farming (Hibbs 1983; Burl 1985; Bender 1986; Patton 1993). Scarre has suggested that the inland menhirs represent the sacralization of an uncleared landscape beyond the limits of cultivation in a social context of widespread seasonal population mobility during the Neolithic (Scarre 2001: 299). Their erection as enduring monuments has been related, in a general way, to changing conceptions of space and time and notions of social identity from the Mesolithic to the Neolithic and to the symbolism of the axe and the body (Thomas and Tilley 1993). More specifically a close association between some with springs and water courses has been noted (Giot et al. 1979). Attempts have also been made to relate the orientation of the broad faces of the stones to the movements of the sun and the moon (Le Pontois 1929). We know that a number were clearly places where culturally significant materials were deposited. A few excavations undertaken around the bases of menhirs have recovered fragments of Neolithic and Bronze Age pottery, fire-reddened stones, charred wood, chips of flint and axe blades but tantalizingly little else (Giot et al. 1979). Some have been associated with tin sources (Le Roux 1999). Others have been suggested to be part of a death cult: memorial or ancestor stones erected in conjunction with the construction of dolmens and passage graves (L'Helgouach 1965; Burl 1985; Bender 1986). In the Morbihan area of southern Brittany it has been demonstrated that decorated menhirs were broken up and re-used in the construction of a number of passage graves (Le Roux 1985; Kirk 1993; Patton 1993; Thomas 1993). It has also been noted that pairs of stones are often strikingly different in their form and dimensions (Giot 1988; Burl 1993), and the anthropomorphic shapes of some have led to suggestions that they might be associated with fertility in a general way, or perhaps represent male or female forms (Le Rouzic 1913; Giot 1988).

Owing to lack of modern excavation and radiocarbon analysis, most menhirs are almost impossible to date with any certainty. Radiocarbon dates confirm the erection of some as early as the fifth millennium BC and others into the third millennium BC (Briard et al. 1995: 54–6; Lecerf 1999). Because of this, and the multiplicity of interpretations possible, any study has to attempt to reflect both the enormous span of time and the changing economic and social circumstances during which the stones were erected and used. Also, regional and local differences need to be recognized and incorporated. What is clear and self-evident is that there can be no single explanation. The stones were (and continue to be) capable of multiple meanings – meanings which changed through time and from place to place. But part of the problem in trying to understand more fully the reasons why menhirs were erected, and what their social significance may have been, stems from the tacit assumption in the literature that these are fundamentally simple monuments about which very little can, in fact, be said at all. Our research suggests the opposite.

Interestingly, menhirs have always been considered as a single generic class. It is quite striking that while there are numerous typologies of megalithic tombs, and detailed discussions of their different architectural forms, none exists for menhirs. They are all considered to be the same. Descriptions of the individual stones often amount to little more than a mention of their height, presumably assumed to be their primary attribute (Burl 1985; Bender 1986; Briard 1990; Giot 1995). Other qualities of the stones such as shape, texture, colour, rock type, presence or absence of weathering lines, cracks, depressions, etc., have not been considered in any detail or systematically studied. Similarly there has been very little analysis of the relationship of individual menhirs in their local setting, regional groupings or wider landscape context.

Our aims in this chapter are threefold: first, we attempt to demonstrate that standing stones are monuments of considerable complexity belying their apparent simplicity of form, and discuss the phenomenological experience of these 'complex' monuments; second, we consider their relationship to landscape; and, third, we attempt to provide some novel interpretations linking the form and experience of these stones to their individual and regional landscape settings. The study is based upon an analysis of 93 stones from western and northern Finistère, Brittany, representing a c. 95% sample of all known surviving stones still standing in this area.

Experiencing menhirs

Most menhirs are unshaped stones. The majority were not therefore intentionally designed and constructed as physical objects to represent a particular set of ideas. This suggests that they did not signify or represent anything in conventional semiotic terms and so we cannot reduce their experience to the level of language. They took on their meanings in relation to the experiences and feelings of those people who lived with them in the landscape through particular modes of encounter and engagement. What we are referring to here are bodily processes of perception and reception through which particular forms of representation and meaning came into being. The architecture of the stones resides in a fusion of their physical form and location or placement in the landscape, the sensual experience of these stones and the ideas and memories, histories and mythologies that became associated with them. Thus a sense of the poetic spirit of a place was created and sustained. The visual encounter of size and scale, shape and proportion was only one experience among many. The nature and character of the raw material, the stones themselves – their colours, the constituent elements of the rock, the personal and intimate experience of touching their surfaces and the aural experience of the sounds emitted when struck or the echo generated from people chanting or drumming in their vicinity – may have been of equal importance. It is also important to consider that such incarnate sensory experiences may have been negatively encountered. For example, the unspeaking, unsinging silence of many stones may have been significant: the fact that they did not echo sounds or resonate when struck. Similarly, the stones do not smell, a characteristic that contrasts with the wooden posts which they might have either replaced or were associated with over time. What we are suggesting is that the 'energy', power and significance of the

stones was derived from an interlinked combination of multiple sensorial characteristics, at least of the visual, the tactile and the acoustic, of which, we would
argue, the first two were primary and dominant in most instances.

The stones also had a significant and less obvious experiential dimension: time.
Physical processes of weathering have gradually altered the form and character of
these stones from the moment of their erection until the present day, accentuating
grooves and depressions and bringing forth irregularities within them. Some have
been subjected to lightning strikes, altering their physical form, and lichen growth
and moss has changed the surface colour and texture. Just as we can recognize
these stones as old from such features, so, in the past, older and newer menhirs
could be distinguished. Some stones were undoubtedly chosen because they
already looked old with a sense of history about them when lying prostrate on the
ground in their prone, unaltered state. At a very localized level, the presence or
absence of trees would, over time, alter the effect of weathering processes on the
rock itself, and this would, in turn, affect the acoustic properties of the stone, as
would the accumulation of lichen and mosses. These changes through time would
be particularly significant where the rock itself is softer, more friable and subject
to frost damage, as in the Montagnes Noires (see below).

The origin of the stones too, whether derived from rocks exposed along the
shoreline, from river channels or estuaries, stream beds or particular rock outcrops,
like time, was an important 'hidden' dimension to their meaning and potency. Each
menhir would have its own origin story, which may have been mythologized over
time or continue to reference the epic work of ancestors. Through time these stories
might have merged and elaborated to incorporate world origin stories and cosmological knowledge.

The sheer size and proportion of many menhirs dwarf people in relation to
themselves, and this clearly had (as it does today) an important bearing on the
manner in which they were bodily experienced. The tallest standing menhir at
Kerloas in the Bas Léon area is 10 m high, considerably more than five times the
height of an average person today. Although it is situated near to the highest point
of the Léon plateau, the origin of the stone is probably riverine, brought from the
Aber Ildut, at least 2.5 km to the west. Similarly, the broadest menhir at Kerscaven,
embedded in a stream with water flowing along its sides, is 5.7 m high or three
times the height of a person. This stone measures a massive 13 m in circumference
at the base with broad faces of c. 5 m. The sheer enormity of such stones and the
acts of their transportation and erection were intended to impress in the past as they
do today. The superhuman effort required in moving these stones suggests of itself
that their choice was carefully considered and that the particular qualities of the
stone chosen were absolutely fundamental. Size is not always significant. Some
menhirs are slim pillars around 2 m in height and 1-2 m wide: modest stones of
bodily scale. Many such menhirs were undoubtably significant not because of their

size but because of their particular shape or the rarity of the stone used and its inherent properties and associations. Obvious examples are the multi-coloured stones and milky white quartz pillars found on the Crozon peninsula.

While most menhirs in Finistère are of unshaped stone, they often appear as if they had been shaped or carved. They must have been chosen because they possessed a particular desired shape (or were ancestrally 'pre-carved') prior to their movement and erection. These unshaped but shapely 'natural' stones all possess their own individuality, and so it follows that no two menhirs are precisely alike. Even those which look similar, on close examination, have their own distinctive individual characteristics making each unique, giving it a 'personality' and thus enabling it to create a distinctive sense of place and social attachment to places in the wider landscape. Such stones would act to sustain a sense of social identity for the people who erected and subsequently lived with them. People would recognize themselves, where they were, and who they were through the material qualities and identity of the individual menhirs.

Size and shape were only two among many specific qualities recognized in the rocks: straight or convex or concave profiles from top to bottom, particular curves, distinctive cracks, weathering lines, depressions, etc., were equally important in the creation of difference, meaning and identity. The major exception to this wider set of characteristics are the axe-shaped menhirs of the Bas Léon area (discussed below). These now beautifully shaped stones were transformed by smoothing, grinding down and significantly rounding the hard corners of the raw material. It was a process which effectively erased their character and individuality of form. The stones became generic cultural symbols whose uniqueness was only maintained by the discrete presence of harder inclusions in the granite or in terms of their sheer dimensions and scale experienced in combination with the wider landscape context.

In respect of the visual and physical shapes of the menhirs, two basic forms can be distinguished: those stones that appear to be static, lacking any sense of dynamism and movement, and those with curved (convex or concave) profiles that give the impression of growth and movement – of kinetic potential. The static forms appear as fixed, rooted or thrust down into the soil. The curved stones, by contrast, suggest upward movement or growth from the soil. We build this basic distinction into an interpretation of the changing meanings of the stones.

Unshaped menhirs may have slightly rounded or sharpish edges. They may have as few as two clearly distinguishable faces or as many as five. The vast majority have four faces, usually two broad faces and two narrow faces, but there is much variation and distinct faces may be lost, or appear so, when one looks towards the top or the base of the stone. Different sides of the same menhir, both the broad and the short faces, may look remarkably different when seen from different viewpoints. A pillar that appears squat and lifeless seen from one direction may appear curved and tapering when seen from another. Weathering lines, cracks and depressions may be present and marked on one side of the stone and not on the other, which may be almost perfectly smooth. The same menhir may, in effect, appear as four or five different menhirs as one moves around it. As one face becomes lost in movement, another different stone is revealed. Such stones are obviously open to multiple interpretations depending on from where they are seen. The tops of these stones may also be markedly different (pointed, square, rounded, notched, angled, etc.) and appear different in form from different directions.

Different colours and staining patterns of the stones are also of significance in many instances. In Finistère these range from milky white quartz stones to grey granites with white quartz crystals or pink quartz crystals to blue-grey or yellowy brown schists to silver grey quartzites lacking any crystals. The texture and feel of the stones may also vary markedly from those that feel coarse to the touch, to others which are as smooth as wax. Sometimes a stone may look smooth and regular in form and profile – even when viewed from a relatively close distance – but feel incredibly rough when touched. Conversely a stone covered with surface cracks and indentations may feel smooth. These perceptive contrasts are often quite striking, adding to the ambiguity of the manner in which the same stone may appear to be a different stone when seen from elsewhere and experienced close to. Some stones even have a grainy texture so that they resemble wood or a scaly surface which looks like bark. The presence of mica crystals, acting like tiny mirrors, may make a dull grey stone gleam and glitter when the sun shines from a particular direction.

The micro-characteristics of the menhirs just described illustrate some of the ways in which individual stones can create multidimensional experiences when encountered. Complex local and intimate experiences are generated through movement towards and around the stones. The stones are dynamic even when they are so obviously fixed.

Menhirs in the Landscape

In this section we present a detailed case study of the menhirs of Finistère, attempting to illustrate some of the points made above in more detail. The menhirs can be subdivided into eight discrete sub-regional clusters (Figs 2.1–2.4), six of which are situated near to the coast, the other two being inland groups of stones. We discuss each area in turn and then compare and contrast similarities and differences between the different groups.

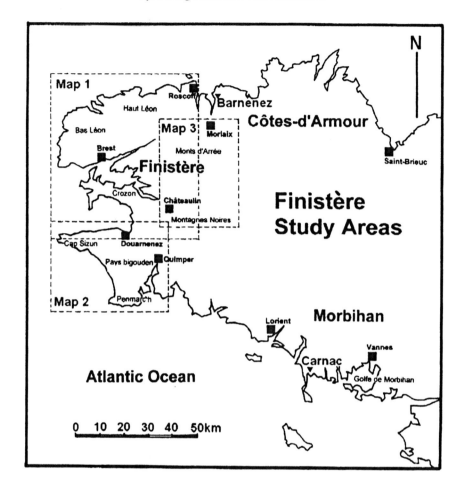

Figure 2.1 Location of the study areas in Brittany.

Bas Léon (Figs 2.2 and 2.5)

In Bas Léon there is a cluster of fourteen menhirs and two double menhir settings in the Pospoder area with a few more isolated stones to the east. The menhirs are of two basic kinds: enormous stones shaped in the form of axe blades with their cutting edges thrust into the ground (10 or 71%) and more irregular unshaped stones (4 or 29%). Half of the menhirs occur in pairs. In these cases an axe-shaped stone is usually placed near to an irregular pillar, except at St-Denec, where three irregular stones originally formed a short alignment, and at Kergadiou, where two massive axe-shaped menhirs occur together. The axe-shaped menhirs are particularly massive, ranging from 3.6 to 10 m in height, dwarfing a person standing at

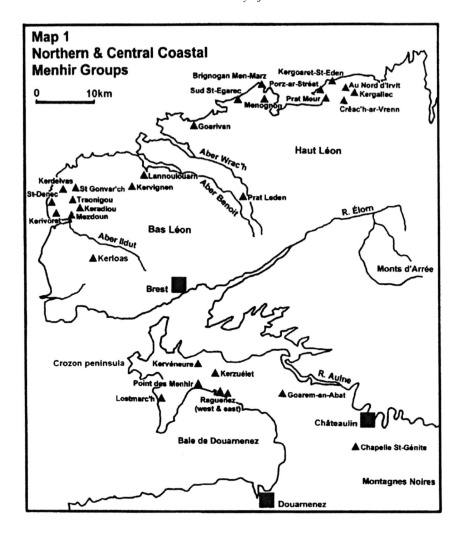

Figure 2.2 The northern and central coastal menhir groups.

their base. The more irregular menhirs are usually shorter, ranging between 3.6 and 5.2 m in height. The axe-shaped menhirs are relatively thin and taper to the top with the wider circumference at their base or blade end. All but the isolated menhir of Kerloas, which is also unusual in other respects, have their long axis uniformly orientated N–S or NE–SW. The theme of the giant axe dominates this group even in cases such as St-Denec, where only irregular stones are found. Here a now recumbent menhir has two hafted axes carved in bas-relief onto the upper facing surface of the stone. When the menhir was standing, the blades of these axes would have been pointing down the stone towards the ground. At Kerivoret the menhir is

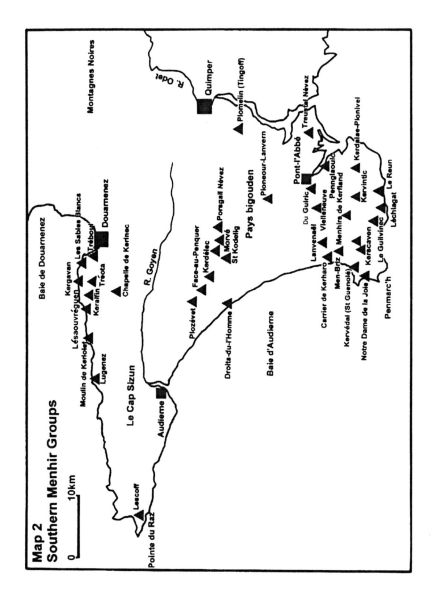

Figure 2.3 The southern menhir groups.

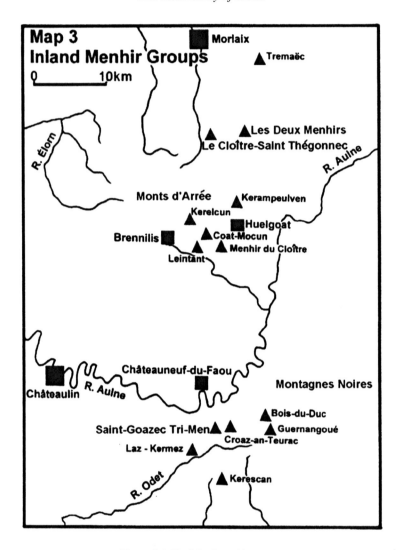

Figure 2.4 The inland menhir groups.

an unshaped stone, but the shape of the stone, when seen from either the west or the east, resembles that of an axe. The sheer size and height of many of these menhirs and the dominance of axe symbolism is remarkable for this group (Figs 2.6, 2.7).

All the stones are of the same local granite, which is very coarse-grained with reddish pink quartz crystals. These quartz crystals may be oblong in form, ranging between 2 and 5 cm long and 1–2 cm wide, or more rounded, square or irregular in form and up to 5 cm in diameter. Thus the huge axe-shaped menhirs appear to

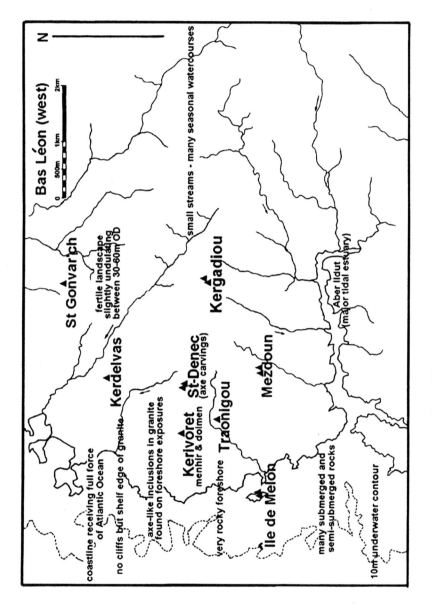

Figure 2.5 Menhirs in the western part of Bas Léon.

Figure 2.6 The Kergadiou menhir, Porspoder, Bas Léon.

the eye to be very smooth and uniform but they feel coarse, sharp and irregular when touched. The sensations of the eye are thus contradicted by those of the hand in a most striking manner. The granite here sometimes has a series of small inclusions of much finer-grained and harder rock completely lacking in quartz crystals and smooth to the touch. These inclusions may be rounded or somewhat

Figure 2.7 The Kerdelvas menhir, Porspoder, Bas Léon, with its axe-shaped inclusion.

irregular in form (like those found on the Kerloas menhir) but much more frequently they resemble axes in form. Usually there are only one or two such
inclusions on one, or at most two, faces of the menhirs but at Kerivoret there are
five axe-shaped inclusions on the north-west face of the stone, up to 50 cm long,
to which the chamber entrance of a nearby dolmen, 36 m away to the west, is

Figure 2.8 Axe-shaped inclusion in the Kerivoret menhir, Porspoder, Bas Léon.

orientated. These smooth axe-shaped inclusions weather at a slower rate than the matrix of the surrounding granite and thus may eventually stand out in relief, emphasizing their distinctive form and presence (Figs 2.7, 2.8). Giant axe-shaped menhirs may thus have smaller axe forms protruding out from the rock matrix. These smooth rock inclusions occur on nine of the fifteen recorded stones in the group (60%). On the present-day coastline, rocks can be seen where the action of the sea is currently eroding these smooth axe-shaped inclusions out of the coarse surrounding granite and completely eroded-out examples of these 'axes' can be picked up on the beach. Thus the sea gives birth to axes out of the living stone.

In Bas Léon we find a majority of menhirs in the form of giant axes and menhirs which themselves have axes of a different stone within them – as well as the axe carvings on the fallen St-Denec pillar. The landscape in which these menhirs are found today is remarkably free of large stones and rock outcrops. Indeed almost the only place where outcropping rocks occur are those exposed by the tides along river estuaries and the shoreline, and in the low coastal cliffs which are today, as in the past, more or less just an erosional surface where land meets sea. At low tide, granite blocks of the same size as the menhirs found in the wider area are exposed, created by the erosion of vertical and horizontal joints in the stone. It seems likely that many of the menhirs of Bas Léon were transported from the Neolithic coast-line or from the ancient pre-Ice Age coastal cliff-edge somewhat further out to the west than today but we think no more than 3–4 km away from most of those menhirs around Porspoder. The stones were thus associated with the beaches, the sea and the smooth 'axes' eroding out of them. Those menhirs with axe-shaped inclusions may have been deliberately chosen because these forms were visible in them. Other large blocks were probably chosen because of the ease with which they could be readily shaped, with stone mauls into giant axes, when erected, their blades thrust down into the ground. This static imagery of an axe blade thrust down into the ground, its kinetic force immobilized, contrasts with that of some of the irregular and unshaped pillars. Cracks, weathering lines, depressions and fractures make these menhirs both appear and feel irregular and rough, as opposed to the axe menhirs, which look smooth and feel coarse. This contrast is further highlighted where, as at Mezdoun and Traonigou, axe forms and natural pillars occur together. At Mezdoun the menhir has a rare example of an irregularly shaped quartz-free inclusion which has a very distinctive star-shaped fracture running across it, giving this stone a most unusual and special character (Fig. 2.9). At Traonigou the menhir appears sinuous in form, bowed at the middle, bulging at the bottom and tapering to a rounded top, as does the southernmost of the three stones at St-Denec. These stones, unlike the giant axes, appear to be growing out of the ground. Their irregu-larity is associated with a dynamic upward movement and they appear to resemble a stylized human form or torso in a process of growth. Such 'growing' stones may contain axe forms within them but have not themselves been shaped so as to be axes.

The axe-like menhirs of Bas Léon, planted into the land, have enormous symbolic power. There is an overwhelming aesthetic force to these stones which dwarfs the human observer. The overriding symbolic theme is one of transforma-tion. Perfect axe blades have been created from originally irregular rocks exposed and eroded by the force of the waves. The process of shaping destroys the individu-ality of the stone and transforms it into a static cultural symbol fixed erect into the

Figure 2.9 The menhir at Mezdoun, Porspoder, Bas Léon.

ground. The irregular pillars, by contrast, retain their individuality of form and have the potential of upward growth and transformation within themselves. The contrast is striking.

Despite the enormous height of some of these menhirs, they are not highly visible landscape markers, with perhaps one exception, the isolated stone at

Kerloas. Set on a localized high point, this stone is visible from the outskirts of Brest 12 km away to the east but it is not visible today from the menhirs in the Pospoder group only 8 km away to the north. It is only the menhir pairs in this group which are intervisible despite the fact that the distances between their locations range from only 500 m to just less than 2 km. These huge stones were not, then, highly visual features in the landscape. They had a localized significance and could only be seen from short distances away irrespective of whether or not tree cover was dense in the Neolithic. The long axis or faces of the stones are not orientated towards any visually significant landscape features. Indeed there is an absence of such features in an area which largely consists of a low-lying and only gently undulating coastal plateau in which the menhirs are situated on flat or slightly sloping land. All are situated c. 200–600 m away from the courses of small streams – many of which only flow intermittently – but they are not situated, as elsewhere, along the watercourses themselves but rather on ground between them. In three cases single menhirs, or groups of menhirs, are only a few hundred metres from springheads. Since we can see that the landscape is generally undifferentiated with prominent natural features, it seems that it is the menhirs themselves which effectively mark it and create distinctiveness and difference within it, but, importantly, this occurs only at a very localized scale. There is a real sense of a local social geography being formed by these stones. Excepting the Kerloas menhir, they do not dominate or stand guardian over extensive landscapes. It is interesting that all the more isolated menhirs in the group are axe-shaped. It is only in pairs, or the short setting of three stones at St-Denec, that the more irregular pillars are found. Movement around in this landscape would have entailed repeated encounters with giant axes, some with axe inclusions inside themselves, but otherwise differing only in terms of sheer size and scale and pairs or short alignments of menhirs containing the more individual and distinct irregular sinuous pillars pregnant with a sense of growth and fecundity. Perhaps the axes had to be planted in order to allow the pillars to grow and give birth to the axe forms inside themselves, perhaps interpreted as a sign of ancestral work, creative force and energy.

Haut Léon (Figs 2.2, 2.10)

In Haut Léon the majority of the menhirs are situated near to the coast in two groups. Those to the west are much more dispersed with distances between the stones of 2 km or more. The menhirs in the eastern group near to Plouescat are more densely concentrated. These are all single stones with pairs of menhirs and short settings of three stones not being present. Despite the relatively short distances between some of them, none are intervisible. None of these menhirs appear to have been shaped and they are all somewhat irregular in form. They differ

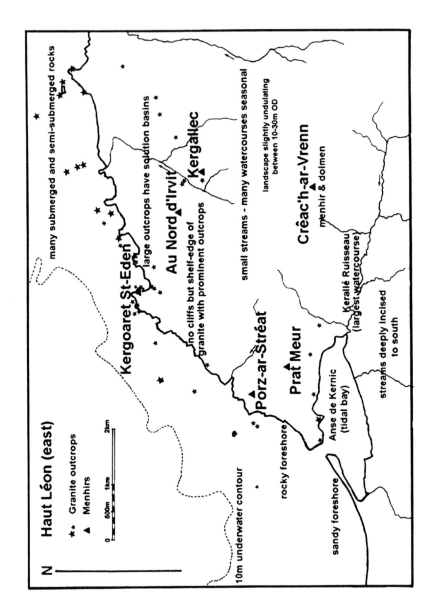

Figure 2.10 The distribution of menhirs in the eastern part of Haut Léon in relation to rock outcrops.

markedly in dimensions: the largest, Men-Marz, is over 8 m high and measures 9.6 m round the base, while the smallest is a slender stone just 2.3 m high. Each of these pillars has a distinctive form and profile and the same stone may look utterly different according to from which direction it is seen. The irregularity and mutable shapes of these pillars contrast markedly with the axe-shaped stones of Bas Léon. The directional orientation of the long or broader faces of the stones also differs greatly, with some being orientated N–S, others W–E or NW–SE. The feature that all share is that they are squat and broad at the base, tapering towards the top. Five are distinctively curved and give the impression of 'growing' out of the soil. Two in the eastern group have distinctive anthropomorphic forms when seen from particular directions. The stone north of Irvit has unusual weathering in the uppermost part of the rock and on the south-east face. This, together with the way the rock thickens markedly to the base of the stone, gives the impression of a standing figure resembling the head and upper torso (see cover illustration). The 6.2 m-high menhir at Kergoaret-St-Eden is by far the most remarkable in the group. It has only three distinct faces. The western face has two distinctive vertical weathering grooves from the top of the stone running down to a horizontal groove about one third of the height down. Otherwise this face is smooth apart from being pockmarked with at least thirty small carved circular cup marks which occur on the lower two-thirds of the stone. Originally, prior to erection, this would have been the side of the stone lying downwards. The eastern face of the stone, now facing a small tidal bay, would originally have been uppermost when the stone was recumbent as it has two irregular solution basins on its face. The lower of these is 0.8 m long, c. 0.6 m wide at its eroding outer lip and about 0.3 m deep. The top solution basin is similar in form but smaller. In addition to these solution basins there are a series of much shallower irregular interconnecting depressions in which originally the rainwater would collect and run into the solution basins. The southern face of the stone has two horizontal weathering grooves on it running halfway across towards the west and a slightly irregular weathered surface above these to the top. Seen in profile from the south-east, the stone resembles a giant face with an eye (upper solution basin), a mouth (lower solution basin) and an ear formed by the two weathered grooves (Fig. 2.11). This face, somewhat resembling an Easter Island statue, melts away into the stone as one moves around the menhir and looks at it from any other direction. There is a clear contrast between the solution basins on the eastern face of the stone, originally water-filled and facing the sky, and the carved cup marks on the western face. The former were perhaps regarded as carvings created by the ancestors. The latter must have been added after the stone was erected, perhaps to strengthen the connection between the creative powers of the ancestors and the work of the local group erecting the menhir.

The stone at Men-Marz, which, as noted above, at over 8 m high, is the tallest in Haut Léon, and one of the tallest remaining menhirs in Finistère, is the only

Figure 2.11 The Kergoaret St-Eden menhir, Plouescat, Haut Léon, from the south-east.

other menhir to possess solution basins. This is a massive triangular slab with one straight short side to the east and a sloping convex side to the west. It appears to be a slender pillar when seen from either of these directions with the western side 'growing' out from the ground, but appears utterly different when seen from the north or the south. The northern face, facing seaward, is indented with six deep

Figure 2.12 The Men-Marz menhir, Brignogan, Haut Léon, northern face.

solution basins and interconnected erosion channels most marked towards the thick base (Fig. 2.12). The southern face, by contrast, is much smoother and regular in form but has a distinctive ledge towards the top. This was the side of the stone that originally lay downwards.

This marked difference between the form and appearance of the pillars is characteristic of the menhirs of Bas Léon and other sub-regional groups in Finistère. The menhir at Menogen has flat southern and northern faces with a distinctive triangular shape. However, the western and eastern shorter faces give the appearance of a pillar that is much more slender and they are more bulbous and irregular in form. The Crêac'h-ar-Vrenn menhir with three distinct sides appears distinctively concave or bow-shaped, tapering to the top and growing out of the ground when seen from the north but as an irregular rectangular form when seen from the west (Figs 2.13, 2.14). Similarly, the anthropomorphic profile of the pillar north of Irvit is lost if one sees it from any other direction than the south-east, and it metamorphoses into a slender pillar when seen from the north The menhir at Porz-ar-Stréat looks utterly different in profile when seen from the north or south and west and east. These stones must have been deliberately chosen so as to create quite distinctive visual experiences when seen from these different directions. Not only are all these menhirs uniquely individual in form but they all look like different stones when seen from different directions. The visual contrast is as great between the sides or faces of a menhir as between the menhirs themselves. This contrast is particularly striking in the cases of those stones that look anthropomorphic when seen from a particular direction or appear curved and 'growing' out of the ground when seen from a particular angle. It is further accentuated by the presence or absence of distinctive grooves, weathering lines, ledges and solution basins on particular faces of the stone. All these features serve to create a constantly changing visual dynamic as an observer walks through the landscape between the stones and moves around them. Indeed, the visual character may have specifically defined how you moved about through and around the local space close to a menhir.

These menhirs with their often rough and indented surfaces appear visually much coarser than those in Bas Léon but the texture of the granite is very different. In the eastern group of menhirs it is fine-grained with densely packed white quartz crystals seldom exceeding 1 cm in size and over large areas of the stone 0.5 cm or less. These stones are rough visually but feel relatively smooth, the precise opposite of many of those in Bas Léon. In the western group of menhirs the grain size of the white quartz crystals is more variable from stone to stone and they are somewhat larger but these stones still feel quite smooth to touch. The small 2.3 m-high irregular and tapering menhir south of St-Egarec is of an utterly distinctive gneiss with no quartz crystals being distinguishable. The stone itself is pink, rather than grey, like the other stones in Haut Léon, with many shiny mica inclusions and appears somewhat grainy in texture. This pillar is much smoother to touch than any of the others. It is also visually 'smooth', lacking cracks, distinctive weathering lines, grooves, etc. It also differs from the other menhirs in the area in that it possesses no short or long faces. Squat at the base, it grows out of the soil.

Figure 2.13 The Crêac'h-ar-Vrenn menhir, Plouescat, Haut Léon, seen from the north.

The landscape in which these menhirs occur is a low almost totally flat or slightly undulating coastal plain with low coastal cliffs crossed by small shallow valleys with streams flowing north or west. Although the menhirs are often only a short distance from the streams, they occur between rather than along the watercourses and they are not associated with springs or water sources. The association

Figure 2.14 The Crêac'h-ar-Vrenn menhir, Plouescat, Haut Léon, seen from the west.

with water is less obvious and direct than in other areas but nevertheless occurs in the form of solution basins in the sides of some menhirs and distinctive weathering lines and grooves in others.

The chief characteristic of the landscape here is the way that it is broken up and articulated by numerous low rock outcrops (c. 3–10 m high). These also occur in the sea to the north of the present-day shoreline (Fig. 2.10). Virtually all of these rock outcrops are very heavily weathered and riddled with solution basins and splayed weathering channels running down the sides of the uppermost stones. The otherwise flat and rather undifferentiated landscape is punctuated by these highly visual features which are absent in neighbouring Bas Léon. They are visible from 60% of the menhirs and they are the likely stone source for most. Distances between most of the menhirs and the nearest rock outcrop are short, varying from between a few hundred metres or less to no more than 2 km. The intervisibility between the menhirs and the rock outcrops contrasts with the lack of intervisibility between the menhirs. It is the rock outcrops, not the menhirs, that visually mark and differentiate the landscape. In a few cases there is a very close relationship between the menhirs and these rock outcrops. The massive menhir at Men-Marz stands immediately to the north of a rock outcrop which was its stone source (it is now quarried away). The menhir at Kergoaret-St-Eden is only 57 m away to the west of a rock outcrop with deep water-filled solution basins. It is also some 250 m east from a more massive stack, now situated on the coastal cliffs, but originally some way inland, which is riddled with solution basins and channels including one stone with thirty well-developed and water-filled basins (Fig. 2.15). A rock outcrop a short distance to the west of the menhir at Kergallec has, in addition to well developed solution basins, a series of small cup marks thus strengthening the association between solution basins and cup marks found on the Kergoaret-St-Eden menhir. Unusually, the menhir north of Irvit has its long axis aligned to a rock outcrop to the south-east which prevents this menhir being intervisible with the Kergallec menhir only 800 m away. The long axis of the menhirs seem not to be directly aligned to rock outcrops in this manner. We suggest that these rock outcrops must have been named places with ancestral associations. Each menhir would have been associated with a particular outcrop, its stone source, in a direct and specific manner. Perhaps erecting the menhirs was all to do with forging a direct and specific relationship with individual ancestors responsible for creating these places and carving the rocks with solution basins. The highly variable and individual character of these stones and the carefully chosen anthropomorphic shapes of some might suggest that they were symbolic tokens or even direct representations of these ancestors enhancing a landscape that the ancestors had themselves made. But they were not intrusive. It was the stones that the ancestors had created that remained the highly visible landscape markers, not the menhirs. Situated on flat or gently sloping land, the menhirs were places from which the ancestral stones could perhaps be viewed and venerated at a distance. If this was the case, then it is likely that ceremonial ways ran between the menhirs and the outcrops.

Figure 2.15 Solution basins in rock outcrop to the east of the Kergoaret St-Eden menhir.

Monts d'Arrée (Figs 2.2, 2.4)

Here there are two groups of menhirs, one to the north and the other to the south of the needle-like spines of rocks forming the summit peaks of the Monts d'Arrée, the highest range of hills in Brittany. All but one are massive stones ranging in height from 4 to 6 m. Whilst these are all unshaped stones, they are nevertheless very distinctive in character. Most are irregular rectangular pillars which taper to the top. Three of those to the south resemble axe blades, either triangular in form or more irregularly tapering to the top. Virtually all appear static in character, fixed into the ground, and in only one case, the stone at Leintant, Brennilis, is there a suggestion of sinuous 'growth' from the soil. Orientation of the long faces of the stones is highly variable and none, except those forming pairings, or parts of three-stone arrangements, are intervisible. In the case of intervisible and paired stones, the dimensions and shapes differ markedly. All except the massive Menhir du Cloître in the south (Fig. 2.16) and one of the menhirs at Plougonven in the north lack distinctive weathering lines or cracks in the stones and it is primarily their shape that distinguishes them from each other. These stones are of the same granite, which is fine-grained with small white quartz crystals generally about 1 cm in diameter. They appear visually 'smooth' and feel smooth to touch.

Figure 2.16 The Menhir du Cloître, Huelgoat, Monts d'Arrée, south-west face.

Three of the stones in the northern group are prominently situated in the landscape and meant to be seen from long distances. The menhir at Tremaëc, south of Plouigneau, is both at the top of a rise and adjacent to a small but strong flowing rivulet. The stone may be marking the water's bubbling source, presently a short distance to the east. The pair of menhirs at Plougonven are situated 50 m away from each other along a narrow ridge top with extensive views south to the jagged outlines of the rock outcrops forming the Monts d'Arrée, which are also visible from the menhir at Le Cloître-St-Thégonnec. Saint-Thégonnec is not highly visible, being situated on a slope to the north of a small area in which there is a notable cluster of small circular rock outcrops, similar to those in Haut Léon, but forming a straggling north–south band about 700 m long with the menhir marking the northern end (Fig. 2.17). These are distinctively weathered and many have well-developed solution basins. They occur nowhere else in the immediate surroundings of the stone and we would suggest that they formed a pathway to the menhir through the landscape. The menhir is also only a few hundred metres from the source of a stream to the east. At this location there appears to be a strong relationship between the rock outcrops, water and the menhir itself.

The menhirs in the southern group occur in a variety of landscape settings. Three occur on localized high points in undulating terrain, one on a gentle north–south slope and another towards the bottom of a slope a short distance from a stream to the north. This menhir at Kerampeulven occurs in an area with many huge rounded grounders which contrast markedly with the vertical poise and linearity of the pillar. We can summarize this menhir group by concluding that the variety of menhir forms is mirrored by the variety of their locations and local landscape contexts. Unlike Bas and Haut Léon, however, there appears no cohesive theme other than one of local distinctiveness and context.

Les Montagnes Noires (Figs 2.2, 2.4)

Here there is a marked concentration of menhirs. The main group is located along an east–west ridge just parallel to the summit areas of the Montagnes Noires. The alignment consists of a single menhir to the east and then two short settings of three stones each. Another partially destroyed setting of three stones occurs at Guernagoué to the east, and there are some more isolated menhirs to the north, south and west of the main group. The furthest stone to the south is a striking 2 m-high white milky quartz block with amber and pink staining. Squat at the base and tapering to a rounded top, it is situated in completely flat land about 5 km due south of the main group of menhirs running along the top of the ridge. Its size is modest and presence undemonstrative. Two distinct deep and smooth holes in the north-east and north-west faces of the stone could be interpreted as possible offering places – receptacles for receiving votive tokens. This stone is remarkable for whilst the surface of the quartz looks cracked and irregular, it is beautifully smooth to the touch with no sharp edges and an almost warm waxy texture (Fig. 2.18). The use of quartz and its extraordinary textural qualities, together with the relative isolation of this stone, make it quite unique. Now, as probably in the past, it is a stone which

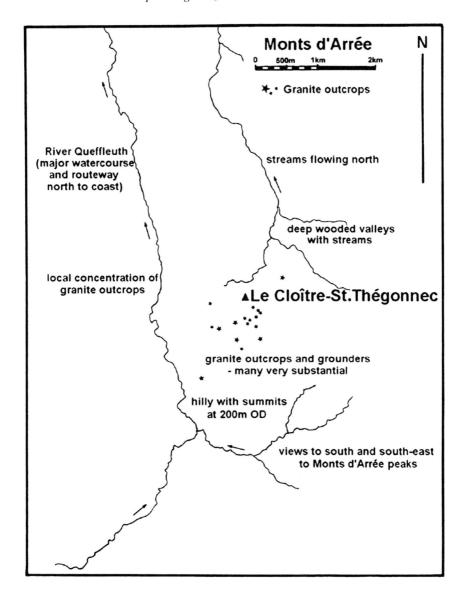

Figure 2.17 The relationship of the menhir at Le Cloître-St-Thégonnec to rock outcrops.

has a wonderful tactile feel. Through these qualities it was perhaps attributed special properties or powers.

The menhirs at the western end of the group are of a very coarse granite, grey with large chunky quartz inclusions of white and rose pink colour, up to 3 × 3 cm and feeling very coarse with a pebble-dash texture. The stone at Kermez is an

Figure 2.18 The quartz Spézet menhir, Kerescan, Montagnes Noires.

irregular roughly rectangular pillar that seems to erupt out of the ground at an angle and then straightens and curves up giving a sense of dynamism and growth. Situated towards the base of a NW–SE slope, there are very restricted views to the SE but there are extensive views up to the Montagnes Noires to the north and the west and east.

The menhirs forming an alignment running along a southern ridge of the Montagnes Noires are composed of an entirely different stone, a soft blue-grey, flaky schist completely lacking in quartz inclusions and both visually appearing and feeling smooth to the touch. This stone has a very fine-grained and striated texture resembling a wood grain, and here the menhirs might well have been regarded as fossilized or petrified trees. The main group consists of a single short menhir at the eastern end of the ridge and two short alignments of three menhirs in the centre and at the western end. None of these, the single menhir or the groupings, are intervisible with each other. They range between 2.5 and 4.3 m in height and all are rather thin, irregular rectangular pillars each with a distinctive shape and form. The easternmost menhir has its long faces aligned east–west in the direction of the ridge top. Two hundred metres to the west there is a short NW–SE row of three menhirs situated midway down a gentle west–east slope running along the axis of the ridge. Today two of these are in a dense wood, the third is exposed in a field. Those in the wood have a scaly surface texture resembling wood bark while the stone exposed to the elements has a perfectly flat and smooth surface. This contemporary difference in the stones indicates in an interesting way how menhirs may have also looked very different in the past when encountered in wooded settings or a landscape cleared of trees. To the north of this group the land rises blocking the view, but there are panoramic views to the west along the ridge top and to the south. To the south-east there are a series of exposed rock outcrops about 150 m away. These consist of exposed low lines of rocks running both parallel to each other and the direction of the ridge. A further 1.5 km to the west at a flat high point on the ridge top there is another, now ruined, alignment of three stones. The one remaining standing stone, 4.3 m high, is the highest in the group (Fig. 2.19). Because these stones are so smooth with a flat surface they have the property to reflect and amplify sound. This phenomenon contrasts with the rough granite menhirs found elsewhere in Finistère, which remain mute, or only reflect sound dully. The amplified acoustics offered by these stones on arrival in their proximity may have played a dramatic part in ceremonies. The sound would define a special area of space close to the menhirs and would seem to enhance their power and potency. Given the special acoustic properties and size of these western stones, we can suggest that these would have been the culmination of processional cere-monies using the ridge and its other stone settings.

To the east another ruined setting of three menhirs at Guernagoué has two stones with cup marks and somewhat ambiguous carvings. One of the fallen stones is distinctively axe-shaped and blue in colour. This stone has numerous cup marks on its upper face. From the stones' location on the lower southern slopes of the Montaignes Noires, there are extensive views to the south. These stones appear isolated and don't obviously reference any prominent feature in the surrounding landscape.

Figure 2.19 The Saint-Goazec Tri-Men menhir, Montagnes Noires, seen from the south.

The Crozon Peninsula (Fig. 2.2)

The surviving menhirs on the Crozon peninsula (Mornand 1998 records 37 certain or probable sites but only seven are still extant) are all rather short irregular or roughly rectangular unshaped stones varying in height from 1.7 to 3.4 m. These menhirs do not dwarf an observer as elsewhere in Finistère. Only the stone known as La Républicaine, the tallest in the group, has a sinuous 'growing' form. The other stones are rather squat, solid and somewhat 'static' in form. The Crozon menhirs are also distinctive because they do not possess the distinctive cracks, weathering lines or depressions found on menhirs in other areas. However, they are perhaps the most differentiated group in Finistère, not because of these character-istics, but rather because of their unusual rock type, their colour, distinctive surface texture and their locations in the landscape.

Three of the seven surviving menhirs are gleaming white quartz blocks. Their surfaces are very irregular, cracked and fractured. Although these stones look extremely jagged and split, the surfaces feel soft and smooth. This is an interesting contrast as quartz is extremely hard and durable. In places it is indelibly stained a pale pink. The isolated quartz menhir at Kerzuélet is 2.2 m tall and is situated towards the top of a north–south slope which runs down to a stream 750 m to the south. The surface is extremely fractured and uneven. It would appear that the finding and setting up of a white quartz stone of this size was a powerful social act in itself as quartz is not found lying about the landscape in the way granite can be found. A pair of similar quartz pillars set only 100 m apart and intervisible with each other can be found at Raguenez. These are located on the southern side of the peninsula and are set high up on the coastal cliffs with stupendous views south across the Baie de Douarnenez. Taking into account post-Neolithic changes in sea level, these menhirs would have been set on the upper southern slopes of an inland cliff over 1 km from the presumed coastline and they may well have been skyline-sighted from a flat coastal plain below. The widest and smoothest sides of these pillars face towards the south and the sea below. This orientation would allow for the widest sides to catch and reflect the sun as it travelled across the sky.

About 4 km to the west of Raguenez, the restored La Républicaine menhir occupies a high point on the coastal cliffs. This stone is a pinky yellow hard schist with a peculiar wormy or brain cortex-like surface texture. Again its broadest and flattest side faces south towards the sea. About 100 m south of La Républicane is a large rock outcrop, now the cliff summit, and the stone found here obviously provided the source of the menhir itself. Looking east from this outcrop there are two strikingly white quartz blocks on the cliffs rising out of thick vertical veins visible in the exposed rock faces. These are in effect natural menhirs which could have been interpreted in the past as being supernatural in their origin. They are similar in size to those at Raguenez, which leads us to think that these may have been set up to emulate the ancient 'natural' stone formations 4 km along the cliff to the west. The menhir at Lostmarc'h is different again, a massive pear-shaped reddish brown hard stone shot through with numerous distinctive white quartz veins. The rock has numerous tiny mica grains which sparkle and glisten in the sunlight giving the stone a shimmering appearance. The stone surface is highly irregular. It both looks and feels rough. Originally part of a series of now destroyed stone alignments, it is also situated on a high point above the cliffs and is skyline-sighted from below to the south with the northern horizon very close by.

The stone at Argol, by contrast, is situated inland some 3.5 km from the coast on the mid-point of a west-east slope. This unusual stone is an extremely hard silver-grey quartzite and incredibly smooth to touch, although the surface of the rock is pockmarked with shallow depressions and slight cracks (Fig. 2.20). The stone feels markedly cool like the quartz menhirs to the west of it. Although in a wood today, the elevated position of this modest menhir – it is only 2.3 m high – would allow for extensive views to the west along the axis of the peninsula and in the direction of the setting sun. Furthest to the east and not accurately on the peninsula proper is the menhir at Chapelle St-Génite. This is a very fine-grained red-brown metamorphosed shale menhir with two broad faces and well-defined edges. It has a markedly flat and smooth surface and differs from all the other menhirs in the Crozon peninsula group in the regularity of its form. This stone is situated towards the top of a prominent hill, the Menez Quelc'h, but, like the stone at Argol, is not itself conspicuous in the landscape. It would seem that both these stones represent places to look out from rather than to be viewed from a distance.

Le Cap Sizun (Fig. 2.3, 2.21)

The menhirs of Le Cap Sizun are strung out in a west–east band on or near to the dramatic northern coastal cliffs of the peninsula. We suggest that, despite changes in sea level, the Neolithic coastline here did not differ greatly from that which is seen today, with seven out of the ten recorded menhirs intervisible with the sea to the north. The menhirs are all of unshaped granite, light grey in colour, sometimes with yellow or pink staining. The white quartz crystals are of a more or less uniform size, rarely exceeding 2 cm in diameter. The stones, usually lacking significant cracks, hollows or depressions, both look and feel smooth. They vary significantly in dimensions. The tallest (now recumbent) is 8 m long and the shortest 1.7 m. The majority are quite massive, between 3 and 5 m in height. They also vary significantly in shape. Half have sinuous profiles as if 'growing' out of the soil. One is of anthropomorphic form (Lésaouvreguen), whilst the remainder are basically triangular in shape or irregular pillars with rounded or pointed tops. The majority have their long faces orientated either NW–SE or NE–SW.

Despite the close proximity of some, none are intervisible with each other. All are situated on sloping land in an undulating low coastal plateau which is inter-sected by small streams flowing north to the sea. At Moulin de Keriolet and Tréota the menhirs are situated near to water sources. It is evident that those menhirs located closest to the sea have their long faces orientated in such a manner as to

Figure 2.20 The menhir at Goarem-an-Abat, Argol, Crozon peninsula.

face out across the Baie de Douarnenez towards the coastal cliffs of the Crozon peninsula to the north, where another series of cliff-top menhirs are found. As elsewhere, it is not the particular orientation of the long axis of the menhir that appears to be important in terms of establishing a sight line across the landscape. Rather, the landscape is 'taken in' by one of the broad sides of the menhir. It is as if the menhir has adopted human form and is acting as a sentinel, looking and facing the wider landscape, on-guard and alert.

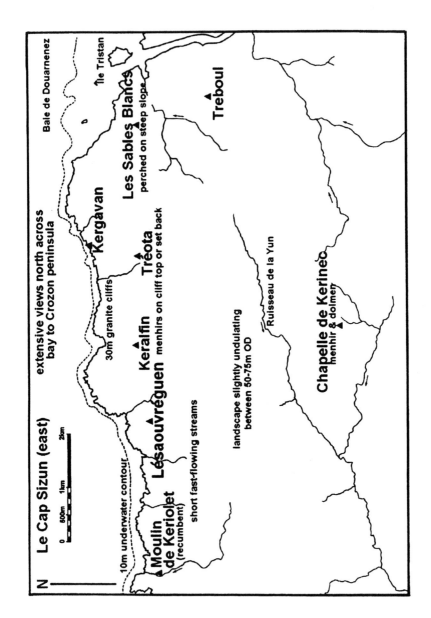

Figure 2.21 The distribution of menhirs in the eastern part of the Le Cap Sizun peninsula, south face.

One of the most massive menhirs is at Les Sables Blancs in the suburbs of Douarnenez. This stone is 5.3 m high and 7.7 m around the base in circumference. It is situated on a very steep slope overlooking the Baie de Douarnenez with its broad face looking outward (Fig. 2.22). The stone has been set upright using a slight backward tilt to counter the natural tendency for the stone to fall forwards downhill. The hillside location emphasizes the prominence of the stone when viewed from below. The broad girth, which widens considerably at a mid-point up the stone, gives the impression of a giant seed being inserted into the ground, the bulging form suggesting the fecund potential for growth and transformation.

The menhir at Lésaouvreguen is one of the few menhirs in Finistère that has a strong anthropomorphic form (Fig. 2.23). It is located on gently sloping ground with excellent views to the sea, which is just 600 m away. One of its smooth broad sides faces the sea northwards whilst its curving sides and hooded head-like top give it the appearance of a sentinel. Similar guardian-type stones are found right on the cliff top at Kergavan and at locations a little further inland at Lugenez and Kerlafin. The stone at Tréota is pointed and has the appearance of being shaped. Its sides seem sculpted in order to make the sides equal in size and shape. The whole effect is powerfully dynamic and suggests a shoot sprouting out of the ground. In contrast the inland menhir of Chapelle de Kerinec is triangular, axe-like and thin with two massive sides each 2.90 m wide. Interestingly, the long axis of this stone aligns to a dolmen intervisible some 120 m to the south-west. The capstone and entrance of the dolmen are orientated to the west and not in the direction of the menhir. This arrangement would suggest that the menhir is referencing the dolmen and not the other way around.

At the very end of the peninsula near the Pointe du Raz is a 1.7 m-high menhir in a garden at Lescoff. This stone differs considerably from the others discussed for this group. It is relatively small and is sinuous in form with a pronounced bend in its shape. The western broad side faces towards the Pointe du Raz some 2 km away to the west. The stone is located on a local high point ahead of a col which cuts across the headland separating the Pointe du Raz headland from the rest of the peninsula. In its human scale this menhir presents itself as a marker delineating the social world from the end-of-the-world landscape of the Pointe du Raz, the land's end of Brittany with the immensity of the Atlantic beyond to the west.

This group of menhirs offers a varied set of interpretative possibilities: the guardian-like sentinels of those near the cliff edge to the seed-like forms of some, to the blade-like symbolism of the Chapelle de Kerinec. This capacity to evoke considerably differing ideas demonstrates the rich repertoire of meaning offered by the stones when examined closely and in their landscape context. It is clear that the menhirs on Le Cap Sizun do not present an overall schema but rather a discrete number of ideas expressed in stone.

Figure 2.22 The Les Sables Blancs menhir, Douarnenez, south face.

Le Pays bigouden (Figs 2.3, 2.24)

A cluster of eight menhirs can be found in an area called Le Pays bigouden between Peumérit in the south and Plozévet in the north. All are situated inland apart from one, the Droits-du-l'Homme, which is located on the present-day

Figure 2.23 The Lésaouvréguen menhir, Poullan-Sur-Mer.

coastline at Lessunus and now transformed into a public monument. The majority
are irregular rectangular-shaped pillars varying considerably in height and thick-
ness at the base. They are all unshaped stones of a grey-pink granite with a high
density of small white quartz crystals, thus both appearing and feeling relatively
smooth. Despite this, several of the menhirs are coarse to touch. Two stones, one

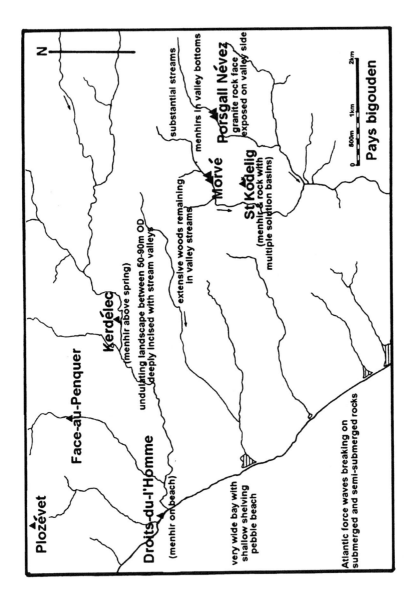

Figure 2.24 The distribution of menhirs in Pays bigouden.

at Morvé and the other at Face-au-Penquer, have distinctive cracks. The menhir at Face-au-Penquer is entirely split vertically through its middle. These aside, the menhirs of this group lack distinctive cracks, hollows or weathering lines. The major differentiating features are their shape and dimensions. Two can be characterized as being sinuous 'growing' forms.

The locations of menhirs in the landscape seem to be strongly related to the presence of water. Le Pays bigouden is a low undulating area incised by numerous heavily wooded shallow or more deeply incised valleys containing small streams. Four menhirs, the most massive, are located in the bottoms of valleys next to or in close proximity to the streams. One of the stones at Morvé is actually in the middle of the stream bed with the water flowing along its long face, while another is a short distance away and only 20 m from the water (Fig. 2.25). These menhirs situated in valley bottoms, despite their considerable size, are completely invisible to the wider landscape. The menhirs at Morvé, only 36 m apart, are barely inter-visible because of the dense woodland growth within the valley bottom. If the vegetative conditions were similar in the past, then this would have created a secretive and mysterious pair of stones deep in the valley cutting, the damp micro-climate of the valley woodland clothing the hard grey stone in a downy cover of green mosses and lichens. These menhirs were not visible from great distances away but would be something encountered along woodland paths in the course of hunting and gathering or walking between settlements. Their locations thus contrast markedly with those situated on the northern coastal cliffs of the Le Cap Sizun and the Crozon peninsula. Although not a dramatic landscape, rock outcrops are sometimes exposed along the valley sides. The menhir at Porsgall Névez (Fig. 2.25) is located besides a stream and close to a 4 m-high and 13 m-long granite outcrop which forms the valley side. Neither the menhir nor the outcrop is visible from outside the valley bottom. The menhirs at Plozévet and Lessunus, while not situated directly in valley bottoms, are also closely related to water. The former is a few hundred metres from a spring source to the south while the latter is situated a few hundred metres from streams flowing to the north and the south. While situated on the beach today, this menhir would have been about 1 km inland during the Neolithic. The menhir at Plozévet is a needle-like stone some 5 m high and is now incorporated as part of a war memorial in the churchyard. The menhir at Kerdélec (today a broken stump) is situated high up on the sides of a valley directly above a spring. The relationship of the menhir at St Kodelig to water is more indirect. Unusually but interestingly for this area, the menhir is situated near to the top of a rounded hill on a very steep N–S slope. The stone is set so that its broad side faces south towards the confluence of two streams 1 km to the south. Just 9 m upslope from the menhir there is an exposed low rock outcrop with two large solution basins with eroding outer lips. Both have channels which drain the water out of the basins down the slope towards the menhir below. The menhir was

Figure 2.25 The menhir at Porsgall Névez, Pays bigouden.

erected next to this special stone with its solution basins in which the pure water from the heavens would collect. It may be significant that the menhir was erected below rather than above the rock in a less dominant position. The menhir seems to be referencing a stone that was already symbolically important with its ability to collect the pure water of the sky. From the solution basins the waters would potently discharge downslope in the direction of the menhir and through the ground to appear in the stream of the valley below. The smooth broad northern face of the menhir contrasts markedly with the fantastic sculpted form of the solution basin stone – an ancestral creation later emphasized and duly enhanced by the presence of the menhir. The inland location of this solution basin stone is rare and this must have added to its significance and local importance.

Penmarc'h and South of Pont-l'Abbé (Figs 2.3, 2.26)

The general area of Penmarc'h is very flat or only gently undulating – mostly 30 m or considerably less above present-day sea level. The land is crossed by numerous small streams and boggy areas which break up an otherwise relatively featureless landscape. The soils vary considerably, with large coastal areas affected by wind-blown sand. The 3.2 m-high menhir at Carrier de Kerharo was until relatively recently buried in sand. None of the menhirs (apart from those in groups) are intervisible and, despite the considerable height of some, they are not highly visible in the landscape. The present-day coastline here is between 1.5 and 2 km, or more, inland of its Neolithic position so that menhirs situated on the coast today would be well inland of their present positions. As in Le Pays bigouden, there is a very strong association of these menhirs with streams and water. Some are situated directly in the beds of streams, while all are situated near to either streams, spring sources or boggy areas (see Fig. 2.26).

There 24 menhirs recorded in the area, including one pair of stones and two short settings of three stones. The stones vary significantly in terms of height (2–7 m), circumference at the base (3–13 m), orientation of the broad face and shape. Three resemble somewhat irregular axes when seen from certain angles. Sixteen are irregular broader or thinner pillars, one is triangular in form and three are much more unusual in form, splaying out to the top. All but three are of the same granite – grey with fine-grained quartz crystals rarely exceeding 2 cm in diameter – and most feel relatively smooth. Three are of fine-grained white granite. One somewhat isolated stone at Ploneour-Lanvern is of a very hard schist with a crystal rod-like structure giving a wood grain effect. This stone stands in a small stream. In a further two instances the quartz in the granite is noticeably coarser and feels rougher. The great degree of variability in their shapes and dimensions is accentuated by the fact that the majority also have distinctive cracks, weathering lines or depressions on one or more faces. Consequently the majority of these stones look very different when seen from different directions. Most (70%) have sinuous profiles giving the appearance of growing out of the land. Menhirs in pairs or short rows all have markedly different profiles, shapes and dimensions. The stones,

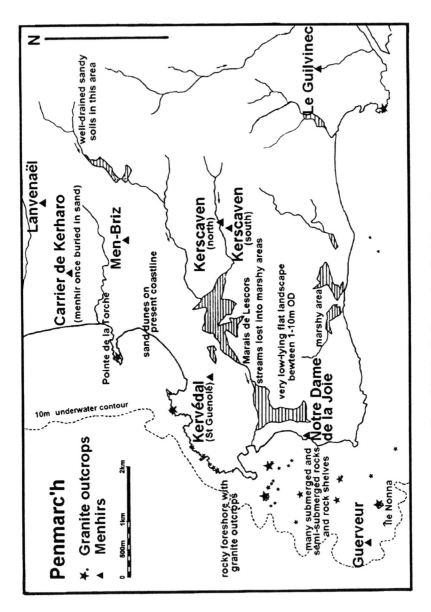

Figure 2.26 The distribution of menhirs in Penmarc'h.

although similar, were deliberately chosen to be different and to contrast with each other. The three stones in the short row at Kerfland are quite remarkable for their degree of variability in terms of weathering lines, cracks, grooves and depressions on their broad faces. It is as if there are twelve distinctive stones here rather than three! The menhirs are aligned in a single row on a north–south axis and are spaced 4 m and 4.8 m apart. The southern two stones have weathered faces on their western sides but are smooth on the east. This is reversed on the northern menhir. The southern stone has a distinctive narrow pointed finger-like top and its overall form is sinuous. The surface is covered with a mass of meandering cracks and fissures. The middle stone has a series of deep weathering lines on its broad eastern face running from top to bottom. In contrast, the western face is virtually flat. The southern narrow face is extremely thin and faces a similar narrow edge on the southern menhir. The wider edges of both stones face away from each other. A similar mirroring between the stones occurs in respect of the highest point of each stone. There is a sort of crude but clear symmetry between these stones when viewed from the side. The northern menhir is set slightly further apart from the other two stones. It has a smooth, almost concave, western face with a vertical deep and wide weathering channel running down through the centre of the stone. Jutting out within this channel are a couple of irregular bosses in its centre. In contrast to the other two menhirs, the eastern side of this stone is smooth. Also unlike the other two stones, the narrow sides are the same width. Both this, the northern stone, and the southern menhir are in direct alignment with the middle stone set slightly to the east. This arrangement means that all three stones can be seen through their alignment when seen from the north or south. What is interesting about this grouping is that, despite the inherent differences between the stones, there is a recognizable attempt to unify them through their subtle arrangement. They are compared and contrasted simultaneously. In contrast to the thin flat slabs of Kerfland, the three menhirs at Plomelin are massive and rotund. They range from 3.7 m to 4.7 m high, the largest with a girth of 8.1 m at the base. Their displaced arrangement strides a fast-flowing brook. Clearly there was a significant relationship between the flow of clear fresh water and stones.

Of the other menhirs, the stone at du Guiric on the outskirts of Pont l'Abbé has a highly unusual form. It is a massive stone 4.3 m high and 8.9 m in circumference at the base. Seen from the south, it splays out towards the top, contrasting with the tapering form of most stones (Fig. 2.27). By contrast, the eastern short face is massively thick at the base, tapering to a long narrow ridge at the top. The top ridge of the stone is arched like an elephant's back and is incised with weathering grooves running downwards from the apex. The stone at Kerscaven, situated in a stream bed, the most massive in Finistère, has a most unusual shape with vast west–east long faces and narrow north–south short faces with a distinctively teat-like or pointed top, directly resembling almost exactly in form the so-called

Figure 2.27 The du Guiric menhir, Pont l'Abbé, seen from the south.

'buckler' or anthropomorphic motif found in engravings on the stones of Breton passage graves (see Shee Twohig 1981). Its sheer scale is difficult to over-emphasize, yet, set in a shallow wooded valley bottom, it could not have been seen in the wider landscape. In contrast to the grounded massiveness of the Kerscaven menhir is another stone some 100 m away. At 7 m high, this is slightly taller but consider-

Figure 2.28 The southern menhir at Kerscaven, seen from the west.

ably thinner with a distinctively fluted and weathered broad western face and a much smoother and more regular eastern face. The visual effect of this stone is extraordinary (Fig. 2.28). It looks like a fossilized plant with frond-like fingers emerging from a solid stem base. The jagged top is suggestive of growth and upward movement.

The tall menhir at Le Ruen, which is 6 m high, has four utterly distinctive faces. The broad southern elevation of this stone is smooth and faces the sea, which is a few hundred metres away. The north broad face has shallow depressions all over the upper part. The narrow eastern side has a series of very deep vertical cracks running right down the edge. This contrasts completely with the western side, which is flat and plain. The menhir is unusually, for this area, situated near to a series of low outcropping rocks to the west, south and east. One of these 7 m to the SSW has a series of shallow and irregular solution basins on its uppermost surface. To the east there is a V-shaped passage grave whose capstones have solution basins on their uppermost surfaces. Adjacent to this grave are a number of large flat stones which have numerous cup marks and grooves carved into them.

Sub-regional Comparisons

There is a very marked difference between the characteristic of the stones in each of the sub-regional groups of menhirs (see Table 2.1). Local sources of rock are used in all cases and there is no evidence of any long-distance movement of stones. From our visual analysis of rock types and nearby stone sources most appear to have been found in the vicinity of where they were erected. Even in cases where you could suggest that the stone was transported over a longer distance this would have rarely exceeded a few kilometres. Also the individual differences between the menhirs in each group, such as the presence of distinctive cracks, weathering lines or depressions, are simply explicable in terms of the character of the local source material available: for example, schists and quartzites in the Montagnes Noires and the Crozon peninsula, differing kinds and qualities of granite elsewhere.

Other differences between the menhirs in each region must reflect the deliberate choices in selecting stones. The menhirs are frequently much taller in Bas Léon and Haut Léon than elsewhere, whilst those on the Crozon peninsula and in the Montagnes Noires tend to be much slenderer pillars. Bas Léon is utterly distinctive in terms of the dominance of impressive axe-shaped menhirs. Elsewhere most menhirs are highly individual in character, with the majority being irregular stones of markedly different form and character. There are no areas without both static and growing forms, but static forms are most frequent in all areas except Penmarc'h, where growing forms dominate. In Haut Léon and Cap Sizun there are equal numbers of static and growing forms. The stones that are most variable in terms of the numbers of distinct faces, and which often look completely different when seen from different directions, are in the Monts d'Arrée, the Crozon peninsula and Penmarc'h, although there is as much variation between the stones within groups as between them. Throughout Finistère there are only a handful of decorated stones and all but a few menhirs are found well away from all other types of megalithic monuments.

Table 2.1 Sub-regional comparisons between the different groups of menhirs.

Area	Ht	Circ.	Grow.	Wealth.	Crack.	Dep.	HtAS	D. St.	D. CC	D. NC
A	5.3	4.8	21.5	6	20	20	53	0.43	2.8	4.5
B	5.2	5.7	50.0	20	20	10	25	0.60	1.1	2.7
C	4.4	5.4	22.3	11	22	11	223	0.48	–	–
D	3.0	3.6	12.5	0	0	12	199	0.88	–	–
E	2.6	3.8	14.3	0	0	0	79	0.67	–	–
F	3.8	4.9	50.0	0	10	0	56	0.40	0.9	1.3
G	4.3	5.0	25.0	12	24	0	49	0.15	3.7	5.9
H	4.0	6.1	75.0	42	38	21	18	0.22	2.3	3.6

Area: A – Bas Léon; B – Haut Léon; C – Monts d'Arrée; D – Montagnes Noires; E – Crozon peninsula; F – Le Cap Sizun; G – Pays bigouden; H – Penmarc'h. Ht = Mean height of menhirs. Circ. = Mean circumference at base. Grow = Percentage of 'growing' forms. Wealth = Percentage of menhirs with distinctive weathering lines. Crack = Percentage of menhirs with distinctive cracks. Dep. = Percentage of menhirs with distinctive depressions. HtAS = Mean height above present-day sea level. D. St. = Mean distance of menhirs to nearest stream or river. D. CC = Mean distance of menhirs to contemporary coastline (no calculations made for menhirs on the Crozon peninsula or the two inland groups). D. NC = Mean distance of menhirs to Neolithic coastline.

Despite the great size and mass of many of the menhirs, most are not highly visible when viewed from long distances. It is as if their presence was known and their encounter anticipated through this knowledge. Visual prominence in the wider landscape was not their principal expression. Today, in a landscape with relatively few trees, none, except those forming pairs or short settings of three stones, are intervisible. In the much more densely wooded Neolithic environment, given even that many menhirs have been removed or destroyed, we can be reasonably certain that all or most stones would not have been intervisible. Rarely situated on high points, but more usually on sloping land or along valley sides, they would have been monuments one encountered while moving through the landscape rather than landscape markers serving to visually orientate movement through it in relation to each other. Similarly, there is no discernible spatial sequencing of the menhirs in the landscape with regard to their shape and form. Precisely where tall or squat, heavily weathered or smoother stones or stones of markedly different shape occur is extremely variable. Likewise, the orientation of the broad face, or long axis, of the menhirs barely has any significance in terms of a relationship with other stones or distinct topographic features of the landscape such as watercourses or nearby rock outcrops. Menhirs do not point towards or reference these local places, and the large variety of orientations do not suggest any kind of celestial theme or astronomical significance. What seems to be important instead is one good broad face of the menhir and what it 'looks' out on, or towards. The narrower side faces are not significant in this respect. This expression can be seen in menhirs located on the cliff tops around the Baie de Douarnenez. Here the stones have their broad face directed towards the ocean.

The impact of these menhirs on the landscape was thus highly localized and furthermore seems to have changed through time (see the discussion below). Generalizing regarding the landscape settings of the stones, we can distinguish five basic sets of relationships in relation to the sub-regional groups of menhirs:

1. *Bas Léon*: The menhirs stand prominent in an otherwise fairly featureless landscape and completely contrast with it. The vertical form interrupts the dominant horizontal of the landscape. They punctuate the landscape and form localized markers, visible today for 500 m or more from certain directions.
2. *Monts d'Arrée and Haut Léon*: The menhirs create a spatial dialectic with rock outcrops that differentiate and break up the land. Menhirs stand apart, separate, but in clear association with these outcrops.
3. *Montagnes Noires and Monts d'Arrée*: The menhirs follow and mimic the lines created by ridge tops.
4. *Crozon peninsula and Cap Sizun*: The menhirs mark points along coastal hills and cliffs.
5. *Pays bigouden and the Penmarc'h peninsula*: The menhirs mark places along watercourses in heavily wooded valleys, remaining virtually invisible until the moment of arrival.

Interpreting the Stones

The post-glacial change in sea level during the Mesolithic, in which the sea rose by around 16 m, must have had a profound effect on hunter-gatherer-fisher populations of coastal areas of Brittany. The impact of such a transformation would have been known about and described through stories much further afield. The marine inundation was a world-event to the Mesolithic populations of western Europe. Towards the end of the Mesolithic, sea level rise had passed its peak and present-day low tide levels had been reached. However, major oscillations in sea level continued throughout the later prehistoric period. There was a major rise in sea level between the Neolithic and middle Bronze Age periods, and subsequent changes have left the Neolithic coastline submerged by around 8 m (Morzadec-Kerfourn 1985; Prigent et al. 1983). The post-Neolithic submergence of the land has resulted in some menhirs, originally located inland, now being situated on or very near the coast. Others are now on islands which were originally part of the mainland, while some have disappeared altogether. It is also important to appreciate that there were also considerable local variations in the effects of rising sea levels which would have resulted in greater social impact in some areas than in others.

In Finistère, post-Neolithic sea level change has had a far greater effect on the flat low-lying areas of Le Pays bigouden and the Penmarc'h peninsula than, it seems, in the areas to the north. In the former the difference between the distance between the menhirs and the present-day and Neolithic coastline differs by as much as 2.2 km. On the Penmarc'h peninsula it may be as much as 6 km in some places. By contrast, the average difference between the menhirs and the two coastlines along Le Cap Sizun is only a few hundred metres. For those menhirs situated along the cliff tops of the Crozon peninsula today the distance from the Neolithic coastline would have been about 1.2 km. Average differences for the menhirs in the Bas Léon and Haut Léon groups are between 1.6 and 1.7 km but at each location the precise variation in the relationship between individual menhirs and the two coastlines differs according to local geographic circumstance.

Recent field walking in Finistère has discovered substantial numbers of Meso-lithic locales in a band about 20 km away from the present coast and other sites up to 50 km inland (Gouletquer et al. 1996). Scarre has interpreted this evidence as suggesting structured seasonal movement from coastal to inland upland areas along blocks of land defined by north–south river valleys (Scarre 2001: 290). A similar pattern of seasonal mobility between inland and coastal areas seems likely throughout the Neolithic, and many of the menhirs may have been erected along and in relation to these paths of movement.

The marine transgression during the Mesolithic and after would have had a profound effect upon the patterns of seasonal movements of the local populations. Those coastal areas most affected by the rise in sea level seem to have been those most favoured judging from the density of menhirs and other monuments (Hibbs 1983: 274; Scarre 2001), assuming we can take monument density as an indicator of such preferment. Rising sea levels would have dislocated the movements and resource exploitation strategies of local communities. Not only would resources and favoured places for settlement be lost, but old familiar landmarks would disappear and new ones would be created. Physical and social geographies would be radically altered in tandem. Old networks of tracks would be replaced by new ones and the life-time biographies of individuals and groups would be substantially transformed. Salt water would pollute fresh water, river channels would become coastal estuaries, rock outcrops would become islands, lagoons would be flooded. Significant local landmarks such as ancient trees would be killed and then washed away. In short, a sense of place as unchanging and immutable, rooted in an an-cestral past which was unalterable, could not exist. Place became transient and always vulnerable to encroachment by the sea. The violence of the Atlantic storm waves pounding the coastline of Brittany today is a fearsome sight and so it was in the past. And who could have told if the sea would ever stop rising? What could prevent the ocean from eating away at the land and disrupting traditional patterns of movement and rest? Hunting grounds and old trees, traditional encampments, rocks and landmarks were lost. The very transformation of the coastal landscape might well have given birth to fundamental set of mythic beliefs among the Mesolithic populations, both passed down and altered from generation to generation. Indeed, the ideological importance of the change in sea level and the disruption it inevitably created for social geographies may have been far more profound than any economic impact. It was the loss of place, and the social relationships and memories rooted in those places, rather than the loss of resources, that would have wrought the greatest changes to society.

The available pollen evidence suggests sporadic and temporary forest clearance during the final Mesolithic and early Neolithic to create pasture and gardens, and we can assume that this process continued on a small scale and may have gradually intensified during the Neolithic, but only in the late second millennium BC (final Bronze Age) does land clearance appear to be extensive apart from in the Morbihan area of southern Brittany, where large-scale deforestation took place during the middle Neolithic (Marguerie 1992). If the loss of land to the sea and the transformation of the coastline had profound ideological effects among hunter-gatherer-fisher populations, we might expect the prospect to be even more traumatic to those who had started to actively invest in the land and were beginning to substantially alter it themselves. In erecting menhirs, communities were tapping into already established ancestral work – markers, such as rock outcrops, or boundaries, such as watercourses in the landscape – and referencing their significance. In Finistère a large number of the menhirs are significantly associated with fresh water. Many are actually situated in stream beds, alongside watercourses or near to springs. Those in Haut Léon are closely associated with granite outcrops with stones riddled with solution basins collecting the purest water of all, that from the heavens. Two are erected from massive stones containing solution basins. A similar association with rocks containing solution basins also occurs in the low-lying area of Penmarc'h. It is perhaps significant with respect to the theme of rising sea levels that the broad faces of the coastally situated menhirs along the cliffs of the Crozon peninsula and along Le Cap Sizun look directly out across the sea. By contrast with the groups of menhirs situated near to the coast, the inland groups of the Monts d'Arrée and the Montagnes Noires are not closely associated with watercourses (see Table 2.1).

One of the reasons for erecting the menhirs in coastal areas may have been for them to act in some way as the guardian spirits of fresh water. They could have acted as means of symbolically stabilizing the land against the future encroachment of the sea. There is an interesting body of folklore beliefs associated with some of the stones in this connection. For example, the huge Men-Marz menhir in Haut Léon is said to have been set up magically by the sister of St Pol. From the moment the stone was erected, the sea became obedient and ceased to devastate the lands of the abbey.

The axe-shaped menhirs of Bas Léon were probably erected significantly later than many of the unshaped menhirs (Burl 1985; Giot 1988) and may be late Neolithic or early Bronze Age in date. In all areas of Finistère (except the Crozon peninsula and the Le Pays bigouden) there are also a small number of triangular or more irregularly shaped menhirs that look like axe blades when seen from one or two sides. These stones were obviously chosen because of their fortuitous resemblance to axe blades, but they often bear little resemblance to the form of an axe when seen from a different direction. This characteristic creates multiple referential potential compared with the carefully shaped stones of Bas Léon. Elsewhere, larger unshaped stones may have suggested the form of the axe when seen from one side or another. The menhirs of Bas Léon were actually shaped into axes, their symbolic blades implanted into the ground. In the course of shaping the stones, their potential for bearing multiple meanings was replaced by one single dominant meaning in these instances. It appears that, as the tradition of erecting menhirs became adopted and widespread, the potential of likening the form of the menhir to the axe reached its culmination after a long period during which sea levels seem to have remained relatively stable. The shaping and erection of the giant axe-like menhirs in the landscape of Bas Léon was perhaps a form of reference to, and acknowledgement of, this creative force of the ancestors, whose own axes had been congealed into the stones and subsequently revealed by the sea. From this origin in salt water, these stones were taken inland to be erected near to the springheads and passages of fresh water, the source of all life.

Conclusions

A significant number of the earlier menhirs in Finistère with their curved dynamic profiles suggest themes of fertility and growth. Perhaps those stones of anthropomorphic form are linked to a theme of human reproduction. Some menhirs can be likened to great bulbous rhizomes being inserted into the ground. The menhirs growing from the soil and nurtured by fresh water would prevent the incursion of the sea. Such a metaphor of growth links the stone with the soil and the other elements, such as fresh water, in a participatory relationship. The stone has its being in and of the desired 'natural' world and 'fleshily' shares in its development. This implies that such stones were considered to be alive, capable of moving, things inherent with creative power growing towards the sky. In some instances the potency of the stones could have been activated by fresh water and thus empowered to repel the marine spirits stealing the land. Fresh water and sea water could be seen as opposites in such circumstances.

By contrast, the erection of the axe-shaped menhirs of Bas Léon may have signified part of a developing conceptual distinction between humanity and the land. A metaphor of organic growth of stones from the soil was replaced by a metaphor of wilful transformation and dominance over 'nature' and 'natural' forces. Unshaped stones were being transformed into axes, their individuality of form and any sense of dynamism removed. Their blades forced down into the ground, these static axe menhirs represented in a basic way an act of force, violence, authority and control, an intervention in the world. Through its clearance and large-scale modification, the land had become transformed from something which was a subject of human endeavour to an object of human authority and control. This may well have been associated with an economic change to a society in which the primary mode of subsistence was now agriculture rather than hunting, fishing and gathering. In a landscape that was cleared for farming, menhirs gained a much greater potential to serve as landscape or territorial markers signifying the affiliation of different groups with discrete areas of land. The significance and meaning of the menhir tradition changed and they became signifiers of people taking control over and laying claim to the landscape and altering it on a massive scale. This stands in opposition to the more ancestral and mythic connections of unshaped stones, whose potential for establishing and maintaining a sense of individual or group difference was considerably reduced. These menhirs, however, might be reindividualized, reworked and transformed into axe symbols themselves through the addition of decorations and plastic forms such as the cup marks and bosses on the menhir at Kerloas. Other axes were by weathering revealed gradually from the very fabric of the stone, grain by grain. These axes could be interpreted as those belonging to either the gods or the ancestors, symbols of their creative power, and these and their number and position would serve to create difference between menhirs. The transformation of the stone brought about by physical activity and social commitment is itself a powerful metaphor for the transformation of old landscape into new.

–3–

From Honey to Ochre

Maltese Temples, Stones, Substances and the
Structuring of Experience

Introduction

The Maltese islands are situated in approximately the middle of the long axis of the Mediterranean about 90 km to the south of Sicily and roughly three times that distance from the African coast (see Fig. 3.1). During the course of the Neolithic, these relatively isolated islands were the site of a temple architecture that is without any convincing parallels elsewhere and has always been a point of fascination. The age and sheer complexity of these monuments, the earliest free-standing structures in the world, provide striking evidence, if any was needed, to destroy the myth of primitivism (Renfrew 1973).

The origins of these temples has always been a primary question. Why was it that on Malta and nowhere else that these monumental structures were erected? Current evidence suggests an initial settling of the Maltese islands around 5500 BC by settlers from Sicily, and Maltese material culture for about 2,000 years remained basically similar to that documented for Sicily and southern Italy. Around 3600 BC the inhabitants began to build temples and continued to do so for over a millennium. The unique character of the temple architecture has been explained over and over again as a product of cultural isolation (Evans 1959; Stoddart et al. 1993; Patton 1996; Bonnano 1996). Renfrew regarded temple clusters as being the territorial centres of redistributive chiefdoms (Renfrew 1973: 168). Each territory might have up to 2,000 persons with a specialized priesthood. Malta's apparent isolation has also provided a ready-made potential explanation for the end of the period of temple construction and use. The fragile island environment with limited natural resources became degraded, creating insuperable economic problems for populations living on scarce resources (Trump 1976, 1981; Renfrew 1973; Malone et al. 1993).

Robb has recently challenged these interpretations, pointing out that Malta was not as isolated as claimed and that a wide network of regional exchanges linked the islands to Neolithic societies beyond: 'Malta's apparent isolation at least partially reflects archaeologists looking at Malta in isolation' (Robb 2001: 189). The boat

Figure 3.1 The location of the Maltese islands.

journey to Sicily could be undertaken in just a few days. High-quality flint, obsidian, hard stone for axes, lava for grindstones, alabaster, semi-precious stones, ochre lavishly used for burial and temple decoration, were all imported, suggesting regular and necessary contacts (*ibid.*: 188). Maltese economic products and technologies exhibit no substantial differences from Sicily and southern Italy, and similarities can be seen in the use of rock-cut tombs for burial, and other related practices. Robb also underlines the almost complete lack of any evidence for either population growth or environmental degradation and economic decline during the temple period. He argues that the unique temple architecture can be understood instead as the cultural construction of difference. The ancient Maltese deliberately created their own world, made themselves different, and the islands themselves were a symbolic resource in this process, sources of ideas, rather than just an environment in which to live. People did not passively slip into cultural difference because of their isolation. They actively created this difference to establish and maintain their own identity:

> islands were key to this process of differentiation, not as environmental determinants, but as ideas. Islands are inhabited metaphors, natural symbols of boundedness and separa-
> tion . . . new social relations emphasizing local originality and distinctiveness were mapped onto the idiosyncrasies of local geography to render immanent the new cultural gap between the group that was in the process of becoming Maltese and the groups in the process of becoming 'others'. In cultural terms, the Maltese didn't live on an island. They built themselves one. (*ibid.*: 192)

Following Robb's cogent thesis, the intention of this chapter is to investigate more specifically just how Maltese cultural difference was established and main-tained through temple construction and use. Investigating the 'idiosyncrasies of the local geography', almost completely ignored in archaeological accounts, which have always focused on the temples themselves, we argue that the idea of building temples developed from an intimate interaction between the Neolithic settlers of the Maltese islands and their new island home. It was a product of thinking place, of creatively relating an architectural order to an ordering of the landscape beyond. Becoming Maltese involved mediating the landscape through architecture so that people could re-think themselves and their place in the world. Tracing the develop-mental sequence of temple architectural forms, we suggest that in the baroque elaboration of the final forms of the temples their meanings became so complex and over-determined that they could no longer serve as meaningful resources for the construction and maintenance of social identities. Knowledge became increas-ingly unstable, and ultimately their cumulative effect was both disorientating and destabilizing. Rather than enabling people to understand place and landscape, a sense of locality and belonging, an interiorized world was created in the temples in which the notion of a wider island identity became imploded into the very form of the monuments themselves. They became dislocated and meaningless in relation to the landscape beyond and in so doing they could no longer relate people to place.

Architecture and Landscape

Around thirty temples are known on the two main islands, Malta and Gozo (Fig. 3.2), and the general developmental sequence of the temple architecture is well established in the literature (Evans 1959, 1971; Trump 1966, 2000). The earliest temples were lobed or trefoil in plan, arranged around a central axis (see Fig. 3.13: A) leading to the development of much more complex and elaborate four-, five-

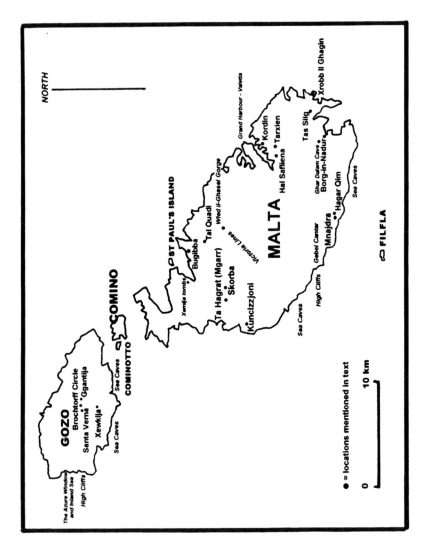

Figure 3.2 The location of the Maltese temples and other places discussed in the text.

and six-apse forms. The majority of the temples stand next to each other in clusters many of which became reconstructed and linked together in various ways, creating a far more complex and intricate series of internal spaces (see Figs 3.6, 3.13, 3.21). They may contain between four and twenty or more differentiated spaces together with passageways and niches with stone tables and 'altars' all enclosed within a massive retaining wall with an external façade and forecourt area at the front. All temples whose development can be reconstructed show a number of remodelling phases, especially in the final Tarxien period (3000–2400 BC).

While all the temple sites are uniquely situated and related to their own landscapes, there are also a number of repetitive features shared by a number of temples which are listed below:

1. An association with the sea and more particularly small off-shore islets, perhaps visited as liminal places during initiation and other rites. In the south, Hagar Qim and Mnajdra both reference Filfla island, from which pottery and other finds from the temple period are recorded (Trump 2000: 110). While probably not settled, this island was certainly visited. On the north coast the Bugibba temple may similarly be related to St Paul's island, clearly visible from the temple site. Some temple locales are directly related to places where one would leave this island world to journey elsewhere. The Kordin temples are near to complex deep-water inlets of the Grand Harbour, Borg-in-Nadur only a few hundred metres from a suitable landing place, as are Hagar Qim and Mnajdra, and Bugibba is even closer.

2. A close association with rivers or wadis (usually seasonal watercourses) that both structure and create natural boundaries in the landscape beyond. Together with the coastline and the escarpment lines of rock outcrops in the north-west of the islands, such as the Victoria Lines, the wadis constitute some of the most dramatic landscape features of Malta with their deeply incised valleys and gorges. Many of the deeply incised wadi courses resemble open-air caves in their narrowing and rising passage, curved and sinuous walls. The sides of the wadis are pockmarked with numerous small caves and rock overhangs and fissures. Sometimes, about half-way up the steep sides, clearly defined ledges occur up to a few metres in width along which one can walk or look down into the hidden depths. Although dry now for most of the year many provided a perennial source of fresh water in the past. The temple at Borg-in-Nadur lies a few hundred metres from the coast but is situated between two wadi channels, one to the east and one to the west. Similarly, Hagar Qim and Mnajdra are coastally situated between wadi valleys to the west and east. The temple site of Kuncizzjoni on the east of Malta is situated between north-flowing wadis. Inland temple locales (i.e. those not situated near to or directly on the coast) are invariably situated along wadi valleys that run down to the sea (e.g. Skorba, Ta

Hagrat and Tal Quadi on Malta and Ggantija on Gozo, which is located on a high plateau area defined by deeply incised wadi valleys to the west and east

3. Only two temple sites occupy *local* high points, Tas Silg and Hagar Qim. The remainder are located on upper or lower hill slopes overlooking either the sea or fertile inland valleys. They are not sited for maximum visibility. Nearby temples in close relationship – such as Hagar Qim and Mnajdra; Ggjantija, and Santa Verna and Xewkija; Borg-in-Nadur and Tas Silg – are intervisible, while Tarxien and Kordin, Skorba and Ta Hagrat may have been. Urban areas or intervening houses now block the view. Smaller temples are more isolated and are not intervisible with other temple locales (e.g. Xrobb Il Ghagin, Bugibba, Tal Quadi, Kuncizzjoni).

4. Pairs of nearby temple sites may be related to each other in terms of higher and lower locations in the landscape, respectively: Skorba and Ta Hagrat; Hagar Qim and Mnajdra; Tarxien and Kordin. In the first two cases the higher temple is to the east and the lower temple to the west. In the last case the higher temple is to the south and the lower temple is to the north.

That these were temples, or ritual monuments, is beyond doubt. The very few domestic structures that are known are utterly different in form and by comparison rather insubstantial oval or round huts (Trump 1966; Malone et al. 1988). Collective burial took place in caves and underground rock-cut tombs. Two huge underground burial complexes are known, the hypogeum of Hal Safliena on Malta and the Brochtorff Circle on Gozo (Evans 1971; Malone et al. 1995). These are almost certainly connected with the nearby contemporaneous temples at Tarxien and Ggantija, respectively, to and from which there may have been ceremonial pathways. Ggantija and the Brochtorff Circle, 300 m apart, are just intervisible. Tarxien and Hal Safliena, less than 500 m apart, may have been so. The entrance to the latter may originally have been provided with an external megalithic façade which would emphasize its position (Evans 1971; Cutajar 2000). Both Hal Safliena and the Brochtorff Circle are on high points in the landscape to the west of the temples. While the dead were being returned underground, these places were conspicuous reference points in the landscape and meant to be visible from some distance away rather than hidden from the temples. Hal Safliena is a maze of underground chambers cut into the rock on three distinct levels in some rooms, replicating details of the temple architecture, but in the negative, created by cutting stone out rather than taking it in. The disarticulated remains of up to 7,000 skeletons have been claimed to have been found there. The Brochtorff Circle, consisting of megalithic stones, enclosed an area of pre-temple period rock-cut tombs entered individually from the surface and an elaborate temple period complex of interconnected chambers associated with elaborate mortuary rituals. While the chambers at Hal Safliena are entirely artificial, cut out of the globigerina limestone, those at the Brochtorff Circle were taken down to embellish natural caverns in the coralline limestone (see the discussion of limestone types below), amongst which shaped megalithic globigerina limestone blocks were strategically placed (Stoddart et al. 1993; Stoddart 1999).

Contextual artefactual evidence for the use of the temples is unfortunately very limited since almost all have been cleared out rather than systematically excavated, Skorba, which is extremely ruinous, and Tarxien being the exceptions (Zammit 1930; Trump 1966; Evans 1971). The main finds include pots and bowls of various sizes and forms, flint and obsidian tools, stone sculptures, obese female ceramic figurines, headless figurines without any clearly defined sexual attributes, beads, axes and axe amulets, and clay and stone phallic representations. Besides representations of human figures, models and carvings in relief of animals, birds and fish have been found. Two friezes in low relief found at the first temple of Tarxien in the left-hand apse depict respectively twenty two sheep or goats and four sheep or goats, a ram and a pig. Elsewhere at Tarxien, figures of humped cattle and a sow suckling her young are carved in relief on a slab of limestone. Representations of snakes occur on two pot sherds from Tarxien and are sculpted in relief at Ggantija. Fish sculpted in relief are documented at Bugibba.

Besides these naturalistic representations, the later temples are decorated with various forms of spiral designs carved in relief and have 'altar' stones and doorway entrances embellished with pit or drill decoration. The sheer complexity and the elaboration through time of the portable material culture of the temples and their internal decorated friezes run in tandem with the growing complexity of their internal architectural spaces.

Topography, Geology and Temple Construction

The Maltese islands consist of two larger islands, Malta and Gozo, and one much smaller island, Comino, situated between the two, together with a number of tiny offshore islets, St Paul's island, Cominotto and Filfla, and offshore rocks (Fig. 3.2). Malta is the largest island of the group, 28 km long and 13 km wide with a land area of only 237 sq. km. Gozo is just over 14 km long and 7 km wide at its widest point with a land area of 66 sq. km and separated from Malta by a sea channel 8 km wide. It is worth emphasizing what a tiny island world this is. Malta is only about the same size as the Isle of Wight in England, and one can walk across it in a day.

Geologically, the islands are gradually being tilted to the east and north-east, so that the highest sea cliffs are found in the west and south-west while ancient river channels are drowned in the north-east, creating the Grand Harbour of Valetta. The lines of the main hills and rock outcrops follow the long axis of the islands themselves, south-east to north-west, becoming more rugged and hilly to the north-west.

These are cut across by the largest river or wadi channels running from south-west to north-east.

The rocks of which the Maltese islands are composed were all laid down during a relatively brief period of the Miocene era. Apart from scattered and superficial Quaternary deposits, they are all sedimentary rocks, The oldest formations are the lower coralline limestone, forming most of Malta's southern and south-western sheer and imposing coastline and outcropping inland along fault lines (Hyde 1955; Pedley et al. 1976). Above these are the softer globigerina limestone formations, blue clay and greensand beds and the most geologically recent formations, the upper coralline limestone. The globigerina limestone outcrops widely in south-eastern Malta and extends over two-thirds of the island's surface, creating a gentle rolling topography with shallow valleys and wide ridges. The upper coralline limestone outcrops cover almost a quarter of the surface area of Malta and Gozo and form the highest points and the most dramatic rock outcrops on both islands. This limestone is important as an aquifer, giving rise to the high-level springs of upland areas of Malta and Gozo. Sink holes and subterranean caverns also occur in the limestone. Two collapsed caverns are of particular note: Il Maqluba near to the south coast of Malta and the Inland Sea at Dwejra on the far west coast of Gozo, where the sea enters a cliff-encircled pool through a narrow cave inlet. Both are huge crater-like depressions with sheer sides created by the caving in of the surface rocks above subterranean caverns. Il Magluba, only 1.4 km ENE of the temple complex at Hagar Qim, is about 100 m in diameter and more than 60 m deep, and is undoubtably one of the most dramatic inland features of Malta. Hyde reports that 'it is said that the sink hole of Magluba is at times filled up to the brim with water after exceptionally heavy rainfall. A few days later all this water has disappeared' (Hyde 1955: 20).

Topographically, Gozo contrasts greatly with Malta. The whole western part of the island is dominated inland by flat-topped mesa-like hills with sharp escarpment edges formed by the outcropping rocks of the coralline limestone. There are many fallen blocks below them and numerous fissures, smaller and larger caves and rock overhangs. Gozo is cut through, like Malta, by a series of wadis which form steep-sided gorges in the southern and western parts of the island. The current state of these wadis, arid and dry for most of the year, is a recent phenomenon caused by over-exploitation and a lowering of the water table through extraction (Haslam and Borg 1998).

The cliffs of Malta and Gozo are rich with sea caves, grottos and arches, some of which have become famous on account of the striking colours of the sea water. The most spectacular of the arches is found near to the Inland Sea on the west coast of Gozo, It-Tiequa or the 'Azure Window' (see Fig. 3.5). This is a massive sea arch which looks like a monumental doorway. Until recently, when a massive piece of rock collapsed, it was almost perfectly rectangular in form (Cauchi 1982: 13).

Both the coralline and the globigerina limestones were used to construct the temples. The qualities of these two very different types of limestone probably cannot be over-stressed in understanding the form and character of the temples themselves. The coralline limestone is extremely hard, resistant to weathering and difficult to shape and work. It varies in colour from white to cream to blue-grey to pink-grey. Being hard and durable, it makes an excellent but difficult building material. As a result of complexes of horizontal and vertical faults, it frequently weathers out into blocks or natural 'megaliths' which lie scattered around on the ground, providing ready-made building material. Through chemical solution, the coralline limestones long exposed at the surface frequently develop a toughened skin, which may be 0.6 m or more deep, known as a tufa mantle (Zammit Maemphel 1977: 28). The weathered surfaces of this stone are often highly irregular in form filled with holes and depressions, giving them a fantastically gnarled appearance (Fig. 3.3).

The globigerina limestone, although technically a limestone deposit, being composed entirely of minute fragments of mollusc shells, in many respects resembles a sandstone. A honey-yellow in colour, it is compact and grainy, soft and easily cut and worked with hand tools to create blocks with an extremely smooth and regular surface (see Fig. 3.23). Unlike the coralline limestone, it naturally lends itself to the creation of geometric shapes and architectural components. Once cut, it develops a relatively hard patina when exposed to the air, but once this hardened surface is broken, it may very rapidly erode away. In many older buildings a characteristic weathering sequence can be seen, an initial honeycombing where the whole surface of the stone becomes riddled with holes, after which disintegration through cavitation and flaking occurs (see Fig. 3.31)

Rough and undressed blocks and slabs of coralline limestone were the sole building material used to construct the earliest of the Maltese temples. In later temples it was still employed as a hard and durable outer casing with the globigerina limestone being used inside the temple spaces. In one of the latest temples to be built or reconstructed, Hagar Qim, the globigerina limestone is also used to construct the external façades. These very different raw materials employed in temple construction contrast with each other in a number of striking ways and can be, summarized as follows:

Coralline limestone	*Globigerina limestone*
Feels hard	Feels soft
Looks cold	Looks warm
Greys to whites to reds to blues	Honey yellow
Irregular shapes	Uniform shapes
Durable	Friable
Gnarled and rough surfaces	Smooth surfaces

Figure 3.3 Characteristic weathering in the coralline limestone.

Natural forms	Cultural forms
High rock outcrops	Lower areas in landscape
Found as megaliths	Must be shaped into megaliths
On the surface	Below the surface
Looks old	Looks new

A very significant aspect of the manner in which the temples were experienced directly relates to the qualities of the stones from which they were constructed, where they were found in the landscape, the origins of these stones, and their associations. All the most dramatic and awe-inspiring features of the Maltese landscape occur in the topography of the coralline limestone. It forms the dramatic and towering sea cliffs of the south and south-west coast, the inland gorges and deeply incised wadi channels that divide the land, the towering linear rock outcrops, the peculiarly shaped mesa-like hills of Gozo, the numerous sea and inland caves. It is at the base of the coralline limestone, where clays occur, that percolating rain water issues forth as springs that are so vital to life on the island. By contrast, the topography created by the globigerina limestone is relatively unmarked and indistinct. Even if caves and arches are sometimes created along the coast, such features are soon undercut, destroyed and washed away.

The very different visual and tactile qualities of the two types of rock are striking. The external architecture of the temple skins built of the coralline limestone look and feel utterly different from the perfectly uniform and regular blocks that could be cut out of the globigerina limestone. In the earlier temples the globigerina limestone tends to be exclusively used for important transition points in the internal temple architecture such as portal doorways and entrance corridors in which bar and rope holes could easily be cut. In some later temples almost everything would be cut from this stone. While the globigerina blocks must have been quarried from out of the ground, the coralline blocks would be collected from the surface and used pretty much as found. The coralline blocks have their own forms and individual characteristics, whereas the globigerina limestone could be cut to standardized and determined shapes as required. The coralline limestone came ready-made; the blocks of globigerina had to be produced. The former is collected as a natural product; the latter is entirely a work of cultural transformation. Any temple built from the coralline limestone even if the blocks were smooth and covered on the inside with *torba*, a form of cement applied to the floor and walls, would look ancient and gnarled on the outside, while the form of an external façade, if made from the globigerina limestone, would look strikingly uniform and new.

No dramatic rock outcrops occur in areas covered with the globigerina limestone. This is gentle rolling terrain, but if the coralline limestone can be characterized as the hard skeletal core of Malta, the globigerina constitutes its flesh. On the coralline limestone only poor thin soils occur, the globigerina both breaks down and can be broken down with effort into an extremely fertile soil on which crops flourish if there is an adequate water supply. It can also crushed to create *torba*.

The relationship of all the older Maltese temples to the landscape was clearly mimetic. They resembled the form and character of the outcropping rocks visible from them in various ways (see the discussion of Ggantija below). In contrast, the façade of the remodelled temple at Hagar Qim, one of the latest temple locales to be rebuilt, was constructed out of the globigerina limestone. It seems to have been designed to deliberately stand out and contrast with its surroundings.

Where did the inspiration come from to build these temples? Two main arguments have been made. One suggestion is that a template or model for the early temples is to be found in the resemblance of their ground plans to figurines depicting the corpulent body of a 'fertility goddess'. The early three- and five-apse temple forms thus represent this goddess lying on her back, with all the implied symbolism of sexuality and fertility. The comparison is indeed striking, but only if we think of the temple in terms of an architectural plan.

The second argument is the suggestion that the form of the temples resemble those of earlier rock-cut tombs. Evans points out that a comparison of the ground plans of the earliest known temple structure at Ta Hagrat, Mgarr, with its lobed chambers, looks very similar to the plans of earlier rock-cut tombs such as those at Xemija. The temples represented an attempt to reproduce the structure of the rock-cut tombs above ground (Evans 1959: 90). This argument has been repeated by others (e.g. Trump 1981; Bonanno 1996). Similarities between the form and architectural structures of the hypogeum at Hal Saflieni and the Brochtorff Circle and the temples have been noted. (Evans 1971; Stoddart et al. 1993: 14). In explicit details of their architectural form such as the cutting of trilithons and niches and corbelling at the hypogeum, these underground labyriths do indeed imitate the temples below the ground. They can thus be considered to be temples for the dead. We know that they were made and used during the later period of temple construction, not before it took place. We also know that the temples were not used for burial.

The argument that the temples were modelled as replicas of rock-cut tombs is based on a comparison of two-dimensional ground plans. While archaeologists often think and draw comparisons in terms of ground plans, it is unlikely the ancient Maltese did so, however. The physical bodily experience of entering the cramped rock-cut tombs is utterly different from the temple spaces. Such a comparison is further questionable when we consider that only two very early temple structures at Mgarr and Kordin, with lobed chambers, actually look, even in plan, like rock-cut tombs. The far more numerous and widespread three-apse temples look rather different. Evans himself notes in respect to this that 'once under way, the development of the temples and their differentiation from the tombs in form made rapid strides' (Evans 1959: 92).

Evans suggests that the idea of cutting underground tombs for the dead may have been derived from an earlier tradition of cave burials. Artificial caves resembling natural caves were thus constructed to house the remains of the dead. The inspiration came from the daily experience and use of caves in the landscape. A similar argument can be made for the form of the earlier temples. They also resemble the forms of caves, but these are not caves which occur above the ground on the Maltese islands, such as Ghar Dalam, which are essentially linear tunnels or otherwise highly irregular in form, but the numerous smoothed and rounded sea caves and arches encountered along the cliffs such as the Blue Grotto just to the east of the temple complex at Hagar Qim with its symmetrically curving arch and internal apses (Fig. 3.4). The rectangular doorway of the sea arch at Dwejra bears an uncanny resemblance to the forms of the temple doorways such as at Ta Hagrat (Mgarr), and both are formed from the coralline limestone (Fig. 3.5). Such comparisons require no plans. They are directly experienced in the landscape. If such an argument is accepted, it establishes a fundamental link between aspects of the land-locked temple architecture and the world beneath represented by the sea. While social identities were being constructed, metaphorically, out of the solid bones and flesh of the land, the coralline and globigerina limestone, as argued above, they also had their origins in the fluidity of the movements of the sea.

Experiencing the Temple Spaces

So far we have made some general observations about the relationship between the constructional form of the temples and their relationship to the land and the sea. Bonanno et al. (1990: Fig. 5) have successfully used access diagrams to represent the changing complexity of the internal temple spaces, but the problem with such an exercise is that it reduces these spaces to another kind of plan even more abstract than conventional ground plans. In the following section we attempt to phenomenologically explore their internal spaces and their physical effects. This is not intended as an attempt to provide anything approaching a full and comprehensive architectural description. That task has already been masterfully achieved by Evans (1971), to whom our account is indebted. It is rather a more limited attempt to consider some of the bodily experiences of moving through and encountering these spaces. At the outset certain problems should be noted. All the temples are in a ruinous state and have been variously reconstructed. They were continually being built and modified throughout the temple period so that our experience of these places is in their final or latest forms rather than in their original manifestation. Today they are light roofless structures open to the elements. Originally they were dim and relatively cool roofed structures amplifying sound from the inside and shutting out sound from the outside. The effects of sound amplification and light penetration illuminating internal paintings (Pace 2000) could have been striking. Similarly, in the Hal Saflieni hypogeum quite dramatic effects of sound amplification have been reported (Mifsud and Mifsud 1999). The only light entering the temple would have been either through the doorway or, in the case of some of the latest temples, also through small 'oracle holes' in the apse walls. Vassallo (2000) has argued that sunlight was directed to specific central and front areas of the temples, while in other areas, such as the inside apses, no light could

Figure 3.4 The Blue Grotto on the south coast of Malta.

penetrate at any time of year. The internal walls would have been plastered with *torba* in some cases, concealing the rough boulders and surfaces visible today in internal walls of some of the earlier temples built from the coralline limestone, although we cannot be sure of the extent of this, and they were probably beautified with ochre paintings and decorations which we know to exist in the chambers of the hypogeum. The portable artefacts are gone, as are internal furnishings made from organic raw materials such as wooden doorways or hide screens. So our sensory experience of these places is both radically different from that of the ancient Maltese and extremely impoverished. We can only really hope to evoke today a few of the visual and tactile senses of place. We discuss three temple complexes, Ggantija on Gozo, Mnajdra and Hagar Qim on Malta. We have chosen these three temple complexes because, relatively speaking, they are well preserved, and their relationship to the surrounding landscape can still be studied. Other temples in Malta are either so totally ruinous that little appears to be gained from this kind of approach and/or they are engulfed in an urban setting, making a consideration of their wider landscape contexts almost impossible.

Ggantija (Fig. 3.6)

At Ggantija there are two temples built side by side within a massive external façade. The larger and southernmost of these is earliest and has a standard form

Figure 3.5 Top: The entrance to the Ta Hagrat temple, Mgarr. Below: The Azure Window, Gozo.

consisting of five apses connected with passageways. One walks up a series of steps into the entrance of the southern temple. The entrance corridor to the temple is well defined by a threshold stone over which one must pass, and a series of eight

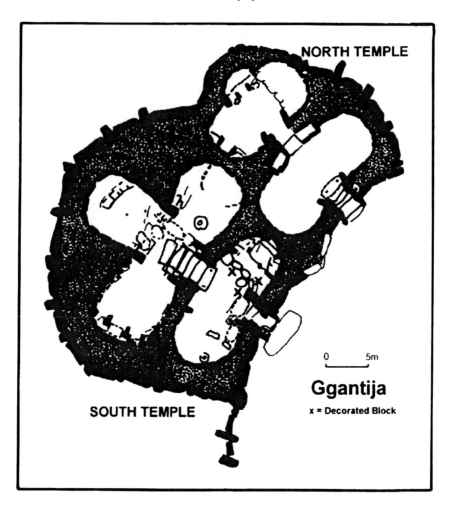

Figure 3.6 Plan of the Ggantija temples, Gozo.

orthostats rising in height from 2.5 m to 3 m as one moves into the temple. The central part of the paved corridor space is deliberately constricted by smaller and lower flanking orthostats which narrow it from 2.10 to 1.35 m at the middle. These are significantly lower (1.8 m) and, if originally capped with lintels, would further emphasize a constricting sense of space. The corridor then widens at the end, with the last and tallest stones set partly behind the others and also forming the corner-stones of the first two apses. The flagstones of the corridor rise slightly as one moves inside, passing through a space which at first constricts, then widens. Walking on a paved floor which gradually heightens, experiencing a roof which is well raised, then lowered, before soaring up at the point where the first side apses are reached – all these features emphasize this corridor space as transitional from inside to outside and are designed to mark this directly on the body as it moves through space. The effect would be far more marked when the temple was originally roofed, involving a movement from light to darkness, from hot to cold, from wind to stillness, from the smells and sounds of the external world to those of the temple itself. From the entrance corridor it is now possible to see all the way to the back of the temple, but the apsoidal form of this space is concealed. Entering into the front rooms of the temples, there is a marked contrast between the left and right apses. That to the left is virtually bare and unfurnished with a simple *torba* floor; that to the right is very elaborated and paved at the back with a raised floor and circular threshold step flanked on either side by decorated blocks with spirals creating a low screen across the apse (Fig. 3.7). These arrangements are only fully visible when entering the central court between the apses. Today the apse walls are irregular and rough in appearance, but excavated evidence shows that originally they were plastered smooth with clay and decorated with red ochre (Evans 1971: 175). The contrast between the rough and irregular external temple façade and the smooth decorated temple interior would have been tremendous. The walls of the front apses soaring up to 3 m or more create an imposing sense of a (domed?) space.

A second corridor leads into the back spaces of the temple, again flanked by orthostats of the globigerina limestone and with a paved floor which gently rises as one passes into the court between the back three apses. These are considerably larger than those at the front of the temple. The apse to the back has a raised floor markedly higher than those to the left or right. Its walls rising up to 5.5 m above ground level are considerably higher than anywhere else in the temple, making an almost overwhelming sensory impression in terms of its sheer size and volume. This space represents the culminating point in the rises of floor and wall levels as one moves through the temple from outside to inside, front to back. Just as the temple floor increases in height, so do its walls, and its apses become larger and wider.

Moving through the entrance corridor, the entirety of the back apse becomes visible, while a full view into the left and right side apses only becomes possible when one moves into the centre of the paved court between them. There is a clear difference here between the left and right apse and again it is the right apse, that is most elaborated. Here a block with a snake decoration, originally part of an elaborate altar arrangement, was found along the south-east wall. The floor is raised at the back with remains of a low kerb, once part of a dais arrangement with a circular stone hearth set into the floor towards the front of the apse. Old prints by Brochtorff (see *ibid.*: Plate 29:1) show that this apse was originally partially blocked and screened by a series of blocks with pit decoration. To enter this space would necessitate stepping up and over these blocks. The left apse is furnished with an elaborate series of niches with capstones running along its back (south-east) wall and with curbstones inset along both side walls (Fig. 3.8).

Figure 3.7 The southern temple at Ggantija: front right apse.

Figure 3.8 The southern temple at Ggantija: altar in the left back apse.

Ggantija south was originally built as a three-apse temple but was modified by the construction of the two front apses. Careful observations by Vassallo have shown that the orientation of the original doorway was such to only allow sunlight to shine through the temple and strike the left-hand side of the back apse at the winter solstice sunrise. When the temple was remodelled, the light hit instead the left-hand stone of the internal entrance corridor from the front to the back room (Vassallo 1999: 45). The visual effects would have been quite striking.

The later northern temple is both considerably smaller and significantly different in form, with the two largest apses at the front, and it lacks a large apse at the back, which has been reduced to a small oval space with a table niche at the front. The floor does not rise up from front to back. This creates a substantially different experiential space for movement in comparison with the earlier southern temple, and this difference must have been deliberately intended. Rather than the temple space opening up, it gets more confined, a reversal of what happens in the southern temple.

The short entrance corridor is not narrowed in the middle by additional internal orthostats and is much simpler in arrangement (Fig. 3.9). The final two orthostats of this corridor are set back from the others, creating a marked opening out of space as one enters into the front room, which is entirely unpaved. These final stones are also significantly higher than the others, an architectural arrangement replicating that found in the southern temple. The front rooms are bare and those to the back reached through passing through a second short entrance corridor only slightly more elaborated. This contrasts with the great degree of elaboration of the front right apse of the southern temple. The floor of the right back apse is raised with a low dividing wall of blocks 0.6 m high, making it markedly higher than that to the left, which has a table niche set against the back wall, replicating those in the back left room of the southern temple but on a much smaller scale (Fig. 3.10).

The only dressed stones in the Ggantija temples are those forming the outer and internal entrance corridors cut from the soft honey-yellow globerigina limestone. These contrast markedly with the form and texture of the coralline limestone blocks, with a pinkish hue, forming the external façade of the temples. The stones forming the façades all have distinctive morphologies because, as noted above, they were used as found rather than being cut and transformed, as was the case for the globigerina blocks composing the entrance corridors. They have numerous deep and rounded holes and fissures, creating a sponge-like and ancient appearance with a coarse, hard and rough surface. Entering the temple corridors thus involves encountering a markedly different kind of stone from that found in the temple façade in terms of colour, regularity of form, relative softness and smoothness to the touch. The internal apse walls are constructed entirely of rough piled boulders of differing sizes and dimensions which were almost certainly internally plastered with painted decorations. These would have both appeared and felt much

Figure 3.9 The entrance to the northern temple at Ggantija.

Figure 3.10 Altar area at the back of the northern temple, Ggantija.

smoother than the globigerina blocks. So movement from the outside to the inside of the temple spaces involved the experience of walls and façades that were progressively smoother, softer, of different colour and more and more culturally elaborated through the addition of decoration: drilled sequences of holes on some of the entrance orthostats and more elaborate spiral and hexagonal designs in the apses. While the temple exteriors were composed of undressed megalithic blocks, the stones inside the apses were entirely smoothed, their shapes and contours and surface textures concealed and replaced by ochre decorations. The temple interiors with regular and hewn limestone blocks and plastered and decorated walls would have appeared both new and artificial. By contrast, the temple façades appeared as old and as a mimetic image of the surrounding landscape.

The outer wall of the Ggantija temples is composed for the most part of massive megalithic blocks with a characteristic arrangement of stones. The lower part consists of large wide slabs with their broad face outwards with projecting pillar slabs set at right angles to them surmounted by layers of horizontal coursing stones projecting inwards to form part of the vault of the temple roof. The largest of the broad slabs is huge: 5.7 m wide and 3.8 m high. Placed to the north and back of the temples, it occurs at the point at which their external façades join. Both temples have their own distinctive inward curving forecourt areas on either side of the entrances, both of which are orientated to the south-east. In front of the buildings there is an artificial terraced platform up to 35 m wide with a vertical drop of 5–6 m beyond. The southern temple has an extended façade of blocks jutting out to the south-west (see Fig. 3.6). This effectively blocks off all views from the forecourt areas to the west across Gozo. The effect of this is to emphasize and highlight Nuffara hill and the ridge running west from Nadur, both to the south-east (Fig. 3.11). The entrance of the earlier southern temple is orientated directly to Nuffara hill, that of the northern temple to the southern end of the ridge. Both Nuffara hill and the Nadur ridge are capped by prominent rock outcrops, and the effect of the extended façade wall of the southern temple is to focus attention through the entrances and forecourt areas to the south and east and to these features of the topography. By far the most important of these landscape features is Nuffara hill, to which the earlier temple is orientated.

Nuffara hill is a flat-topped hill 'island' with steep sides and distinctive cliffs riddled with fissures and small caves or overhangs which jut out just below the top. These are formed of the hard coralline limestone. There are a series of such distinctive mesa-like hills across Gozo to the west which give the island an utterly distinct identity compared to Malta. However, Nuffara hill is the most easterly of these hills. The external wall stones of the Ggantija temples, when seen from upslope to the north, bear an uncanny resemblance to the cliffs of Nuffara hill, the temple in effect becoming a visual metaphor for this striking hill beyond and across the valley from it (Fig. 3.12). The Ggantija temples themselves are situated near the

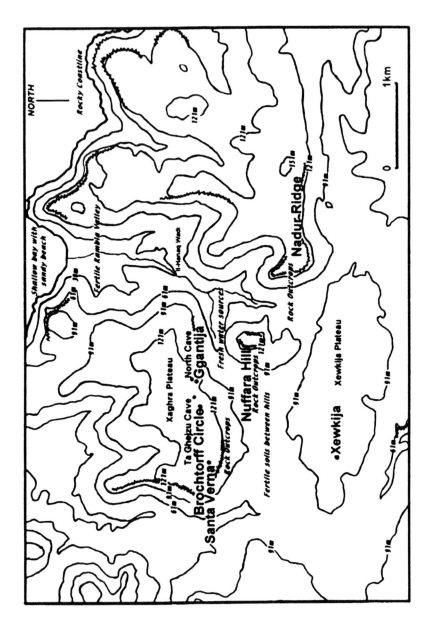

Figure 3.11 The landscape around the Ggantija temples.

Figure 3.12 The back of the Ggantija temples and Nuffara hill with its exposed rock outcrops.

very top of a west–east ridge in a location where cliffs typically occur, and indeed rock outcrops are visible to the west and east of the temples along the same or only slightly lower contours. Seen from the top of Nuffara hill about 800 m to the south, the temple itself resembles a series of outcropping rocks along the edge of the ridge on which it is situated. The exterior, of the temples thus mirror features of the surrounding landscape, which in turn mirrors them in a double relation of mimesis (Fig. 3.12). The internal temple space, by contrast, deliberately creates another world with few direct referents to the outside. While the Brochtorff Circle is intervisible with the Ggantija temples, any view to it is completely blocked off from the forecourt area. There is no reference to this probable resting place for the dead of Ggantija.

Mnajdra (Fig. 3.13)

The three temples at Mnajdra are located on a gentle sloping shelf of land between sea cliffs to the south, and the hill top rising to the north. They are highly visible from the sea but concealed from the north inland. Views to the west and east are also restricted by rising land. The nearby temple complex at Hagar Qim is just visible on the skyline 500 m to the east. By far the most dramatic feature of the landscape setting of these temples is the presence of Filfla island 5 km away off the

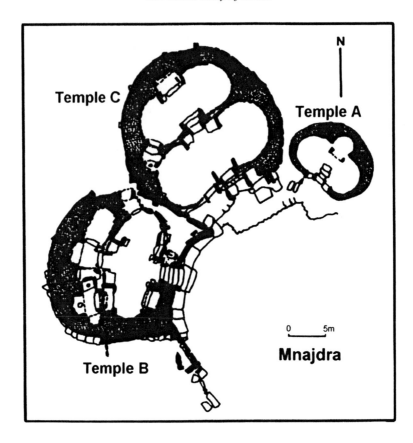

Figure 3.13 The Mnajdra temples.

coast, and there appears to have been a special relationship between this island and
both the Mnajdra and Hagar Qim temples.

The earliest temple at Manjdra (Fig. 3.13: A) is of simple trefoil plan with apses
to the left and right of the entrance and a rounded chamber at the back. There is a
niche to the left of the entrance set into the outer wall in the position one would
expect to find altar arrangements in other temples between an inner and outer
court. The entrance is orientated south-west and looks directly out to the island.
This directional orientation of the temple entrance to face towards an important
feature in the wider landscape is similar to the earliest temple at Ggantija with its
relationship to Nuffara hill. The entrance orthostats, about 1 m high, are elaborated
with pit-drilled decoration on their outer faces and with parallel lines of pit-drilled
decoration along their internal faces replicating the orientation of the entrance to
the island. They are low, requiring stooping to enter the temple. The floor of the
interior is partially paved in front of the entrance and the dimensions of the floor

Figure 3.14 Mnajdra: Temple A, view through the entrance.

stones widen, emphasizing the apses stretching to the sides (Fig. 3.14). Having passed through the entrance, the entire internal temple space is visible except the rounded chamber at the back, which is partially screened behind blocking orthostats covered with drill decoration. The reconstructed walling of the apses, of rough boulder construction, and the chamber at the back lack orthostats today.

Temple B is by far the most elaborated of the three and its form was altered in the process of constructing temple C. The external façade of this temple, lacking in the other two, is massive and designed to dwarf a person. It is made of the local coralline limestone that outcrops on the temple site. The six façade stones, three on either side of the entrance corridor, about 2 m wide and 1 m thick, are pitted with numerous larger and smaller holes and depressions. Coupled with the irregularity of their form, this again makes an overriding impression of an extremely ancient structure. Even when the temple was newly constructed it would have looked old from the outside. An outer platform of footing blocks at the base of the façade emphasizes the height of the stones, 2–3 m, which are capped by massive horizontal coursing blocks.

Standing outside the temple in the forecourt area, the view to Filfla island is completely blocked by the façade. The entrance is orientated due east looking out across the sea. As opposed to the two other Mnajdra temples, there is a clear elaboration of external space and the forecourt area is at least partly paved (Evans

1971: 96). The nearly 4 m-long elaborate entrance passageway emphasizes the transitional experience of moving from the temple exterior to the interior. It is paved throughout and continually broadens towards the interior. The external entrance slab has a striking natural vein of dark quartz meandering across its surface, and resembling a serpent. It must have been chosen and placed here because of the presence of this inclusion (not mentioned in the literature). Four pairs of orthostats make up the walls, the first three of which rise to a height of 2 m. The first pair of entrance orthostats are thick and made of coralline limestone, rough and pitted. These contrast with the rest of the orthostats made of the globigerina limestone, which are thinner, smoother and very regular in form, their honeyed yellow surfaces contrasting both visually and to the touch with the pinky grey of the coarse coralline limestone orthostats.

The innermost orthostats jut out into the first room and are huge pillars, 4 m and 3.4 m high respectively. At the end of the entrance corridor there are two small steps down into the first room of the temple. There is a significant contrast between the sheer sense of space in this first room (14 m long and 7 m wide) compared with the comparatively restricted entrance passage. The remarkably uniform walls rise up to 4.3 m, made of vertical slabs of globigerina limestone up to 2 m high and capped with horizontal lines of corbelled blocks of the same limestone. The whole aspect of the stones composing the back wall of the front room presents a unified façade of what effectively appears to be a temple within a temple. Ahead is another elaborated trilithon entrance with passageway beyond framing a view to the back of the temple. To the left there is a portal entrance from the front apse to the back of the temple hewn out of a slab elaborately decorated with drill holes.

Immediately upon entering the front room from the entrance corridor, the first unusual detail that becomes apparent, looking to the right, is the presence of a small rectangular window hole cut through near to the base of one of the uprights next to the central stone of the apse. This is recessed and resembles a stone-cut temple entrance in miniature (Fig. 3.15). Moving into the space of the front room and looking further around to the right, one is then able to observe another partially blocked niche hole cut through near to the base of another orthostat and next to it a simple portal entrance to another room located within the mass of the front wall of the temple. Three steps lead up to this room through a rectangular portal entrance cut through another orthostat, and a view into it is almost entirely obscured (Fig. 3.16).

There is an interesting structural contrast between the left- and right-hand apses of the front room. To the left the orthostats are not perforated with holes. The portal entrance to the back room is immediately visible ahead on entering the room and highly elaborated both by drilled decoration and the provision of an external trilithon façade. To the right the portal entrance is hidden in the front wall and one must turn round to see it on entering the front room. It lacks an elaborated façade and

Figure 3.15 Mnajdra: Temple B, front right apse: orthostat with incised hole.

Figure 3.16 Mnajdra: Temple B, front right apse: doorway through wall.

decoration. This hidden entrance is in a place in which one would least expect to find it.

The connecting entrance passageway to the back chambers of the temple is significantly shorter than the outer entrance. It is flanked by pairs of upright slabs of the smooth globigerina limestone widening out to the back to create an expanding sense of space. On either side at the front it is flanked by two altar-like arrangements consisting of horizontal blocks covered by drill decoration on their front faces seen from the front room and on the sides flanking the passage. Behind are uprights set broadside on and flanking them are two further uprights jutting out into the front room and running parallel with the line of the corridor. These are both decorated but in markedly different ways. That to the left is densely covered with drilled decoration of the same type as that used on the façade of the portal doorway. The one to the right is less densely drilled with smaller holes set further apart. At the winter solstice sunrise, light enters diagonally through the temple entrance and falls on the left 'altar'. At the summer solstice sunrise, the light overshoots this altar to illuminate the decorated portal entrance to the left (Vasallo 2000: 34).

Moving into the back room from the interconnecting entrance corridor requires stepping up over a threshold stone. Straight ahead is a roughly rectangular altar area covered by a table slab supported by two pillars. At the end of the entrance corridor one only has a partial view into the left and right apses of the back room, which are smaller and far more irregular in form than those in the front room. It is only when entering into the space of the back room that the entirety of the right apse becomes visible. This is a roughly semicircular space with a raised floor 0.4 m higher than that to the left and in front of the entrance corridor. It is bounded by a stone step. The space to the left is blocked by a double-pillar table.

To enter the back space of the temple to the left requires crawling through the elaborate drill-decorated portal entrance leading off from the back of the front left apse. The arrangement of the stones set inwards creates a perspective of exaggerated depth. Their specific arrangement being set inwards from the outside creates the same visual perspective as the staggered inward-set orthostats on either side of the entrance doorway corridors leading from the back to the front room and out of the temple. From such a perspective this is a doorway turned inside out (Fig. 3.17). Passing through, one enters a small rectangular area with three recessed niches to left and right and, at the back, with table altars. The back niche has a stone slab resting on a single central rounded column. The left niche has two stone tables resting on pillars, one raised above the other. The top, bottom and edge of the lower table are covered with pitted drill decoration. The niche to the right now has a floor consisting of a single slab, but, according to the excavator, it probably had tiered tables (Evans 1971: 98).

From the right front apse one must crawl into another room through an un-elaborated portal doorway at the front of the temple which is extremely irregular

Figure 3.17 Mnajdra: Temple B, front left apse: doorway with pitted decoration through to the back of the temple.

in form. This room is formed between the internal wall of the apse and the outer façade wall of the temple. The floor is 0.7 m above that of the floor of the front room of the temple, from which this area is completely hidden. Kneeling down, one is able to observe much of the front room of the temple by looking through the rectangular window opening cut through the orthostat next to the entrance portal without being seen from the temple space. Immediately to the right of this entrance portal is a hidden pillar niche with an external trilithon doorway into it (Fig. 3.18). In the north-west corner are the remains of another pillar niche.

The outside of the back of the temple was originally built in the style of those at Ggantija with slabs arranged alternately with broad and narrow sides facing outside, although much of this no longer survives today. Some blocks, as at Ggantija, are massive. In the north-west corner of the external wall face where it butts on to the middle temple there is a small external room originally entered through a doorway. From here one can see down and across the front room of the temple through the small window cut through the orthostatic wall face.

The third temple or middle temple at Mnajdra (Temple C) is considerably simpler in form and arrangements. If it ever had an external façade, it is now completely destroyed. The floor level lies 2–3 m above that of Temple B. Its entrance is orientated south-east towards the sea but any view from it of the small

Figure 3.18 Mnajdra: Temple B, interior of hidden room reached through the doorway in the front right apse. Note rope holes.

island of Filfla is blocked by the curving façade of Temple B. The entrance is markedly different from the norm. The principal entrance was through a porthole doorway measuring 1.2 m wide and 1.6 m high. The short entrance passage widens with staggered orthostats into the front room, which is remarkably spacious: 16.5 m long and 7.5 m wide. The connecting passage to the smaller back room (13.7 m long and 6 m wide) is flanked by altar arrangements on either side. Otherwise the front room has no furniture. At the winter solstice sunrise, light coming through the portal doorway hits the left altar stones (Vassallo 2000: 34). Perhaps significantly in relation to the last observation, the only decoration within the temple is a small temple representation engraved into one of the orthostats forming the left-hand altar facing the entrance corridor to the back room and meant to be seen from it.

Standing in the front room, this entrance appears to be of simple form with two flanking orthostats. However, passing through it, the structure is revealed as a complex staggered arrangement of three orthostats which become progressively higher and wider as one moves towards the back room. The internal orthostats of the external temple entrance, by contrast, get lower as one enters into the first room.

Walking into the smaller back room, one faces an hexagonal shaped niche with a horizontal cover resting on vertical slabs flanked by two taller pillars. The apse

Figure 3.19 Mnajdra: Temple C, right back apse with hole cut in orthostat.

to the right has no stone furniture. The principal detail of interest here is an opening cut through one of the central orthostats recalling those found in the right apse of the front room of Temple B, but this hole in the orthostat does not connect or relate to any hidden room lying beyond the internal façade (Fig. 3.19). It mimics the position of those in Temple B. In the far left corner of the left apse there is a portal entrance to a small hidden room through which one must crawl. The presence of this room is not apparent until one enters into the left apse from beyond the corridor area, and its presence is entirely unexpected (Fig. 3.20). There is a great contrast between the elaboration of this left apse with its hidden room and the simplicity of the right apse. The cut portal stone is designed so as to obscure a view beyond it from the centre of the left apse. Crawling through the hole one faces a table altar supported by a central tree-like pillar with thin supporting pillars at either side.

The two large temples contrast with each other in a striking manner. The middle temple, C, has an austere simplicity of form with its wide-open room and apses with little internal architectural elaboration or decoration. By contrast, Temple B is extremely elaborated with its hidden rooms, elaborate portal doorways, raised floors, windows cut through orthostats, decorated stones, imposing external façade and table altars. It seems clear that some, if not most, of this internal architectural elaboration occurred at the same time as Temple C was being constructed. This

Figure 3.20 Mnajdra: Temple C: porthole doorway leading to room with pillar altar in back left apse.

allowed the remodelling of the temple, which may originally have been as simple internally as Temple C.

Moving into and around and encountering architectural spaces clearly has direct physical effects on the body and creates a set of expectations with regard to future encounters. Someone experiencing the internal spaces of Temples A and C at Mnajdra might become utterly confused and disorientated on entering Temple B. In Temple C there is only one hidden room at the far back of the temple space to the left. In Temple B there are a multitude of unexpected places and features to be encountered. Rather than simply moving from front to back down a central corridor, one can move from front to back through different doorways and seemingly through the very front walls of the temple itself from its inner to outer skin. One can observe without being observed from both inside and outside the temple space. While one can move relatively freely down the central corridor, movement into other spaces requires stooping and crawling, moving up and moving down.

Today the roofless temples are light and airy. If we imagine them roofed and dark, lit internally with flickering flames, we must picture a radically different form of experience. The external entrance corridor in Temple B is provided with rope and bar holes, as is the internal entrance corridor. The entrances to rooms 3 and 5 have rope holes and are cut so as to allow wooden doorways or screens to be fitted. Different parts of the internal temple space could thus be closed off or opened at will according to circumstances. It could become many different spaces which could be revealed or hidden, on different occasions. Temple C offered few such possibilities, but here the principal entrance, a porthole doorway, is what one would normally expect to find inside rather than outside a temple. The corridor from the front to back room is furnished with rope holes to enable it to be blocked. Otherwise such features are missing and would hardly be required.

No doubt at some stage in the early Tarxien period the three temples were the centre of a complex of rites. Temple A seems to celebrate the relationship to Filfla island, which was symbolically connected with the temples. Temple C appears to be a relatively open and public place for ceremonies and rites. Temple B, on the other hand, may have been intended as a reserved space for special ceremonies (see discussion below).

Hagar Qim (Fig. 3.21)

By contrast with Mnajdra, the main temple complex at Hagar Qim has a baroque degree of elaboration. It stands on a hill top and is thus a conspicuous local landmark with the land dipping away in all directions, only rising to a slightly higher point a few hundred metres to the south-east, the site today of a restaurant. From the temples there are extensive views to the south across the sea, where Filfla island is conspicuous. To the south-east the coastal cliffs where the deeply incised Wadi Babu meets the sea are prominent. To the east there are extensive views across the coastal ridge to the heights where the Wardin Tower stands some 4 km away. Looking west, one can see as far as the distinctive high ridge of Gebel Cantar, again about 4 km distant. From both these heights with distinctive rock outcrops there are extensive views across Malta and beyond. Mount Etna on Sicily can be seen on clear autumnal days (information from local bird hunter). Inland to the north, views are much more restricted as the land begins to rise up a short distance from the temple. A view across the inland landscape to the north does not appear to be have been at all significant (Fig. 3.22).

In relation to these heights, and to the sea, Hagar Qim can be conceptualized as being poised between the heavens and the sky and the depths of the sea, its position on a lower coastal rise in the landscape mediating between the two. The main entrance passage to the main temple itself is orientated north-west to south-east. From the north-west end one looks out and *up* to the rock outcrops of Gebel Cantar. From the south-east end one looks *down* to the entrance of the Wadi Babu and the bare coastal cliffs where fresh water meets the sea. The contrast between the extensive visual field of Hagar Qim and the limited one from Mnajdra is quite striking.

By comparison with most other temples on Malta, whose external façades were constructed from the coralline limestone Hagar Qim would have looked strikingly

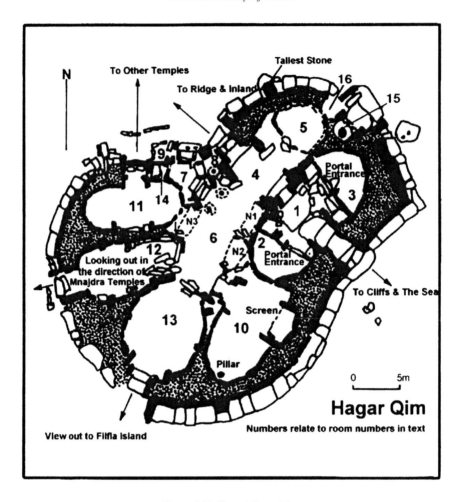

Figure 3.21 Plan of Hagar Qim.

new when first constructed, as the stones making up the façade are cut from the soft globigerina limestone, and are remarkably regular in appearance. It is only the subsequent extreme weathering of some of the orthostats on the seaward end of the façade that gives parts of the temple façade today its somewhat fantastic appearance. The globigerina blocks used to construct parts of the temple interiors at Mnajdra probably came from the same local source. Both temple complexes thus have a common source of origin in the very stones used to build them and were probably used by the same local group in calendrical and other rites with ceremonial pathways connecting together the upper and lower temples. Hagar Qim, like Mnajdra, was radically remodelled during the course of its use, so much so that the basic plan of entrance corridors and side apses becomes almost entirely lost in

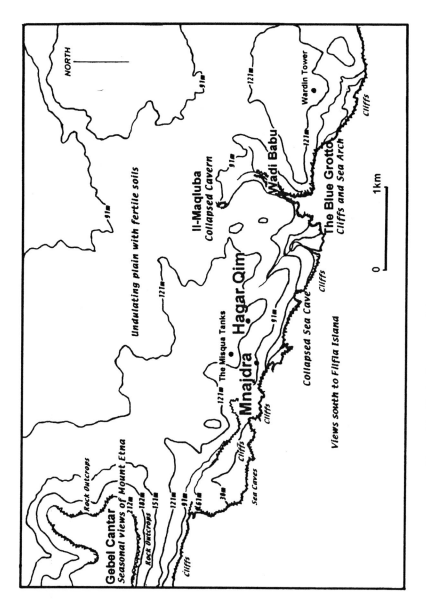

Figure 3.22 The landscape around the Mnajdra and Hagar Qim temples.

Figure 3.23 The façade and south-east entrance of Hagar Qim.

an internal maze of rooms and spaces and niches and passageways of entirely different form coupled with various entrances and exits from different parts of the complex.

On the south-east façade of the main temple there is a deliberate gradation in size of the orthostats serving as a funnel effect to emphasize the entrance (Fig. 3.23). One remarkable feature about this temple is the corridor which passes straight through it which would have made this passageway, when unblocked or shuttered, unusually light and transparent. From the south-east entrance a long paved corridor leads to the first room, widening out into this internal space. Straight ahead and to the left and right of the second entrance corridor ahead there is a standard 'altar' arrangement. The area immediately in front of the altar to the left seems to have been of great significance since this contained a relief-decorated stone with a double spiral, and a free-standing 'altar' stone sculpted with floral decoration (Fig. 3.24). A number of human figurines were found here. Vassallo has shown that the sun's beams at the midwinter solstice sunrise strike precisely this area of the internal temple space (Vassallo 2000: 45). Both the semicircular apses leading off to the right and left of the front room are entirely screened by stone slabs and in each there are portal doorways which could be closed and barred. Two hidden and secretive spaces thus occur immediately upon entering the temple, which, when compared with the wide-open apses of the front rooms of other

Figure 3.24 Hagar Qim: room 1, left side.

temples, appears as strikingly confined. The portal doorways between the screens are set asymmetrically in relation to each other. The one to the left (Fig. 3.25) is set towards the beginning of the dividing screen, that to the right towards the end. This first room is the most elaborated in the temple in terms of both the internal architectural arrangements and decoration.

Figure 3.25 Hagar Qim: portal doorway in room 1 to room 2.

Both portal doorways are raised about 0.5 m above the floor and require crawling to pass up and through them into the raised spaces beyond, which now lack any furniture. The stones making up the external walls of the apses are very irregular in form, reminiscent of those found in Ggantija, contrasting with the carefully constructed screen, and they had *torba* floors contrasting with the carefully paved court between them. The entrance corridor into the next room is slightly raised above the paved court of room 1 and the *torba* flooring of room 4. Straight ahead is the second external north-west entrance to the temple, which is unusual in form in that the orthostats are arranged so that the entrance corridor widens out both to the exterior and to the interior, rather than in the typical manner, which is to widen out into the interior only. The arrangement of the stones thus emphasizes the highly distinctive character of having a second entrance in this position. The south-east and north-west entrances to the temple differ markedly in form in other respects. The south-east entrance is longer and lower, the north-west entrance shorter and higher. The effect of the arrangement of orthostats at the north-west end is to let more light into the external space and a wider view to the landscape beyond from the entrance corridor.

To the right a low curtain wall defines room 5. This is markedly different in character from rooms 2 and 3. The external walls consist of well-fitted orthostats with lines of horizontal coursing blocks above. In front of these there is a semi-circular arrangement of slabs and a low screen or curtain wall dividing this room off from the court apart from a central entranceway with a paved slab off which one steps down into this space. What is being created here is a well-defined roughly circular space within a pre-existing apsoidal space, demarcated on all sides. While the floors of rooms 2 and 3 are higher than the court and the presumed ceiling would have been lower, in room 5 the floor is lower and the ceiling is higher. Rooms 2 and 3 are totally screened from the court while room 5 is only partially screened.

Opposite the entrance to room 5, in the external wall orthostat a semicircular hole has been pierced all the way through, allowing communication with the outside of the temple, where there is an external niche in the wall (Fig. 3.26) interconnecting with another (Fig. 3.21). This is a permeable space as opposed to one sealed off and hidden. Light shines through the hole on the summer solstice sunrise (Vasallo 2000: 45).

From the court area (4) one can look straight down room 6 to the left. This space contrasts markedly in form with 5, being long and roughly rectangular in form. Entering this room, two deeply recessed covered niches are visible to the left and one to the right, together with an entrance passageway flanked by elaborate stone table pillars to room 7 (Fig. 3.27). Steps are visible going up to the concealed room 10.

The entrance to room 7 is further elaborated by orthostats decorated with pitted decoration which are angled so the space widens before being narrowed by ortho-stats set sideways to confine the entranceway, which is paved. One must move up over a threshold stone and stoop to enter this space. The whole of room 7 is raised in relation to room 6. Looking straight ahead, one has a partial view of a niche to the left of the entrance and a further niche straight ahead elaborated with drill decoration (room 9). After entering the room, the presence of another table niche,

Figure 3.26 Hagar Qim: view into room 5 from room 4.

Figure 3.27 Hagar Qim: view from room 6 into room 7.

to the right, becomes apparent. From room 7 another space leads off to the right (8), originally provided with its own doorway covered with drill decoration and painted red (Evans 1971: 85). This space is a pillar niche framed at the back by the massive orthostats of the passage doorway with a stone pillar and table slab, a space in which one can stand fully upright having crawled through the doorway. Another niche (9) leads off from room 7 to the left with a small window doorway only 0.6 m wide, a space into which one could see but probably not enter. The labyrinthine bewildering complexity and the depth of this arrangement of niches and different spaces leading off each other is completely unexpected in room 6.

Room 10 is raised 0.7 m above room 6 and is now entered by a series of five steps. It is provided with a short entrance corridor of staggered orthostats widening out into the internal space in the usual manner. One enters a wide apsoidal space curtailed to the left but extensive to the right where a rounded pillar of coralline limestone now stands in the middle of the side wall. It is uncertain if this position is original or whether it once stood hidden in the niche (*ibid.*). Straight ahead is a screened polygonal chamber with a narrow portal doorway with an external threshold pavement through which one must crawl.

The remaining rooms in the temple complex can only be entered from the outside and are not linked together. The entrance to room 13 is directly orientated so as to face Filfla island about 5 km distant. It is provided with substantial threshold steps which one must walk up before stepping down into the ovoid chamber. All the orthostats and pillars of the walls, alternating and projecting into the chamber on the right-hand side, are massive (2–2.5 m high and 1–2 m broad), giving a tremendous sense of volume compared with many of the other cramped interconnected temple spaces. The internal architectural arrangements of stones here are reminiscent of those to be found on the outside of the Mnajdra and Ggantija temples. It is effectively a space turned outside inward. Room 12, of similar form and construction to 13, is entered from the west. The view from the doorway is towards the Mnajdra temples and the sea beyond.

The entrance to room 11 is orientated due north so as to face towards another smaller and now very ruinous temple complex. The room in shape and appearance resembles the typical front room of a temple with left and right apses of approximately equal size and altar-like arrangements at the back with pitted decoration, where what appears to be a typical corridor passageway which might lead through into room 12 is blocked by the stones used to construct that space. The floor of this space is significantly raised in relation to the outside, and to enter it requires clambering over a blocking stone set on edge 0.7 m above the ground surface outside. To the right of this entrance is an external niche built into the temple wall (14). It is positioned opposite room 9. While access to the latter is extremely complicated, involving going through a succession of enclosed spaces, access to the former, from the outside, is immediate.

This temple complex is the most elaborate of all those found in Malta, with the exception of Tarxien, but in many respects space is structured at Tarxien in a relatively simple and predictable manner. Here three temples are conjoined and one moves from front to back through a succession of apses which become smaller and more constricted. What makes Tarxien distinctive is that the middle temple of the complex has six apses. Hagar Qim must have clearly been constructed and reconstructed over a long time period. It seems most likely that there were originally two temples on this site, each with a front and back room with side apses. Rooms 1–5 and part of 6 would originally have constituted one temple space with a niche at the back where the present second entrance is now located. The other temple would have consisted of room 11 and another room where 12 is situated. Rooms 12 and 13 represent another period of rebuilding during which room 6 was remodelled and spaces 7–10 were probably created. Room 5 must have been remodelled in conjunction with the construction of the external wall niches 15 and 16.

Whatever the precise sequence of construction, the end result is a complex of almost bewildering architectural complexity, one in which it would only be too easy to get lost, confused and disorientated. As at Mnajdra, the internal space of the temple complex was mobile. Entrances and exits, all provided with rope and or bar holes between the different spaces and the inside and the outside, could all be blocked or opened at will (Fig. 3.28). Every time you entered this temple there remained the possibility of encountering and being led around a different kind of space. And, of course, not only could the physical space of the temple be altered in terms of the possibilities for moving through its spaces but so could the positions and relationships of its portable furnishings of artefacts. Pots and figurines and statuettes, plaques and sculptures could be moved and secreted in different niches in different positions. Thus there were infinite possibilities for creating different and unpredictable architectural effects, and associations between things, all played out in a realm of variable light and darkness, shadow and sound. The sheer solidity and seeming permanence of the temple façade masks an internal performative space that was flexible and mobile in character. According to what kinds of rites were being undertaken, the temple spaces could be changed. So one can imagine rites associated with the passage of the seasons and the agrarian cycle, rites concerned with water, rites concerned with birth, fecundity and reproduction, initiation into different ranks or statuses and for the ancestral dead. As the temple spaces became more complex in time in tandem with the elaboration of the portable material culture and decorative art, the possibilities for manipulating space and creating contrast and surprise increased. It was only the latest temples to be built, or reconstructed, at Mnajdra, Hagar Qim and Tarxien that have 'oracle holes' allowing things to be passed from the inside to the outside, allowing the possibility of manipulating smaller portable artefacts during ritual performances. The rites

Figure 3.28 Hagar Qim: bar and rope holes in orthostat at north-east entrance.

associated with the temples were not inflexible but must have been constantly changing and developing.

In the final stage of the building of Hagar Qim almost every normative expectation of what a temple space is likely to be is disrupted. Thus the internal spaces of rooms 12 and 13 resemble other temple façades. Room 11 resembles the front room of a standard temple, yet where it should lead to a second space it is blocked off. The apsoidal spaces of the front room of the main, and probably original, temple complex are entirely screened off. There are two entrances rather than one and a series of intricate and secret spaces leading off the second courtyard to the left. To the right a structure is built within a structure and communication is possible with external niches and shrines letting in light, air and sound. Such a complex structure could never have been planned. It grew and accumulated in a contingent manner as the original space of two separate but adjacent temples was altered and conjoined. An initial simple and repetitive plan became exceedingly complex and reticulated. The bodily effect of moving through the new temple spaces, whose form could be altered at will, would be disturbing. One would rapidly loose a sense of orientation and direction and be continually surprised by the elaborated network of chambers, passages, niches and internal spaces. The apsoidal form of the traditional temple space is only retained in one area but even this, because of the high screens and the position of the entrance portals, is disrupted and the basic form is only really apparent looking at a plan. It is not experienced bodily. So, effectively, Hagar Qim is a temple in which the internal space has become so elaborated as to lose all resemblance to the other temples. Parts of it are inverted and, relatively speaking, it is a temple open to the wind with light and air penetrating the complex structure. It creates cognitive dissonance. That this is a markedly different spatial form is perhaps deliberately masked by the precision of a 'modern' façade of neatly fitted and dovetailed globigerina limestone blocks. The pure and refined regularity of form seen on the outside belies the incredible irregularity encountered on the inside.

Similarly references to and relationships with the wider cultural and topo-graphic landscapes are far more complex than at other temple sites. The multiple entrances to the temple relate both to the land and the sea, to distant rock outcrops and the island of Filfla, to the Mnajdra temples below and adjacent temple sites. Significant stones in the façade relate to the cardinal directions. The tallest stones are in the northern and southern façades, the broadest to the east, while on the western side there stood massive carved figures (only the stump of the stone remains in the wall next to the entrance to room 13).

On the top of the hill 200 m to the north of Mnajdra and about 500 m to the east of Hagar Qim are the Misqua tanks (Fig. 3.22). It has been argued that they are almost certainly Neolithic in date (Zammit 1994: 64; Trump 2000: 116). These are six enormous bell-shaped pits cut into an exposure of coralline limestone pave-ment. The largest is 3.4 m long, 1.5 m wide and up to 2 m deep. The others are only slightly smaller and a central pair interconnect. They are intervisible with Hagar Qim but not Mnajdra. Today they serve as water cisterns and are used to irrigate the surrounding fields. It has been assumed that in the past they also served this purpose, providing a water supply for the temple builders, but this use might be quite recent. We know that the fate of the bones discovered at the hypogeum of Hal Saflieni was to serve as fertilizer for the fields, and something similar could have occurred here in the more distant past with the burials being cleared out and the chambers used to collect water instead. These tanks may well have originally been the burial place for the temple builders at Hagar Qim and Mnajdra. Their location on top of a hill replicates the locations of the hypogeum and the Brochtorff Circle and places with rock-cut tombs such as Xemija (Evans 1971: 112ff.). Their distance from the two temple sites is also typical.

Hagar Qim is a temple which, rather than having limited references and relationships, in effect tries to do everything at once. It is a grandiose act of totalization, a supreme attempt to integrate geographic, social and cosmological spaces into a single structure. Significantly, Hagar Qim is the last and final act of the temple builders to control and dominate their world before these places were abandoned. It represents a baroque elaboration of the temple form and in becoming so it destroys the very thing it attempts to achieve and incorporate, namely a sophistication and elaboration of the original idea. So Hagar Qim destroys the very tradition on which it was founded.

Bodily Effects of the Temple Spaces

The temples were clearly designed to have theatrical bodily effects. They were transformers of experience and performative spaces. The main ways in which these effects were achieved were through the following:

1. Forcing changes in physical bodily posture: being able to stand upright, having to stoop or having to crawl, moving up and moving down.
2. Changes in volume: contrasts between wide-open voluminous spaces and narrow confined spaces.
3. The successive darkening of space and the changing effects of light and the amplification of smell and sound. The experiences created in the temple transformed the experience of the everyday into an experience of the unworldly, evoking a sense of the infinite and eternal.
4. Tactile impressions: the smoothness of the globigerina limestone and the roughness of the coralline. A contrast between the *torba* plastering and the globigerina stones within the temples and paved flooring and *torba* flooring. The feel of the dot and drill ornamentation around the portal doorways and entrances would have created another important tactile sensation.
5. The manipulation of perspective. In the internal temple spaces distances often cannot be accurately discerned or judged. What may be in reality a short

Figure 3.29 The end of the decorated frieze in the front left apse at Tarxien, with ram with face turned towards an observer and pig and goat behind seen in profile.

distance away can appear to be much further away through the narrowing and widening of exits and entrances, The portal doorways both frame and hide what is beyond. Entrances to inner parts of the temples through which one must pass may sometimes invert architecturally familiar external entrances with the orthostats arranged so as to be staggered outwards to the front rather than inwards to the back, which is the usual fashion. Similarly, internal rooms can resemble external façades,

6. The creation of special visual effects through light and sunlight, art and decoration. The front rooms of the main western temple at Tarxien are striking in terms of the animated effects of the elaborate spiral forms carved in relief, and in terms of the unique depiction of friezes of animals. Indeed Zammit commented that these internal decorative features seem to have been of more concern to the Tarxien temple builders than the architecture of the temple itself (Zammit 1930 cited in Evans 1971: 135). In the left front apse one of two decorated friezes with animals consists of six animals facing right, i.e. into the temple space. From left to right they are a procession of four goats with straight horns, a pig and a ram with curled horns. The leading ram in this frieze, quite remarkably, disengages to look out directly at an observer (Fig. 3.29). This iconographic moment is significant in transforming the depiction of the animal form from a somewhat passive iconic stylistic expression into a living and three-dimensional beast with which one engages visually. The ram's face meets the observer's face eye to eye, and so has an especial impact fixing the moment of encounter to an eternal now. That this frieze depicts a sacrificial procession seems highly probable. Zammit, excavating this temple, found within niches in its deep recesses numerous quantities of bones from goats, these apparently having been the principal sacrificial animals (Evans 1971: 120). In the opposite right apse

Figure 3.30 Tarxien: right front apse: spiral decorated altar with concealed hole.

flanking the internal entrance corridor there is an elaborate spiral decorated altar. The front is decorated with a double row of branched spirals resembling the curling horn cores of a ram. In the middle of the lower row of spirals there is a carefully concealed cut hole with a lunate plug with the same spiral motif (Fig. 3.30). Removing the plug, Zammit discovered within the altar cavity hole a curved flint knife and charred animal bones of sheep/goat and oxen along with pot sherds (*ibid.*: 121). Surmounting this altar is a miniature trilithon with an opening through which the charred animal bones and horn cores appear to have been thrown. The curling horn cores of the ram may have had a special significance suggested perhaps by their similarity to some of the curving spiral designs found here and by the fact that some appear to deposited in special ways. In the hypogeum a plugged concealed 'rope hole' in the floor of one of the principal rooms (the so-called 'holy of holies') contained two goat horn cores (*ibid.*: 54).

Architecture and Cosmology

We now turn to a more general consideration of the temple architecture and its links with landscape and cosmology. A number of structuring principles can be suggested, which we shall now examine in greater detail.

Dualism

An all-pervasive dualism is to be found on both a macro and a micro scale. There is the dualism of the major Maltese islands themselves, Gozo and Malta, which in turn relates to the cardinal directions west and east. There is the dualism of the two types of stone used to build the temples relating to outside and inside and the dualism of pairs of temple locales in the landscape that in turn relates to upper and lower (see above). Within the temple complexes we characteristically find two main temples placed side by side as at Ggantija, (see Fig 3.6) Kordin III, Mnajdra (see Fig. 3.13), Ta Hagrat and Skorba, but this is an asymmetric dualism in that one temple, the western of the pair, is always larger and more internally elaborated. The only exception to the size rule is at Mnajdra, where the eastern temple is larger but is much less elaborated than the western temple. Within the temple spaces there is the obvious dualism of the symmetrical apses and altar arrangements on either side of the entrance corridors. The internal structuring of the apses is again asymmetric. Either the right or left side will be more elaborated, and this usually alters as one moves from the front to the back rooms.

The theme of dualism and pairing extends more generally to most other aspects of Maltese material culture. Table niches with two covers, one placed above the other, are found in pairs. Models of phallic niches were found at Tarxien with the inset phalluses in pairs. Twin seated human figurines have been found in a burial deposit at the Brochtorff Circle (Stoddart et al. 1993). Double vases are known from the temples. Spirals carved in relief are consistently paired and/or arranged in two parallel lines. A pair of humped-back cattle depictions occur at Tarxien, as do paired lines of sheep or goats (see illustrations in Ridley 1976; Evans 1959, 1971; Pace 1996).

Ethnographically, one might expect this dualism to be related to principles of social organization, perhaps a dual kinship structure with two clans being related to each temple complex. The asymmetry found in other aspects of the temple architecture might suggest senior and junior clans maintaining and using the temples with differential access to them. Cosmologically, this would relate to the domain of the living and the temple spaces and the sea and the caves of the underworld to which the remains of the ancestral dead were returned.

Movement

We have described the interiors of the temples as mobile spaces that could be changed at will according to circumstances, all surrounded by a solid static exterior wall, The mobility of the temple as a mediator of experience can be directly related to certain aspects of the island world itself. First, there are the obvious cultural connections between the peoples of this island world and peoples from the outside, discussed by Robb (2001) and Grima (2001). These in turn find their analogues in the natural world. Malta is well known for its fierce winds that blow from different directions at different times of the year, (see Fig. 3.1) all of which are named today and have their own characteristics: the Majistral from the north-west, the Punent from the west, the Lbic from the south-west, the Grigal from the north-east, and so on.

Malta is on one of the main migration routes of birds from Africa to Europe during the spring and autumn (see Fig. 3.1). Today the islands are visited annually by more than a million finches, half a million songbirds and thousands of birds of prey and herons. Hundreds of thousands end their lives there. Exhausted after a long flight, they make easy prey for the numerous Maltese shooters and netters. The spectacular seasonal arrival and departure of these birds, almost all of which are exotic non-native species, is one of the wonders of this island. The arrival and departure of the birds from the south or the north are annual events which would have punctuated the year for the ancient Maltese, as they do today, with different bird species arriving and leaving at different times. For the ancient Maltese, a north–south axis was a line of ancestral origin. They came from the north. The many depictions of birds found in the temples attests to their ritual significance. Small clay figurines, pendants, stone carvings, incised decorations on pottery vessels, all depict birds and must have evoked the significance of directional movement, the narrative theme of going away and returning. A seemingly static island existence was in fact continually punctuated by the visible presence of movement and change. If identity was rooted by the solidity of the temples in the land, it was also connected with movement to and from the outside world. In mythic thought this might be cosmologically linked with the movements and directions of the wind and the waves, the sun and the moon, the migration of birds and the local growth cycles of plants, with the flows of life. Reassurance of the continuation of life is found in repetition and regularity both in the temple architecture and in the predictable changes in the natural world.

The primary axis of orientation of the entrances to the majority of temples, and of the internal entrance corridors, was on a north-west to south-east line (Stoddart et al. 1993: Fig. 10). It has been argued that this was because of the importance of the manner in which light entered internal areas of the temples at sunrise and sunset on astronomically significant days of the year and in particular at the midwinter solstice sunrise, as mentioned above (Ventura and Tanti 1990; Fodero et al. 1992; Vassallo 1999, 2000). This obviously implies that astronomical observation was the key to alignment. But this was only one factor among many, and it is a component that is not replicated in several temple sites. We have suggested that what landscape features could be seen out from the entrance was also of considerable significance. Stoddart et al. have suggested that looking towards the entrance of the monument from the forecourt area was of equal significance, and that 'a more probable orientation for the vast majority of the congregation would have been towards the focus of liturgical intensity, that is to the interior of the monument itself' (Stoddart et al. 1993: 16). They suggest that temple priests might have elaborated 'a protected and exclusive astronomical lore derived from over the shoulders of the congregation' (*ibid.*). While temple 'priests' might be interested in solar alignments, etc., the congregation gathered outside the temple façade would have understood the significance of the entrance orientation of the temple in a more general way. It can be interpreted as an orientation towards Sicily, thought of in terms of ancestral origins. Following this point, the acts of both entering and exiting the temple would be following an ancestral path of movement and origin.

The Land and the Sea

Grima has argued that the relief representations of fish at Bugibba and of sheep, goat and pig at Tarxien may symbolize two cosmological domains of utmost significance in an islander's cosmology: the land and the sea (Grima 2001: 56–7; see also general discussions in Broodbank 2000: 21ff. and Helms 1988: 24). Grima notes that some reliefs with interlinked running spirals are associated with the spatial setting of the entrance court to a few of the temples, particularly with boundaries marking the central court off from lateral side apses or doorways. The elaborated decorated side apses of the front room at the western main temple at Tarxien are bounded off from the court between them by rows of running spiral designs on blocks. Depictions of animals occur behind and inside the apses, and other types of spiral designs which differ significantly in form and in their branching lines suggest tree or plant forms (Grima 2001: 58; see also discussions in Evans 1971: 120 and Ridley 1976: 23–5). A separation is therefore created between the internal space of the apse, representing the domain of the land, and the court area, representing the domain of the sea, flanked by lines of running spirals. Grima notes that for the latter at Tarxien 'there is a consistent emphasis on horizontal repetition and regularity, with individual spirals retaining the same form, size and topological relationship with other spiral elements, across the whole interlocking composition' (Grima 2001: 58). He suggests that they may represent the waves of the sea, marking transition points between the different internal spaces of the temple, the central court and the apses. Ridley has also noted the similarity of the form of some of the spiral designs at Tarxien to waves – 'the spirals with their "horns" may also have suggested the waves with their crests' (Ridley 1976: 26) – as well as noting the similarity of others with trees. Grima points out that the 'grafitti' boat representations at Tarxien marking a stone adjacent to an entrance doorway, which also occur in the front apse to the left, and a boat-shaped threshold stone lying across the entrance to one of the side apses at the Kordin III temple are also placed in boundary areas in the temple, at the junctures of different domains: 'land' and 'sea'. He concludes that 'the crossing of spaces and boundaries within these architectural spaces may not only have recalled the islanders' experiences of land and sea, but could also have given meaning and order to those experiences' (Grima 2001: 62). That this is so is beyond dispute. But while a design, such as the spiral, seems ideally suited to represent something rather amorphous like the waves of the sea, it can also metaphorically link different domains rather than simply serve to demarcate and separate them. We can see tree-like or plant-like forms in different types of branching spiral designs, waves in others, and the curling horn cores of sacrificial goats in others, as we have already suggested above. The spirals prob- ably had many different referents as polysemous symbols and thus had tremendous evocative power and cosmological significance in the ritual and mythic world of the temples. In this respect it is interesting to note that the Kordin boat was reported by Ashby, who cleared the temple, as having been found with a stone rubber inside it used for grinding grain (Evans 1971: 23). If this was the case, the grinding of grain in a boat-shaped threshold stone again directly links the opposed domains of land and sea and might in turn hint at an originary ancestral journey bringing grain to Malta over the sea. A further connection might be found in the forms of the temple roofs. It seems probable that most were covered by a mixture of corbelling and timbers which may have resembled in inverted fashion the planking of boats.

Monumentalization and Miniaturization

A striking feature of some aspects of the material culture of the temples is the occurrence of the monumental and the miniature together. Entering the first temple at Tarxien, the remains of a colossal obese skirted statue can be seen in the first right-hand apse, which originally must have stood over 2.5 m high. Stumps of similar statues are known from Hagar Qim. Within the temples themselves numer- ous tiny human figurines have been found. Here there is clearly an exaggerated sense of scale in relation to the human body from the huge to the miniature. Similarly, the temples are monumental structures but within them have been found tiny models and engravings of temples. The stone table temple altar niches find their counterpart in clay models. Huge stone and ceramic vessels are found in the temples which may be up to 1 m high and have a counterpart in tiny miniatures, little more than a few centimetres in size. Ground stone axes of standard size have duplicates in tiny axe pendants and there are miniature figurines depicting birds and the animals used in sacrificial acts: oxen, pigs, sheep and goats. If the construc- tional forms of the temples are in effect landscape miniatures, as argued above, and if their all-pervasive dualism suggests a mimetic relationship both to the very island topography in a basic way, and to its coralline bones and globerina flesh, such a relationship is duplicated in the material forms found within them. That which effectively mediates between the macro and the micro, the monumental and the miniature, is the experience of the human body itself in action and movement both inside the temples and outside in the landscape.

Transformation and Transformative Substances

We have argued that the temples are fundamentally to do with the manipulation and transformation of human experience. They condense the island geography, they transform materials, space and time. In effect they construct the people who constructed them. We have also argued that the experience of the temple spaces, and of the world outside, was fluid and subject to both repetition and change, a process of being and becoming. The transformation of human experience, altered states of consciousness and knowledge, was, on the other hand, produced by the synaesthetic effects of the temple architecture and the manipulation of artefacts within them. The miniature human figurines found within the temples and in the underground burial places are startling in their variety and forms and poses. A few are clearly fat female forms but the majority have no obvious indication as to whether they might represent males or females. Phalluses, rather than being marked on the bodies of these figurines, become detached as sculptures and models. Figurines show a variety of styles of dress and headdress. Some represent markedly different body postures: some stand, some are sitting; others appear to be sleeping or reclining, such as the famous 'sleeping lady' of the hypogeum. Perhaps most remarkable of all are the large numbers of headless figurines on which there are clear attachments for heads to be fitted. There are also large numbers of heads which might be fitted to different figurines. All this evidence seems to directly imply states of transformation of the human body: different forms, different postures, changing or interchangeable identities in which different heads might be attached to the same figurine. Furthermore, study of a cache of figurines found together at the Brochtorff Circle (Stoddart et al. 1993: 11) has shown that various states of manufacture or sculpting of the rock are represented. Some are more finished than others. The transformation of human states seen in the iconography of the figurines is perhaps a token of self-recognition and self-consciousness of this processual character of individual identity. They can be related to transformative substances used to induce these changes. Consideration of this in turn also brings us back to consider further aspects of the temple architecture.

Blood and horn   Animal sacrifice, the collection of blood, eating meat, and the curation of scorched bone and horn cores, the enduring parts of the animal, was an important part of the temple rituals. All these animals were domestic, found outside the temples in the landscape beyond. The sheep and the goats would be likely to graze much further afield from the settlements, on hill tops and rocky areas; the pigs and the cattle would require much more tending and control and would be found much closer to the dwellings and temples. Different domestic animals would therefore have different degrees of closeness or association with people, and those at the greatest distance, the sheep and the goats, and especially the male ram, seem to have been the most significant in sacrificial acts. Since no proper analysis of the animal bones found at Tarxien has been carried out, we do not actually know what, if any, proportion of pig or ox bones are represented in the finds. We do know that ram horn cores were curated. There is no evidence for the curation of ox horns in special places in the temples. If the male goat was the principal sacrificial medium associated with the ritual transformation of people from one state to another, it is interesting to note that this involved the use of the most 'wild' of the domesticated animals, furthest removed from humanity. On a small island the 'wild' is likely to have been conceptualized in terms of the 'beyond'. Could this be part of the significance of the remarkable frieze found at Tarxien with the pig, a symbol of domesticity, mediating between the sacrificial ram at the front and the lines of goats with straight horn cores beyond, a differentiation between the relatively wild and the relatively domestic, between animals most closely associated and living with people, and those furthest removed and therefore having a greater degree of spiritual power?

Water   Water is another agent of transformation and a medium for movement. Fresh water has always been a key concern and a perennial problem on Malta. The arrival of the autumn rains would have been one of the most auspicious events in the agrarian calendar. Along the convoluted wadi channels, numerous circular swirl holes occur, formed by the grinding actions of stones. These bear an uncanny resemblance to the deep 'libation' holes found outside the entrances and forecourt areas to some of the temples and sometimes inside. They suggest the collection of holy water to be used in the temple rituals, just as it is venerated today by the Catholic church with special water chapels such as St Paul's church located underneath a rock overhang along the Wied il-Ghasel gorge (Haslam and Borg 1998: 148). This water, source of all life, comes from and is associated with springs arising from the coralline limestone and running down the deep wadi gorges to the sea. This suggests an association between fresh water and this limestone, and indeed the pockmarked spongy appearance of the rock itself is suggestive of water and water action, as opposed to the dry, crumbling and sandy appearance of the globigerina limestone. So we can suggest that the two types of limestone are material metaphors for wetness and dryness which in turn relates to the temple exteriors and temple interiors and the day-to-day experiences of life in this island world with its dry and rainy seasons.

Honey   The ancient Maltese almost certainly collected honey and used it in the temples. It was the ancient Greeks who first called the islands Melita, meaning honey, after the intensely rich and sweet variety produced by the wild bees. Bees often live in cave entrances and therefore have a direct association with the underworld and the caves used for the burial of the dead. Ethnographically, we know that honey, the subject matter of numerous myths, is a preeminent ritual substance, a passion for which is unequalled among other foods, and people are prepared to take almost any risk for the sake of collecting it for use in honey festivals, associated with states of ritual transformation (Lévi-Strauss 1973).

Anyone today can observe the manner in which the globigerina limestone, when exposed to the weather, may rapidly decay and develop a honeycomb pattern (Fig. 3.31). That the ancient Maltese would observe these effects is without doubt. Except at one of the latest temples to be rebuilt, Hagar Qim, the globigerina limestone was reserved for the temple interiors. Altar arrangements on either side of entrance corridors from one part of the temple to another, internal portal and trilithon doorways and niches in recesses are often decorated with dot or drill depressions of various densities covering the entire surface of the stone. This beautifies it and transforms the appearance and texture of this honey-coloured stone. This transformation of the honeyed stone has the effect of making it appear like weathered stone, i.e. old stone, but the transformation effected is cultural and much more regular.

If some of the spirals in the temples represent the ceaseless movement of the waves of the sea, always and forever, a constant reminder of the eternal, perhaps these decorated stones are symbolic representations, meant to resemble honey-combs and honey. Honey would be used in the ritual transformation of states, one to another, and in the temples one passes through honeyed doorways, from one place to another.

Ochre   Another preeminent transformative material was undoubtably red ochre. Sprinkling liberal amounts of red ochre over the bones of the deceased was part of common burial practice in the underground world of the rock-cut tombs and at the hypogeum of Hal Saflieni. The quantities used were such that this material was described as blood by workmen clearing sites in wet conditions (Evans 1959: 135). Ochre was also used to decorate the hypogeum and the temple walls and to paint figurines and ceramics. It was probably used for personal body decoration on special occasions. An exotic substance, all this ochre was imported from Sicily as none occurs on the islands. Maniscalco (1989) has argued that it was imported in

Figure 3.31 Characteristic weathering sequence of the globigerina limestone seen in a wall in Valetta with honeycombing, cavitation and flaking.

special vessels. Honey, a local exotic raw material and highly prized food, was no doubt also contained in special vessels.

Decorations on the ceilings of some of the rooms of the hypogeum consist of interconnecting branching spirals, circular designs and polygonal forms. In room 20 Evans comments that the designs 'are somewhat angular, which gives them a polygonal appearance. The whole has a cellular effect, rather like a honeycomb' (Evans 1971: 51). Indeed this is the case, and while the ceiling of this chamber resembles a honeycomb, the decorated upper portions of the walls are covered with two rows of spirals connected to the ceiling decoration by vertical lines (Fig. 3.32). The connected spirals, resembling curled ram horns, are very similar in form to those found on the special altar at Tarxien with the sacrificial animal remains and the plug hole (see above). This suggests a direct link, as we might expect, between goat sacrifice and the ritual use of honey. Both were connected with states of transformation. But if we understand the spirals as being polysemous symbols and

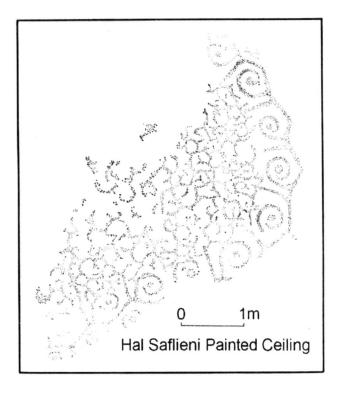

0   1m

Hal Saflieni Painted Ceiling

Figure 3.32 The Hal Saflieni painted ceiling. After Evans (1971).

also having metaphorical referents to the movements of the waves, we have here a striking image of a honeycomb above water, a material metaphor for Malta, the islands of honey, floating on the sea.

From honey to ochre: food for the living, food for the dead   Comparing two of the primary substances used as mediums for the transformation of ritual states in the temples we may arrive at the following distinctions:

Honey	*Ochre*
Wet and viscous	Dry and powdery
Transparent	Opaque
Local	Exotic
Made by bees often high up	Found below in the ground
Yellow	Red
Colour of stone	Colour of blood
Edible	Inedible
Present	Past

Smells of death,	Used to decorate the living,
Eaten by the living	Sprinkled over the dead

Honey is a natural food, made by the bees. As Lévi-Strauss (1973) has noted, it is something almost too cultural, a 'pre-cooked' substance, ready to eat, but untouched by fire. Ochre, on the other hand, is a cultural product that has to be ground down to form a powder and mixed with water to form a bloody coloured paste for painting. Honey is often found in nests high above the ground; ochre must be dug out of the ground. Honey is a product of insects, which, like humans, have an intensely social life and are organized in hierarchies of workers and drones. The cellular geometric architecture of the bees finds its counterpart in the architecture of humans. Ochre is not made by living creatures but may be a powerful symbol of the blood of ancestral creation, thus honey is of the present and ochre is associated with the past.

In the temple rituals honey and ochre were no doubt associated with cults for the living. In the rock-cut tombs and the hypogeum they were associated with cults for the dead. If the honey of the bees was eaten by the temple initiates, perhaps the copious amounts of ochre found with the dead suggest this was their food and nourishment. Ochre, with its exotic origins in Sicily coupled with perhaps a notion that this was ancestral blood created when the world was made, was thus a peculiarly appropriate substance to sprinkle over the dead, who smelt like honey, a primary medium eaten by temporal initiates passing through life and towards death. The blood of ochre was brought along the old ancestral path of movement across the sea. The honey was collected from its own originary island source. Ochre was thus associated with movement and the sea, honey with stability and the new island home. Ochre, an exotic ancestral substance, was linked with honey, a special island substance. Both were rare materials, difficult to obtain, and this involved human hardship, the sea journey and the potential danger of interactions with other peoples, climbing rocks and trees and the battle with the community of bees. The bodies of the deceased buried in the hypogeum, like all dead bodies, would have given off a somewhat cloying sweet smell like honey: the scent of honey is linked with the scent of death. Just as we can regard the redness of ochre as an obvious metaphor for the blood of life, the blood of death, the taste and smell of honey also link the two domains in a powerful way, but synaesthetically.

Conclusions

Differing social interpretations of aspects of the architectural spaces of the temples have radically different implications with regard to who had access to them. In one view, the majority of people were excluded from the temples, which were the domain of a specialist priestly elite (Stoddart et al. 1993; see also Bonanno et al.

1990). In another view (Evans 1996; Grima 2001), passage through the temples was part and parcel of group identity and rooted in ritual practice in the temples. In our view, passage through the temples was an essential element in constructing individual and group identity, but it was restricted as well. The point was not to prevent access to the temple but to carefully control the manner in which the temple spaces were experienced. Preventing access would have made the temple irrelevant to most people's lives. Certain parts of the deep temple interiors would only be accessible to a few. Other areas would be more or less public and open to all. It seems pretty clear from considering the internal details of the temple architecture that the most public areas were the court areas immediately in front of the entrance or entrance corridor as you entered the temple. It is precisely these areas that are the most highly decorated at most temples and where one finds the majority of the naturalistic motifs at Tarxien and the greatest number of decorated stones at Hagar Qim. It is also these areas that would be most illuminated by sunlight shining through the doorway, as discussed above. The ever-darkening and increasingly constricted temple interiors, restricted by bars, curtains and doors, from front to back, imply greater secrecy and control.

We can surmise that ultimately the temples were embodiments of ideas, material metaphors through which the island world and that beyond became known. They created the landscape through its domestication and incorporation into a social and cosmological world. There can be little doubt that they served to demarcate claims of belonging to the land and were situated within the landscapes customarily used by different social groups. Knowledge of and relationship to the land was a process never completely articulated or finishing, changing as the temple complexes were built and rebuilt and related to each other. Such knowledges would have been constructed as stories to be passed down from one generation to another. The power locales in the landscape, the caves, rock outcrops, sea arches, wadi gorges, giant sink holes, etc., would be systematically related to the local ancestral genealogies of the temple-using group. There were the teachers and the taught, and some of the taught became the teachers. The most intimate and deepest recesses of a temple might only be entered and known to only one or a few ritual specialists, public areas to all, or most. A person's entire life might involve being shown and initiated into different areas of the temple according to status and gender, rank and age, through the medium of animal sacrifice, imbibing blood and honey, drinking the pure water of the heavens, and being decorated with ochre. As one became older and went through various initiation ceremonies, new areas of the back spaces of the temples and their contents would be successively revealed. It is in this temporal expression of a journey through life to the afterlife that the full meaning and significance of the temple architecture and its portable elements would be successively revealed. The recessive spaces and intimacies intensify, shrink and diminish as a metaphor for life.

Somewhat ironically, something along these lines happens today. Tourist groups, up to twenty at a time, are usually led through the temples by guides who impart knowledges. Those tourists at the front can see and hear much less than those at the rear. Temple guards restrict access and maintain surveillance at the sites. Rope barriers prevent entrance into most of the apses and temple niches so that the tourist parties only encounter central parts of the monuments. There is much that they cannot see or encounter. Consequently, their experience and knowledge always remain filtered, limited and partial. Archaeologists, such as ourselves, given permission, and allowed free access everywhere, become the new temple 'priesthood' able to make up our own knowledges and tell our own stories rather than having to listen to those told by others.

$-4-$

Frozen Waves and Anomalous Stones

Rock Carvings and Cairns in a Southern Swedish Landscape

In the far south-east corner of Sweden, near to the small port of Simrishamn, there are a well-preserved cluster of Bronze Age rock carving sites together with one of the densest barrow concentrations in southern Sweden. The carving surface at Järrestad is one of the largest and most elaborate in the country. Only 15 km to the north is the Kivik grave, the largest and most monumental cairn in the whole of Scandinavia, with a unique, elaborately engraved internal cist that nestles next to the Baltic coast. It is associated with an elaborate stone ship setting, numerous small cairns and two funerary longhouses to the south. This chapter is an attempt to reinterpret these important features of the archaeological record both in relation to their landscape settings, and to each other.

The Study Area

The study area (Figs 4.1, 4.2) extends for 25 km north–south and to a maximum extent of 14 km west–east. It can be divided into two parts of roughly equal size. The southern half is an open, almost treeless landscape and much of it today consists of an extremely fertile and productive undulating agricultural plain. The northern part is much more heavily wooded with poorer soils, higher hills, and is much more starkly undulating, broken up with smaller and larger hills and ridges which are often quite sharply pronounced. The topography here is highly varied and tightly localized, creating a sense of enclosed intimacy compared with the wide vistas of the south. Here there are numerous small enclosed worlds bounded physically and visually by ridges, hills and knolls, and these are often limited to a kilometre or less, except on heights overlooking the Baltic Sea. The most signifi-cant of these is the horst ridge of Stenshuvud, rising to height of 97 m above the Baltic, from which there are sweeping views inland across a broad-leaved forest and out across the Baltic to the north, south and east. From the top the Danish island of Bornholm is visible to the south on clear days. But this hill is effectively a seamark rather than a landmark, only appearing prominent when seen from Vik to the south or Haväng to the north, along the coast, or out to sea. This northern

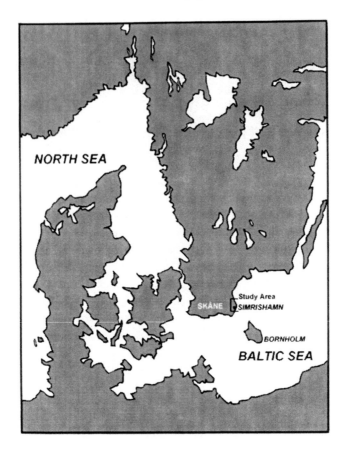

Figure 4.1 The location of the study area in south-east Sweden.

landscape is dissected by numerous small fast-flowing streams running from west to east. The underlying geology is granite.

The southern part of the study area is characterized by a number of distinctive topographies:

1. Running for 4 km along the coast from Simrishamn in the north to Brantevik in the south and in inland areas around Järrestad and Gladsax there are areas characterized by large exposures of white Cambrian sandstone pavements with thin or no soil cover. Rough grass and scrub provide only rough grazing. The Cambrian sandstone also outcrops along the coast at Vårhallarna, Baskemölla and Vik, north of Simrishamn. The surface character of these sandstone pavement areas differs locally. Just to the south of Vik the 60 m-wide geologically celebrated 'Parson's bathtub' occurs in the rocks on the foreshore. Here concen-

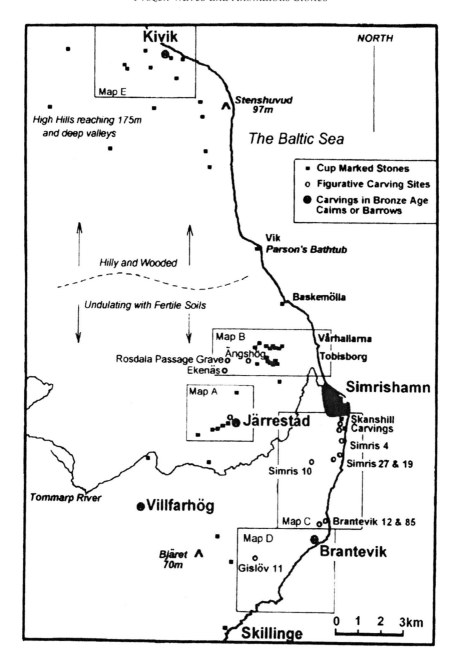

Figure 4.2 The distribution of stones with figurative carvings, cup-marked stones and carvings in Bronze Age barrows or cairns in the study region.

Figure 4.3 The Parson's bathtub, Vik.

tric waterfilled rings of stone bear a striking resemblance to a massive ring cairn with a central human-sized cist-like depression (Lindström 1967; Carserud 1992: 49) (Fig. 4.3). The pavements exposed at Brantevik and Vik have numerous marine fossil inclusions and a rough surface. Between Simrisham and Brantevik, the pavement has an entirely different character. Here it forms extensive glassy ice-like sheets dipping down into the sea, from which they are highly visible.

2. Extensive areas of the agricultural plain extending around Hammenhög to the west are almost completely flat or only very gently undulating.

3. Numerous small bogs and depressions affording rough pasture break up the arable landscape.

4. The majority of the plain is characterized by gentle rises, low spurs, depressions and knolls.

The differences in height in this entire southern area are generally slight. At 70 m the hill of Bjäret is the highest point, but many other short ridges and knolls rise to 50 m or more. In the south-east of the study region, from Simrishamn to Skillinge, the land rises markedly from the sea, forming a somewhat irregular coastal ridge separating a narrow coastal strip of land to the east from the inland agricultural plain. The only watercourse to drain this area is the Tommarp river, which flows through the centre, cutting more deeply into the plain in its eastern lower reaches, where it meanders in a relatively deep valley before it reaches the sea north of Simrishamn. There is a fairly well-defined northern boundary to this undulating plain where the woodland cover becomes extensive with the hills rising to 80 m or more, reaching 175 m at the highest point in the far north-west.

The northern and southern landscapes of the study region thus constitute significantly different worlds and in agricultural terms one is rich, the other is poor. One way of describing this area is to say that there is a distinctive northern and southern world, another is that there are distinctive coastal and inland worlds within each. In the past the major route of communication between these worlds would have been along the coast. To reach the great Kivik grave in the north from the large barrows in the south would only be a matter of hours. The sea connected, while the land separated, different communities.

Qualities of Stone

The presence of rock carving sites has been known and documented since the mid-nineteenth century. Since then there have been a number of important publications and surveys. The first attempt to comprehensively survey and document them was published by Althin (1945), followed by a new survey and documentation of them by Burenhult (1973), and the recent work of Coles at the largest site, Järrestad (Coles 1999). Welinder (1974) published a quantitative survey of the frequencies of motifs on the sites as known then. Since the date of Burenhult's publication two major new carving sites with figurative designs have been discovered (Strömberg 1985: 72–7; Broström and Ihrestam 1998). An extensive new survey and inventory of rock carving sites in the whole of the southern part of the study region has been carried out (Broström and Ihrestam 1996), resulting in the discovery of large numbers of previously undocumented cup-marked stones and a few new sites with figurative designs. In terms of our knowledge of the locations of carving sites, and in terms of their standard of published documentation, we have an excellent record with which to work.

The overall emphasis in most previous research has been to achieve an 'object-ive' documentation of these carving sites, so Burenhult criticizes Althin's work as too impressionistic and his documentation of Järrestad is in turn supplemented by that of Coles, who reveals further details. Althin's, Burenhult's and Welinder's studies are principally concerned with chronological questions rather than the structuring and meaning of the designs. Randsborg (1993), by contrast, provides an important and major iconographic study of the Kivik grave, but while discus-sing far-flung evidence elsewhere in Scandinavia, such as the Sagaholm barrow in Småland, he does not relate the decorations of the Kivik cairn in any detail to the much closer carving surfaces to the south. Coles' reinterpretation of Järrestad, in turn, is not linked to a detailed consideration of other carving surfaces in the area nor to the Kivik grave. Here, and building on these previous studies, we attempt to draw the various strands of evidence together to provide a fresh interpretative account relating the various carving sites both to each other and to the locations of Bronze Age barrows in the landscape.

All the carved rocks with figurative designs occur in the southern part of the study region, where there are three carved rocks of major significance with the greatest frequency and variety of designs. A further three rock surfaces possess smaller numbers of designs. Numerous other carved rocks have only a few figurative designs or are decorated exclusively with cup marks (Table 4.1; Fig 4.2). In the northern part of the study region only cup-marked stones occur and in much lower frequencies than in the south, although this may be partly attributable to lack of recent survey work. Apart from their presence on exposed rock surfaces, cup marks also occur on the upper surfaces of the capstones of middle Neolithic dolmens and passage graves. Figurative carvings occur uniquely on the capstone of the Rosdala passage grave. Carvings are also documented in the stone cists or stone settings of Bronze Age barrows and cairns, notably at Kivik in the north and at three sites in the south (Table 4.1; Fig. 4.2). They thus occur on a variety of media: on exposed rock outcrops, on monumental stone tombs of middle Neolithic date and in Bronze Age barrows and cairns, on both 'natural' and 'cultural' stones and, from a Bronze Age perspective, on contemporary and preexisting monuments in the cultural landscape.

In the north all the cup-marked stones are granite. In the south all the figurative carvings on exposed rock surfaces, with the exception of Gislöv 11 and Simris 10, which are engraved in granite, occur on the white Cambrian sandstone. The cup marks on the capstones of the passage graves are also on granite, with the exception of those on the Rosdala passage grave. The figurative designs and cup marks on the nearby stone at Ängshög are on the top of an enormous isolated granite block. Most of the recently documented stones with cup marks, away from the coast, occur on granite boulders.

The contrast between the Cambrian sandstone exposures and the granite surfaces and blocks on which the carvings occur is of great significance, although it has not been discussed in the archaeological literature, where the qualities of the rock, or even the rock type, are rarely mentioned. The rock surfaces have been regarded as a kind of blank slate on which the carvings are inscribed and their qualities effectively ignored. Althin's representations of the carvings are in the form of water colour painted drawings in which the rock surface becomes reduced to a white two-dimensional background. Burenhult used a different method of technical documentation involving covering the surface of the rock with water-soluble white paint, which was then wiped clean, leaving the paint in the cracks

Table 4.1 Frequencies of designs on the rock carving sites in the Simrisham area, excluding sites with cup-marked stones

	Rock	Circles	Circle/cross	Animals	CM	Boats	Humans	Axes	Feet	Shoes-soles	Other
Coastal locales											
Skanshill group	CS	1	–	–	2	4+	–	–	–	–	Two frame figures
Simris 4 group	CS	1	–	–	10	11	–	14	–	–	
Simris 19	CS	10	6	2	10	45	3	53	–	–	Oval frame design; omega design; 1 snake; conjoined wheels
Simris 27	CS	–	4	2	8	27	3	4	–	–	
Brantevik 12	CS	–	–	–	9	–	–	–	–	3	
Brantevik 85	CS	1	7	–	46	9	1	1	–	–	Oval frame design
Inland Sites											
Simris 10	G	–	–	–	–	11	6	–	–	–	
Gislöv 11	G	–	2	–	39	12	–	2?	–	–	
Järrestad	CS	2+	9+	3	338	29	1	4?	96	90	6 horse riders; 3 spirals; 2 snakes
Rosdala	CS	1	1	3	90	8+	–	6?	–	–	
Ekenäs	G	–	–	–	242	–	–	–	–	3	
Ångshög	G	–	–	–	542	2	–	–	–	9	3 snakes/meanders

Rock type: CS = Cambrian sandstone; G = Granite. CM = Cup marks. For locations of sites, see Fig. 4.2

and carvings and the unaltered surface clean. This was then rubbed with black oxide and the colour contrasts created on the surface were then traced and photographed with superimposed 1 m grid lines. This resulted in the representation of much starker and less 'romantic' images than those produced by Althin but set against the rock similarly represented on large-scale plans as a stark white background. Their representations very effectively highlight the carved images but utterly decontextualize them from the rock itself. This gives their plans of the rocks a somewhat surreal quality standing in opposition to the bodily experience of visiting them in the landscape. The precise two-dimensional diagrams give no indication of the textures and qualities of the stones, their cracks, colour and surface morphology. Coles' documentation of Järrestad is based upon paper rubbings and he represents them in relation to both minor and major cracks breaking up the carving surface. This represents a major and important attempt to recontextualize the images back in relation to their original rock context and in this respect is a clear advance on the documentation of both Althin and Burenhult. However, the rock is still necessarily flattened out in his plan as a uniform two-dimensional surface in which the only feature of the rock surface itself which is regarded of importance is simply the presence or absence of cracks breaking it up, and the scale at which his plan is published makes it difficult to use and impossible to verify details in the field, in contrast to Burenhult's plans. On Burenhult's plans of Järrestad some carvings appear that are missing on those of Coles, and vice versa. None of these authors discuss the colours and manifold sensuous qualities of the rocks. These are eliminated from the accounts.

In this study we have used the documentation of both Burenhult and Coles, which is of a technical standard which probably cannot be bettered. In a sense the goal of attempting to document these carvings 'as they really are' will always be a delusion. Choices always have to be made as to what to include or exclude, and seeing a plan can never substitute for the experience of the rock in the landscape, the kind of understanding, which we attempt to at least evoke in this account, that results from bodily interaction with it.

Rock carvings only become images when they present themselves purely to our vision, i.e. as sheer visual forms instead of being intimately related to the qualities of the rocks themselves and their landscape contexts. Often in the field, to 'see' a design is to simultaneously feel it, to trace its outlines with the fingers. If we regard rock carvings as just visual things, we tend to abstract their appearances from their material existence and their relational significance to the sensuous qualities of the rocks themselves. The reason for the abstracted documentation of the rocks is not hard to surmise. Archaeologists have only been interested in the carvings themselves. The rock itself is regarded as making little or no contribution to the meanings of the designs but instead becomes only a source of worry and difficulty: might this crack be part of a design? Has surface erosion or destruction removed part of this carving? What was the original form and how does this relate to what is visible today? So the rock surfaces themselves as a resource for understanding what the carvings might mean have been entirely ignored, with the exception of Coles' recent work at Järrestad. In this study the aim of the analysis is effectively the reverse. It is an attempt to understand the carvings in terms of the experiential qualities of the rocks themselves and to make this, and bodily interaction with the patterning of the designs across the rock surfaces, a starting point for their reinterpretation.

The white Cambrian sandstone rock on which all the major sites with figurative designs occur is both unique and striking within a Scandinavian context. Outside this tiny corner of south-east Sweden virtually all documented rock carvings occur on various types of granites which may be relatively coarse or fine-grained in surface texture and range in colour from shades of dull grey to brightish pinks. By contrast the surfaces of the Cambrian sandstone rock exposures are sensuously smooth and glossy to touch. In places the rock feels like glass. The surfaces gleam in the sunlight and glisten in the rain. The rock surfaces are rarely pure white, except when seen from a distance. They range in colour from an off-white creamy surface, to shades of silver and blue-grey. In places the rock surfaces resemble in surface texture and quality old or dead ice, ice that has been warped and stressed, fissured and exposed with time, like the ice that forms today in the winter along the coasts and across the northern part of the Baltic Sea. On these icy surfaces the carvings frequently appear as rough grey indentions in a waxy white context.

Today the whitest and 'purest' of these rock surfaces are those at Järrestad and at Simris 19 (Fig. 4.4). The feet of many visitors effectively keep these rocks white and shiny, whereas a rock surface such as Simris 27, rarely visited, is overgrown with turf, grey and dirty-looking by comparison. This suggests that the rock surfaces in the past either would have had to be maintained or were kept clean through being visited on numerous occasions. The exceptional qualities of this stone have long been recognized and the sandstone exposures have been extensively quarried, no doubt destroying many carving sites. Many of the buildings and most of the cobbled streets of Simrishamn use this material. The rock is both dense and incredibly hard, and, like marble, cold to touch. To carve these rocks at all was itself an act of technological achievement at which we can only marvel: a magical act. The exposures of the white Cambrian sandstone pavement along the coast, when seen from the Baltic Sea, might have appeared to the prehistoric populations as huge fields of inland grounded ice: resistant, permanent, perhaps in some way representing an ancient world, an inland frozen sea on which the ancestors had once walked.

Apart from its coldness and icy appearance, the Cambrian sandstone rock outcrops have another remarkable quality: they incorporate in places multiple stratigraphic layers of fossilized wave impressions similar to those that form in the

Figure 4.4 The rock surface at Simris 19 looking towards the sea.

sand on the beach today, throughout the area in which they outcrop. Today the fossil waves are only prominent in quarry sites where top layers of stones have been removed. They may be seen down on the foreshore 200 m to the south of Brantevik harbour and again further to the south. Here there may be up to a one metre distance between the wave crests, huge compared with the rippling wave effects formed by the waters of the Baltic today, indicating that when they were created 570 million years ago they were of oceanic dimensions – huge surf waves (Carserud 1992: 71; Hamberg 1990). The sea that created these gigantic waves lay to the south and the beach was orientated in a west–east direction (Carserud 1992: 71). The beach today at Brantevik runs north-south and the waves come in from the east. This means that the ancient fossil waves run down towards and disappear into the Baltic at right angles to the waves breaking on the shoreline today. The fossil waves of the past are an inversion of those seen in the present and they were a product of a huge stormy sea, contrasting with the relative calmness of the placid land-locked Baltic today, where grass and trees can grow next to the very edge of the ocean.

In the course of our study of rock carvings and barrow sites we have noted the presence of numerous places where these fossil wave formations in the rocks are clearly visible elsewhere in quarry exposures at Simris 4, about 20 m away from nearest rock carvings (Fig. 4.5), around the Tjuvastenen, a quarried block and local

Figure 4.5 Fossil waves in the Cambrian sandstone exposed in a quarried area adjacent to the Simris 4 rock carvings.

landmark to the north, across extensive inland areas of the exposed sandstone pavements north of Simrishamn, around Bäckhalla valley (Bäckhalladalen), to the south of the major carving site of Järrestad, and in rocks exposed by the sea at Branterör. Where the rocks have not been quarried away, these rippling wave effects are less obvious, as a result of the subsequent effects of glaciation. They have only a muted presence or are entirely absent in places where the rock has been planed more or less flat. Notably they run right across the major rock carving site at Järrestad, and part of the recently discovered and exposed carved rock surface at Brantevik 85. Single large wave-like ridge and dip effects occur on the rock carving sites of Simris 27, Simris 4 and Skanshill.

Experiencing Carvings and Barrows

The cold icy rock surfaces quite literally represent a frozen sea, a sea that is now on the land and reverses all the major characteristics of the present-day sea. This is a world which is, in comparison, upside down. The silent waves on this frozen sea are fixed and do not move. Static and arrested forms, they lack all the qualities of sound, colour, constant movement, viscosity, the smell and taste of salt and seaweed associated with the living sea. The coldness, whiteness and static nature of the rocks makes the use of metaphors of dead ice and frozen waves apt descriptions of their symbolic qualities, and, we will argue, these were qualities of the rock recognized in some places by the Bronze Age rock carvers and are part and parcel of the meanings of the designs.

All but one of the rock carving sites with figurative designs occur in two different zones in the landscape, along a coastal strip from Simrishamn in the north to Brantevik in the south and inland to the south and north of Gladsax (see Fig. 4.2). In addition to these there are groups of inland and coastal cup-marked stones. We will discuss each of these areas in turn.

Coastal sites

Simris 27   This is a large rock exposure measuring about 23 m north–south and 12 m west–east. It is situated on the midpoint of a gentle west–east slope running down to the sea which is visible about 250 m away to the east. The land rises up quite steeply in the form of a ridge about 100 m to the west of the rock, blocking views inland. The rock itself is visible from only a short distance away in all directions and only a few of the carvings are visible from a distance of more than 10 m. Today the carving surface is situated on the margin between arable land to the north and rough grazing land to the south. No other carved rocks or Bronze Age barrows are visible from here. The rock dips gently from north–south and from the north-west to the south-east. In terms of the rock slope there are two main carving surfaces, one at the northern and one at the southern end of the rock. The northern part of the rock is virtually flat, dipping only slightly to the north. The southern end dips much more steeply to the south-east. In the approximate centre of the carving surface the rock dips steeply down, resembling a large wave when seen from the south. The surface of the northern part of the rock has a series of cracks which run north–south, dividing the rock into panels within which the designs have been carved. These cracks continue across the southern part of the rock but here the cracks run down the rock as well as across it.

Six groups of designs can be distinguished (Fig. 4.6). At the north-east end of the rock there are four ships all moving to the north or right, parallel with the present-day coastline to the east. Below these, to the east are four paired ceremonial axes, arranged in symmetrical opposition to each other, three of which are borne by human figures. In the approximate centre of the rock there is a large circle cross, positioned on the 'wave' that runs across it here, where the angle of slope is steepest, associated with a group of boats and two smaller circle crosses. These boats are also moving parallel to the coast, some to the right and some to the left, with the exception of one boat moving east or down the rock. They appear much more animated than the boats at the northern and southern end of the rock, which

Figure 4.6 Carvings on the Simris 27 carving surface.

all move in the same direction: north, or to the right. A fourth group of carvings below this to the east consists of eight boats and two animals situated on a virtually flat area of the rock below the wave above and at its lowest exposed point. Four of these boats are moving parallel to the coast, three to the right and one to the left. Two boats move towards the sea to the east and two away from it. The fifth group at the southern end of the rock consists of a large ship moving to the right and other fragments of designs that may also be boats. At the top of the rock there is another circle cross and a boat moving right.

All the designs on the rock can only be seen at its approximate centre where the largest circle cross occurs. Designs at the southern and northern ends of the rock are not intervisible. On this carving surface there is an obvious emphasis upon pairing and symmetry: the opposed ceremonial axes, the boats in pairs and groups of four, the four circle crosses, the pair of animals (deer?) facing towards the group of boats at the bottom of the rock, the circle crosses themselves divided into four. The overall spatial arrangement replicates the overall theme of twos and fours with two groups of designs at the northern end of the rock and four others towards the south. But there is also an interesting asymmetry between the four opposed axes with only three axe bearers. All the boats are differentiated from each other in style. There are no two identical forms. All with the exception of five in the middle of the rock move left (five) or right (twelve) across the rock, parallel with the present-day coast. All those moving down the rock occur in the centre immediately above and below its steepest angle of dip. There is a clear separation on the rock between the panel with the axe bearers and that with the boats, and, in comparison, the former are very shallow carvings.

All these designs are meant to be seen from below the rock to the east, except for the boats in the centre, which, to be seen the 'right way up', must be viewed from the north or south. It is interesting to note that no designs have been placed so as to be seen from above the rock to the west.

Simris 19   This rock is situated a few metres away from the present-day shoreline, which, unlike most other areas of Sweden, stood at approximately the same position in the Bronze Age as today, with subsequent land uplift being minimal (Fig. 4.4). The rock carvings stand out as white against a silverish grey background, or alternatively, as a darker and rougher pecked surface. The rock slopes slightly from the west down towards the east and the sea. No other carved rock surfaces or barrows are visible from it, and the rock itself is only visible from a short distance away (50 m or less) except when seen from out to sea. Today it stands as a sadly marooned block on the edge of an extensive quarry site and cut off by the coast road from the beach. This means that it is not possible to experience the carved rock surface today as once intended. Indeed the present carved surface may once have formed part of a much more extensive distribution of carved rocks to the west, north and south. On the lower part of the rock there is a central depression lacking carvings, which are arranged in groups in a roughly circular fashion around it. The very top (western) part of the carved surface is virtually flat and clearly differentiated from the carved areas below. The entire carved rock surface is visible from any point on its perimeter, from which one can see clearly, or less distinctly, all areas with carved designs. So there are no distinct visual fields here as at Simris 27. The entire carved surface opens itself up to an observer at once, without requiring movement. While the rock itself would be visible from a long distance away out to sea the presence of carvings would not be apparent until reaching it.

The rock surface is criss-crossed by a series of deep cracks (Fig. 4.7) which run west–east down it and diagonally from the NE–SW and NW–SE. The carvings are positioned within these natural panels, rarely overlapping the major cracks. The obvious way to approach these carvings is from the beach and to move up and around the rock surface to the highest point in the west. Overall the rock carving surface is dominated by two motifs – boats and axes. The majority of the boats, unusually, flow down and up the rock surface, towards and away from the sea, contrasting with those at Simris 27, situated 450 m away to the south-west. The boats are arranged in groups with the axes. The orientation of both requires constant movement around the groups of designs in order to see them the 'right' way up. Viewing these rock carvings requires a kind of spatial dance. There is no one and obvious viewing angle as at Simris 27. This requirement for circular movement is reinforced by the arrangement of the carvings around the central depression. A participatory work of movement is needed in order to view the

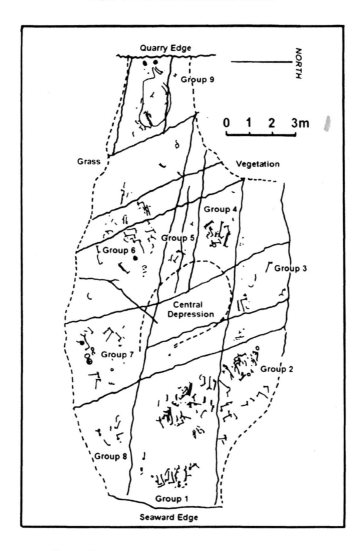

Figure 4.7 Carving groups and major cracks on Simris 19.

motifs 'properly'. While the surface at Simris 27 encourages a static and fixed gaze from off the rock below, these carvings invite one to move in and amongst them around different parts of the rock, which all visitors to the site characteristically do.

There are nine major groups of carvings together with a few more isolated motifs (Fig. 4.7). The first group at the very bottom of the carving surface includes a boat moving down the rock towards the sea, four hafted axes which appear as upside down when viewed from below and off the rock, others of different form which appear the right way up, pecked circular designs and conjoined circle crosses (chariot wheels?). There is also a highly distinctive omega-shaped design identical in form to those represented on the bottom of Slab 8 of the Kivik grave (see below).

Group 2 has one of only three human figures on the rock, a phallic axe bearer with the gigantic axe blade turned towards the sea. The axes dominating this group have their blades orientated in a startling variety of different directions – north, south, west and east – whereas all the boats are travelling towards or away from the sea. Some of the axes are clearly paired, and at the eastern end of the group the hafts of two axes are placed so as to run directly parallel to a boat. Other motifs include cup marks, conjoined wheels and circular designs. Group 3 consists of three axes and an axe blade all facing north and parallel to the coast and a boat moving towards the sea. Group 4 is made up of four boats, two moving down the rock, one across it and another diagonally to the south-east. The axe blades are orientated south, east and south-east. Two circular designs here, one outlined and another entirely pecked out, might symbolize the sun and the moon, and this could indicate movement of the boats by day and night (see discussion on page 197–8). There is a possible human figure near the centre of this group. This is a dense and very deeply pecked group of carvings in which the directionality of the boats in combination with the axe blade orientations create a striking effect of whirling circular motion (Fig. 4.8).

Group 5 consists of two or three axe blades orientated to the east and north. Group 6 is a more open, less densely packed group with two circle crosses, seven boats and seven axes. The axe blades face south and east and the boats flow up and down the rock. Again, to see these designs 'properly' requires constant circular movement around them. A second phallic axe bearer occurs here this time with the axe blade facing south, in a diametrically opposed direction to the one present in Group 2. In this group all the boats can be seen the right way up when seen from the southern side, contrasting with the arrangements found in Groups 2 and 4. Group 7 consists of six axes with their blades facing south, north and east together with six circles and circle crosses and an animal. The boats have disappeared. In Group 8 there are conjoined circles and axes with their blades facing east and south.

An interesting potential narrative theme can be read into this spatial arrangement of groups and motifs. In Group 1 there is a clear emphasis on parallelism between the boat and the axe hafts and there is a pairing of axe forms with blades facing in the same or opposite directions. The motifs in this group can all be seen 'properly' from either the west or the east side and their arrangement appears static. Group 2 is much more dynamic and vibrant, with axe blades orientated in all directions and axe and boat pairings. Group 3 appears static with a pairing between a boat and an axe and all the axe blades facing the same direction: north in opposition to the boat moving east. Group 4 gives a whirling impression (Fig. 4.8). Boats and axes do not run parallel to each other. Some axes are paired, the boats are not.

Figure 4.8 Simris 19: the carvings in Group 4.

In Group 6 axes and boats are relatively disentangled or disengaged from each other. At least two axes appear to be paired. In Groups 7 and 8 the boats are absent and the axes are no longer paired. It is as if we have here the choreographed steps in a dance movement with moments of pause and vitality, forms coming spinning together and forms being split apart, pairing and separation. In the course of this movement the phallic axe bearer moves from facing east to facing south and both the axe and the phallus increase in size. While axes are clearly paired, except in the final stages of this dance, the boats are not and the axes 'dance' much more vigorously. Some axe hafts and boats parallel each other in Groups 1 to 3, form a whirling motion in Group 4, and thereafter become separated and flung apart.

Group 9, the final Group, is clearly separated from the others on a flat ledge of rock at the top western end of the carving surface. Here a unique and deeply carved frame design occurs, open to the west. Other designs here consist of boats, circles, circle crosses and an animal (horse?) overlapping the frame design. This has been interpreted as a death shroud or cloak (Almgren 1960: 19; Malmer 1981: 54) but an alternative, and more contextualized understanding of it in relation to the landscape, is that it is a schematic representation of the Baltic Sea with its opening to the west. The boats here move away or towards the sea and diagonally across the rock. To see them right way up requires moving around the frame design. A meandering snake-like motif is attached to the keel of the largest boat. Axes are completely absent from this group and there is no pairing of the boat designs. This group may have been added to the rock at a later stage. It does not appear to be integrated with the circular arrangements or the putative narrative themes of the other carvings on the rock.

As at Simris 27, all the boats are highly differentiated and no two are identical in style. While all the boats are different, the axe forms are very standardized. Large-hafted ceremonial axes dominate but there are at least two other simpler axe forms represented in Groups 1 and 2. The presence of the axe bearers on Simris 27 directly connect it with Simris 19 but on the former rock the axes and boats are completely separated and the majority of the boats run parallel with the sea rather than towards or away from it.

Simris 27 and 19 are the two largest coastal rock carving places. There are a number of others which have both fewer designs and design associations. North of these carved surfaces a string of smaller carving surfaces are known and documented. At the far northern end of the distribution there are four minor carving sites. Two consist of single cup marks, another has two unique (for Skåne) frame figures, and a fourth boats. Different types of motifs are not being combined on these rocks and they occur in low frequencies. The locations are intervisible, but not the carvings themselves. Here the white sandstone pavement dips gently to the east and the sea, which is visible, but not the shoreline. Here the waves can be heard breaking on an invisible shoreline from which one would have had to move between one and two hundred metres upslope to reach the carvings. At Skanshill three of the boats occur on a wave-like dip in the exposed sandstone pavement on the steepest area of the rock. About 500 m to the south of this group there are a number of other carved rock surfaces at Simris 4. Here individual motifs are characteristically combined and/or paired (Fig. 4.9). The northernmost group of three carved panels consists of axe and boat designs. In Group 1 an axe and a boat are superimposed at right angles to each other. In Group 2 two boats flank the haft of an axe. A third boat is separated. In Group 3 an axe haft and boat overlap. The five axe blades are orientated in all cardinal directions except to the west. These motifs require motion around them in order to see them right way up. All these three groups of motifs are intervisible and occur in areas of the rock exposure free of cracks. Here the rock slopes in distinctive directions. The northernmost group is on a rock surface sloping gently east and towards the sea. This group is highest. The central group is positioned on a west-facing slope and the southernmost group on an area of rock sloping south. So the way the rock slopes reinforces the spatial divisions between these carvings. South of this group of panels other carved surfaces occur. These are less complex and consist of single or paired boats, paired circle crosses, cup marks and isolated axe and ship motifs.

To the south of the major carved panels at Simris 19 and 27 two rock carving surfaces occur at Brantevik. Two adjacent small exposures of flat rock at Brantevik

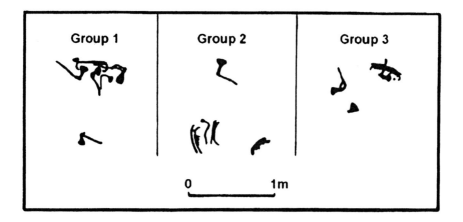

Figure 4.9 Simris 4: carving groups. After Burenhult (1973).

12 are pecked with 35 cup marks and five cup marks and three deeply cut foot soles. At Brantevik 85 a large carved stone surface covering an area of 30 m² was exposed from turf cover in 1985. The rock surface here is very irregular. The western part is lower and broken up by a series of undulating irregular wave-like depressions. The principal area with the carved designs to the east is smoother and more extensive. The surface here is pockmarked with numerous fossil depressions. The groups of motifs are widely spaced out in groups across the rock surface. Group 1 consists of a circle cross and two cup marks situated towards the northern end of the rock exposure. Nine metres to the south is a single boat. This has to be viewed from the west to be seen the right way up. Five metres to the south of this is another single boat which must be seen from the east to appear the correct way up. A further 7 m to the SSE of this is a very large frame figure resembling that on the far western end of Simris 19. This is open to the north. In and around it are 42 cup marks. To the south of it there are two boats. Group 5 on the north-west section of the pavement consists of a human and a boat design. Group 6, six paired circle crosses, and Group 7, four ships, an axe and two cup marks. The rock exposure is thus straddled by two design pathways of very different form leading towards the dominant frame figure at the southern end. The orientation of this (north–south) inverts that of the frame figure (west–east) on the rock at Simris 19.

Inland Sites from Tobisborg to Rosdala

From the coast near to Tobisborg, where it outcrops at Vårhallarna, there extends a large area of exposed Cambrian sandstone pavement about 2 km inland to the west. This area is marked by two corridors of cup-marked stones, one a northern

group, running approximately west–east and another, a southern group, running
north-west to south-east (Figs 4.2, 4.10). Spread across and resting on the surface
of the sandstone pavement are numerous granite boulders, glacial erratics left
behind with the retreat of the ice sheets. These are generally of fairly small
dimensions, no more than 2-3 m in diameter and 0.2–0.8 m high. It is these granite
boulders rather than the sandstone which are decorated exclusively with cup
marks. There may be as few as one or two cup marks on a stone and up to thirty.
The majority are only decorated with a few cup marks. These cup-marked stones
are fairly regularly spaced across the landscape and appear to mark passages
through it from the end of the Bäckhalla valley inland. They roughly delineate the
margins of the area of sandstone pavement to the north and south-west. Here the
soils are very poor and thin and the area only provides rough grazing, contrasting
with the arable land to the west and south. These cup-marked stones are modest in
dimensions and not highly visible in the landscape. Only a few are intervisible. The
fact that they are decorated at all only becomes apparent on reaching them. The
entire area is gently undulating with small knolls and rock outcrops breaking up the
otherwise flat surface of the pavement. All the cup-marked stones occur relatively
high up above the point where the Cambrian sandstone dips down more steeply to
the east towards the sea. Walking up from the sea, you arrive at this higher inland
landscape with the two corridors through it marked by the decorated stones. What
is interesting here is the occurrence of these cup marks on the granite boulders as
opposed to the Cambrian sandstone, the preferred medium for carving elsewhere.
These boulders stand out in colour, form and surface texture, being much rougher
to touch. Their presence in a landscape dominated by the sandstone pavement is
clearly anomalous and this may have been recognized. For a novice to find and
follow the stones would require being guided and led through the landscape. They
appear to mark passages or routes through it.

It is only at the western ends of the distribution of these stones that the first
barrows occur in the landscape together with stones on which figurative designs
occur. From the decorated stones and graves in the west the only granite stone with
figurative carvings is visible in the distance at Ängshög (Fig. 4.10). This, by
comparison, is a huge coarse-grained pink granite block resembling a pulpit, about
5 m in diameter and 1.6 m high, situated in a virtually flat landscape. Its uppermost
flat surface is decorated with 534 rounded cup marks, eight oblong depressions,
nine foot-soles, three stave designs, one simple single-lined boat design and part
of another, and three meandering snake-like designs (Broström and Ihrestam 1996,
1998). Such is the size of the stone that none of these carvings are visible from the
ground. To see them requires clambering up the steep sides of the stone. This block
effectively marks the culminating and terminal point of the corridors of cup-
marked stones traversing the Cambrian sandstone pavement. It also marks the
margins between arable land to the west and pasture to the east, the point at which

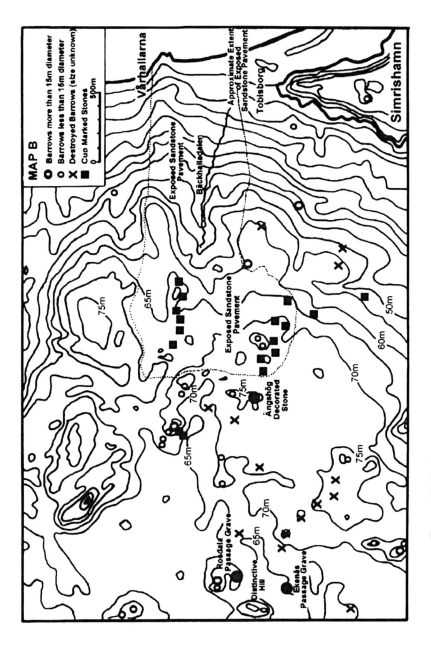

Figure 4.10 The distribution of Bronze Age barrows and cup-marked stones north of Simrishamn.

both the natural and cultural landscape change. To the west large numbers of barrows now straddle the landscape also forming corridors through it. It is as if these barrows now replace the cup-marked stones as landscape markers.

The barrow lines, in turn, terminate further to the west. Here there are two Neolithic passage graves. Two of the surviving granite capstones of the southern Ekenäs passage grave are covered with cup marks. Over 240 are recorded together with three foot-soles. The northern passage grave at Rosdala (Gladsax 18) is surmounted by a massive Cambrian sandstone block, 2.5 m in diameter and 1.8 m high, which stands out in a striking manner in the surrounding landscape. This is decorated with eleven ships, five or six axes, a circle cross, one circular figure, three animals, carved lines and ninety cup marks (Figs 4.11, 4.12). Just as the decorated granite stones stand out as being anomalous on the Cambrian sandstone pavement areas on which they occur to the east, this huge block surmounting the passage grave stands out in an area where the Cambrian sandstone no longer outcrops. It must have been transported either from the Cambrian sandstone outcrops over 1 km to the east or, more likely, from a moraine ridge 200 m away to the west.

All the carvings occur on the eastern side and the top of the capstone facing the sunrise which illuminates them. Standing outside the original entrance to the passage leading to the tomb chamber, only a few of the lowest carvings are visible. They are clearly positioned so as to flow across the eastern side of the roof block and not towards the original entrance to the tomb, indicating that the block was decorated with the figurative designs long after the entrance passage was blocked and hidden. The cup marks which occur on the very top of the stone may, as elsewhere, be of Neolithic date and contemporary with the construction and use of the tomb. The boats all move to the right or from south to north across the block or parallel with the coast to the east. All but one of the axe designs cluster around the large circular figure on the top of the stone with the boats arranged below, except for one boat overlapping with the circular designs and axes. These are simple hafted axe forms contrasting with the ceremonial axe designs which dominate on the carving surfaces at Simris 19 and 27 by the coast. They are of the same type as a group of four axes which occur on the inland site of Järrestad just over 2 km to the south. At least two of the axe blades are orientated so as to face right or north, the same direction as the boats are travelling.

From the Rosdala passage grave the huge granite block marking the end of the corridors of cup-marked stones would (were it not for farm buildings) be clearly visible 1.3 km away. To the west of both tombs, 200 m distant, is a prominent moraine ridge that forms a very distinctive localized feature of the landscape. This blocks all views to the west. From it there are extensive views in all directions, except to the north, where the landscape becomes heavily wooded. From here one looks down to the two passage graves, the strings of Bronze Age barrows to the

Figure 4.11 Cup marks on the top of the capstone of the Rosdala passage grave.

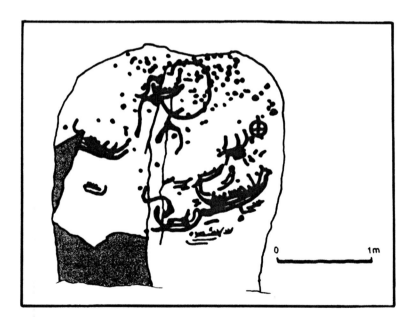

Figure 4.12 Carvings on the capstone of the Rosdala passage grave. Shaded area: stone broken. After Burenhult (1973).

east and the large decorated granite block in the field at Ängshög. The two passage graves are sited at the east towards the northern and southern ends of the ridge, which is composed of a mixture of granite and sandstone boulders, visible in places along it. The form of the ridge itself is rather unusual in the local landscape, and this feature alone provides it with an added significance. It physically marks the western limit of a localized group of carving places and barrow sites, perhaps a distinctive social territory consisting of arable and rough grazing land extending from it to the sea, 4 km away to the east.

Gislöv 11　The rock carving at Gislöv 11 is one of only two places on which figurative carvings occur on a flat granite rock exposure. The granite here is fine-grained, contrasting with the coarse-grained granite of the cup-marked stones to the north of Simrishamn. The carved rock is situated high up in the landscape on a north-east to south-west coastal ridge with extensive views over the sea to the south and east and inland to the north and north-west. Although it is situated only 0.75 km from the nearest coastline, it belongs to a different physical and conceptual world compared with that of the coastal carving sites from Simrishamn to Brantevik. The coastal strip cannot be seen from the carving site and the sea is only experienced in a general sense rather than in any specific way. It cannot be smelt or heard.

The carved rock is unusual in two other respects. It is located in the middle of arable land, and it is situated next to two large barrows also occupying the ridge summit. Unlike the barrows, visible from a considerable distance away, the carving surface remains invisible until one stands next to it. A crack divides the carving surface into a north-east and south-west panel (Fig. 4.13). The north-east panel consists of boat designs and cup marks. The larger south-west panel is dominated by a very large and central circle cross around which a series of boat designs and ambiguous boat/animal forms appear to circulate in different directions. Attempting to see these motifs 'right way up' requires circular movement around the periphery of the designs in a similar fashion to viewing the designs at Simris 19. Linked wheels or circle crosses and axe forms also appear to be represented here but the style of execution of these designs, much coarser and lacking in finesse, contrasts greatly compared with those down by the coast.

At the south-west end of the exposed rock there is a linear arrangement of cup marks. Just 3 m to the south are the remains of a damaged barrow. The mound of this barrow would have probably originally extended 5 m to the north. If this was the case, the carved stone would have appeared from underneath the barrow mound with the cup marks leading towards the central series of designs.

Simris 10　At Simris 10 a similar situation occurs. Here figurative carvings were made in a coarse-grained grey granite rock outcrop. Broken fragments are now in

Figure 4.13 Carvings on the rock surface at Gislöv 11. After Burenhult (1973).

the museums at Lund and Stockholm. The carvings were discovered in connection with the removal of a barrow, Toreshög, in the 1850s and appear to have been covered underneath the edge of the barrow mound. Later they were removed in connection with the quarrying of millstones on the site (Althin 1945: 94–5). On one of the preserved fragments there is one ship figure, on the other five elaborate boats and a number of cup marks. The boats on this stone are orientated at radically different angles from each other and one boat is superimposed across parts of two others. The whole impression is one of a whirling circular movement similar to the boat depictions around the circle cross at Gislöv 11 and in some of the groups of boats and axes at Simris 19.

Simris 10, situated on a small rise and in view of the sea 1 km away to the east, is in a similar landscape location to Gislöv 11. These are the only granite rock outcrops to have had figurative designs on them and the designs on both appear to have been partially or completely concealed by Bronze Age barrows that must have been erected later. Might this indicate that at some stage during the course of the Bronze Age the presence of these figurative designs on the outcropping granite, as opposed to the white Cambrian sandstone, became deemed inappropriate, or was it because the designs had lost their meaning and significance?

Järrestad   The most westerly exposures of the Cambrian sandstone pavements occur in the Järrestad area, 5 km inland from the sea. Here by far the most complex rock carving site in the study area is located. Apart from the major carved panels at Järrestad, seven other carved rocks have been recorded in the immediate locality to the south-west. All these are simple cup-marked stones. Most only have a few cup marks and are not highly visible landscape markers. These decorated stones, at first of rough granite, and then of the white quartzite, form a corridor through the landscape about 1 km long from the south-west to the north-east towards the major carved panels (Fig. 4.14). These stones may have marked the processional way to the place. The frequencies of the cup marks on the stones increase in an interesting way as one moves towards it from those with only one or two cup marks at the south-west end of the distribution, to those with between ten and forty examples, to the surface at Järrestad 4:2 with over 100 cup marks. These occur on a smooth Cambrian sandstone rock outcrop covered with numerous distinctive fossil impressions that resemble bird's feet, like those in the decorated pavement at Brantevik (Fig. 4.15). Sometimes the fossil imprints were used as starting points for the grinding of the cup marks. The rock here is almost perfectly smooth. Sloping to the south-east, it lacks any discernible wave-like marks.

From this point you look down on the great carved rock at Järrestad, which from here itself resembles a huge dipping wave. The Järrestad rock outcrop forms part of a low NW–SE ridge. Immediately to the north the land dips gently away and then rises gently. To the south the land dips away to rise up again to another ridge with sandstone outcrops forming the southern skyline and blocking views of the landscape beyond. To the west the land dips away to an area that was formerly a small bog before rising again to another area with sandstone pavement outcrops, while to the east the land falls gently away to undulating terrain. The views in this direction are most extensive and the sea can be glimpsed on the horizon. Although the carving surface can be seen from as far away as 2 km to the east from the top of the large barrow at Kvegshög and from a few barrow sites along the coastal ridge at Ö Nöbbelöv 3.5 km to the south, from elsewhere it is relatively invisible. It is not visible from barrows and grave sites situated much closer to it. Walking to the rock in the immediate environs, from the north the exposed pavement area is invisible from more than 20 m away. From the east the rock first becomes visible from only within about 50 m. It is visible from greater distances away from the exposed sandstone pavement areas to the south and the south-west. None of the carvings themselves are readily apparent until the rock itself is reached. Both the pavement itself and the carvings on it thus seem peculiarly isolated and remote.

The rock exposure measures about 35 m across from the west–east and 17 m north–south. It has been quarried on the western and north-western sides. Most of the carvings are concentrated in an area measuring 9 × 17 m on the western side of the exposed pavement. Seen from the south, the rock appears as a domed surface rising up beyond an observer. Standing on the southern edge of the rock, the top is effectively skylined, blocking off all views of the landscape beyond. This concentrates and limits the visual field to the rock itself in a striking manner, whereas, from all other directions, the rock is seen as part of a wider landscape context. This suggests a concentration of the visual field from the south looking up at the rock.

The rock is broken up by a series of major and minor cracks plotted by Coles on a new and detailed plan (Coles 1999: Plate 1). These cracks divide the rock into

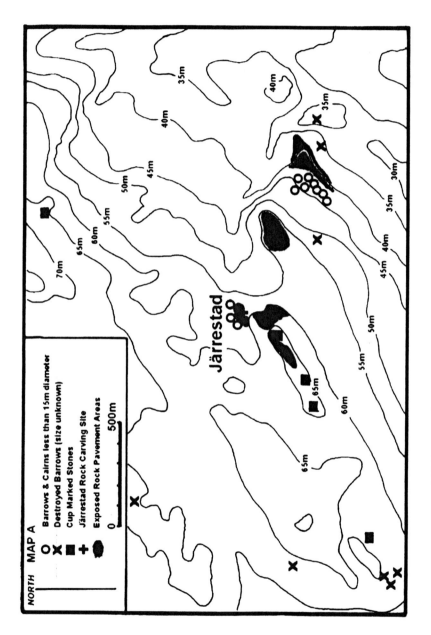

Figure 4.14 Barrows and cup-marked stones in the vicinity of the Järrestad carving locale.

Figure 4.15 Exposed area of rock pavement with fossil impressions to the west of the Järrestad carving locale.

a series of major and minor panels in which the carvings occur. Some of the carvings cross or make use of the minor cracks in the surface but respect the eight major subdivisions created by the major cracks. Although larger and smaller cracks similarly subdivide the carving surfaces on the major sites of Simris 19 and 27 by the coast, they do not appear to have the same significance as at Järrestad in relation to the organization and grouping of the designs (see the discussion on pp. 158–64).

The flattest and smoothest part of the exposed rock surface at Järrestad is at the western end of the rock, where the vast majority of the designs occur. The rock exposure has a distinctive wavy appearance on the eastern side, particularly in the north-eastern corner. From here, the entire surface of the rock can be seen to rise and fall like the waves of the sea (Fig. 4.16). In the main carving area on the western side, presumably subject to the greatest glacial pressure and erosion, this wavy undulating appearance of the rock is less pronounced but is nevertheless present across the entire rock surface. In all there appear to be about twelve waves or ripple effects on the eastern side of the rock which become less distinct as they continue across the rock surface to the west. When sitting or kneeling at the base of the rock pavement to the south, this rippling effect is much more readily apparent than when standing, and to a casual observer the western side of the rock would appear virtually smooth (as it is described and represented in archaeological

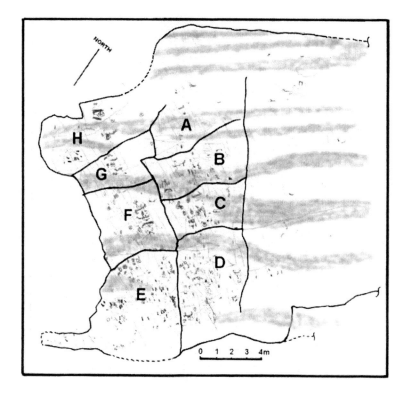

Figure 4.16 The frozen waves discernible on the Järrestad rock carving site. Shaded area represents the troughs of the waves. Major cracks are shown and carving groups defined by them.

publications). The waves run in a north-east to south-west direction across the slope of the rock surface, i.e. towards and away from the coast and the sea, an inversion of the present-day waves that form running from north to south and breaking on the eastern coast. At their most pronounced in the north-east part of the exposed rock pavement the wave crests are about 3 m apart and the dips are about 0.8 m wide and 5 cm in depth. The major cracks running down the rock surface cut across these waves, while some of those running across the rock tend to occur along the bottom of the dips in the waves. Towards the bottom of the western side of the exposed rock surface below the large human figure, this wavy, undulating character of the rock is now lost but would probably be apparent underneath the present turf cover. The rippling wave effects cutting across the rock surface are clearly discernible from all sides of the rock surface if one looks across the rock from one side to the other. The effect is lost if instead one focuses attention on individual carved designs or groups of designs, which have, of course, been the sole feature of interest to contemporary visitors and archaeologists. So the wavy morphology of the rock is a subtle feature of the rock surface only present when

Figure 4.17 The swimmer at Järrestad.

one looks at the rock itself rather than the designs carved on it. But once this quality of the rock is apprehended, the experience of the rock becomes animated in a way in which the background form and the images become fused together to create new meaning.

The single most striking feature of the Järrestad rock is the sinuous presence of the large human figure on it, known as the 'dancer' and always assumed in the literature to be male (Fig. 4.17). This is by far the largest and most dominant single image on the rock surface. It is the only human figure on the carving surface that appears as a single figure rather than as part of another design. It occurs low down the slope of the rock to the south-east. Coles describes the 'dancer' as follows:

> The narrow upper body is separated from the heavier lower body by an uncarved band like those seen elsewhere on large carvings of identifiably-male figures. The slender and long legs have knees bent and the feet appear to be in a ballet-like position; the whole figure is confidently carved. The arms are bent and hands upraised with only the thumbs distinguished. There may be bands around the upper arms. The head is birdlike and pugnacious. (Coles 1999: 177)

He then goes on to discuss possible appendages such as a short sheath which might help to date the 'dancer'. At no point does he discuss whether this is an appropriate term. Looking at this strange image in the context of its occurrence low down the rock below the waves of a fossil sea, we would suggest the appropriate description is that of a swimmer. The extended sinuous legs and arm positions suggest a swimmer in movement through, or beneath, the water, and, as Coles himself states, there is nothing to suggest that the figure is male. If there is a ballet here it is definitely of an aquatic kind!

Apart from this dominant figure, the rock carving surface at Järrestad is dominated by images of boats, naked feet and shoe soles (see Table 4.1). The vast majority of the feet and shoe-soles point down and follow the slope of the rock while the boats run across the slope, the majority riding on the wave crests parallel to their direction. They travel across the rock surface either towards the left or the right, towards or away from the real geographic direction of the sea, riding along the rock waves, which are an inversion of the present-day waves on the coast. As at the other rock carving sites, all the boats are highly individualized in character. No two are identical in form. The majority of the boats are meant to be seen from below or downslope, but some appear 'upside down' and need to be viewed 'right way up' from above, or from the perspective of the feet and shoe-soles. The boats are sometimes paired with each other in an obvious way, one below the other, and also occur in groups of four. Only a couple at the north-east and sparsely decorated end of the rock move downslope.

Many of the feet and shoe-soles are clearly paired, with matched left and right pairs being clearly distinguishable. Overall many more right than left feet are distinguishable in a ratio of about 2:1. The naked feet particularly cluster around the swimmer. They vary in size from those the size of a child's foot to those of an adult. Smaller and larger feet occur together. Many of the shoe-soles are similarly paired, and these, too, vary in size from small to large examples. As with the naked feet, far more right than left shoe-soles are represented. Virtually all the shoe-soles either point downslope or their directionality is ambiguous. This contrasts with a minority of the naked feet that sometimes point unambiguously upslope.

Besides these motifs a number of rarer forms occur: spirals, snake-like meandering designs, six small horse riders, ambiguous conjoined shoe-sole/circle cross motifs, a few animal designs and four representations of what have been variously suggested to be hafted axes, sickles or simplified lurs (Coles 1999: 176).

Coles has drawn attention to the manner in which the major cracks cutting across the carving surface effectively divide it into nine or so major panels (see Coles 1999: Plate 1 and Fig. 4.16). One major north-west to south-east crack separates the rock exposure into two halves. Virtually all the carvings are to the south-west of this crack apart from some naked feet, boat and possible animal designs. In this area two boats moving downslope rather than across the rock are represented together with others moving left and right across the slope. A matched pair of feet point up slope at the top end of the rock directly towards a small barrow above it. Otherwise the feet, both individual lefts and rights, point downslope.

The rest of the carving surface has four major panels on the north-east side and at least four (depending on how you define and trace a major crack) on the south-west side. Each of these panels has its unique combination of motifs and, as Coles notes, 'its own restricted range of images with little cross-referencing to adjacent panels' (*ibid.*: 174). On Fig. 4.16 these are labelled A to H.

Panel A (Fig. 4.18). This consists of five scattered boat designs, some with clearly distinguishable human crew, two isolated right and left shoe-soles moving down the rock, a matched pair of left and right feet, three right feet moving down the slope and a left and a right foot towards the top of the panel pointing, unusually, across it, together with low numbers of scattered cup marks. There is little sense of any structure or order apart from the opposition between most of the feet moving down the rock and the boats across it.

Panel B (Fig 4.18). Here at least three boats traverse the rock. Two are upside down, seen from below. Here a group of four ambiguous axe or lur designs create a unique signature. These overlap with pairs of matched left and right feet pointing downslope (Fig 4.19). The axe/lurs are hafted so as to point to the right and need to be seen from below, i.e. in the opposite direction from the feet with which they are associated. There are two left shoe-soles. At least seven others appear to be rights (one with toes) (all shown on Burenhult's but only some on Coles' plan). All point downslope. There is one possible animal design but this resembles a boat when seen from up the slope. Scattered cup marks occur. Otherwise the surface is dominated by naked feet. One right foot points upslope, the rest point downslope. Only a couple of the feet appear to be left, the rest are right. The only clear pairs are associated with the axe/lurs. Cup marks occur across the entire surface.

Panel C (Fig. 4.20). This has a unique signature of conjoined shoe-soles that also appear to resemble circle crosses ambiguously elongated downslope. There are at least nine of these pairs. Otherwise there are a number of shoe-soles pointing downslope and naked feet. The latter are unpaired left or rights and all but one face upslope. At least two boats travel across the rock, below each other, one to the right, the other to the left. The largest is very deeply engraved. Cup marks are scattered over the surface.

Panel D (Fig. 4.20). This panel has the greatest number of cup marks anywhere in the rock and some are clearly arranged in linear series down the rock slope and following the lines of cracks. One grouping has been claimed to resemble the plan of a longhouse with its posts (Capelle 1991: 132), but such an abstract bird's eye 'plan', while familiar to the eyes of archaeologists, is unlikely to have had such visual resonance in the Bronze Age. These arrangements of cup marks create the unique signature on this panel. Other motifs here are five boats, the lowest utterly distinctive in form. Two are 'upside down'. At least ten shoe-soles, two of which are paired, point downslope. Paired feet point downslope and individual unpaired left and right feet point both up and down the slope.

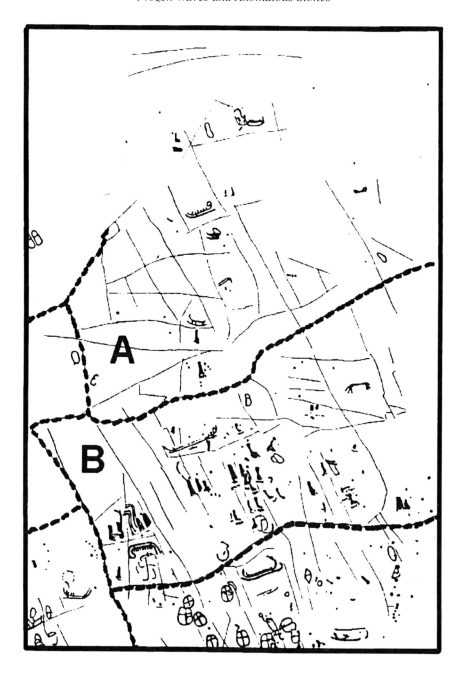

Figure 4.18 Järrestad: carving groups A and B. After Coles (1999).

Figure 4.19 Järrestad: feet, axe/lurs and boat, cupmarks and boat on part of carving area B

Panel E (Fig. 4.21). The unique signature of this panel is the swimmer. There are also three small horse riders, a meandering snake design, many scattered cup marks, feet and shoe-soles. Boats are conspicuous through their absence. The feet cluster around and to the left or south-west of the swimmer. Of these only four (two individual lefts and two rights) point up the slope. The rest, either paired or individual feet, point downslope. Right feet are more frequently represented than left. A couple point across it. All the shoe-soles appear to face downslope either as pairs or as single designs. Cup marks punctuate the surface everywhere.

Panel F (Fig. 4.21). This has at least six boat designs, one of which, the lowest, is moving unusually up or down the slope. The others move across the slope to the right or the left. Two have what appears to be rigging, the lowest of which appears upside down when seen from below. These boats, utterly different from any other boat representations here or elsewhere, represent the unique signatures on this part of the carving surface. A few individual right and left feet are represented pointing up and down the slope. Otherwise individual and matched pairs of shoe-soles occur (apart from a couple of individual lefts and rights moving across the slope), all moving downslope. Small numbers of cup marks scatter the surface.

Panel G (Fig. 4.22). The unique signature of this panel is the presence of conjoined spirals and a third with an emerging snake-like line. There are also two small horse riders, a pair of shoe-soles, three scattered individual shoe-soles and

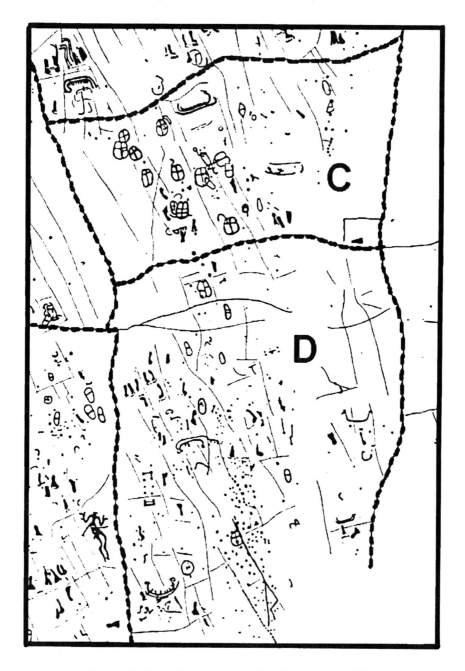

Figure 4.20 Järrestad: carving groups C and D. After Coles (1999).

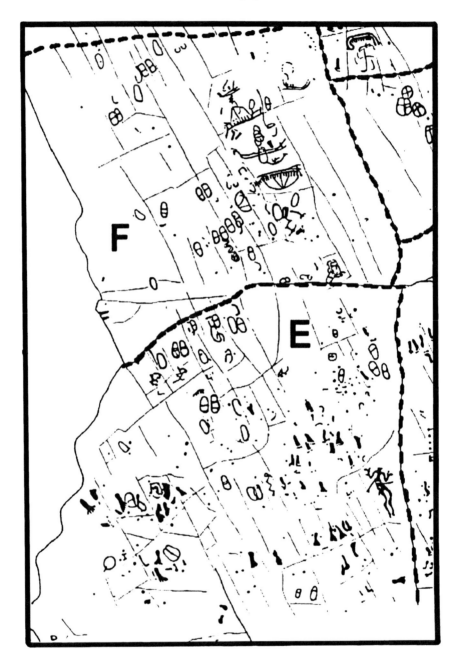

Figure 4.21 Järrestad: carving groups E and F. After Coles (1999).

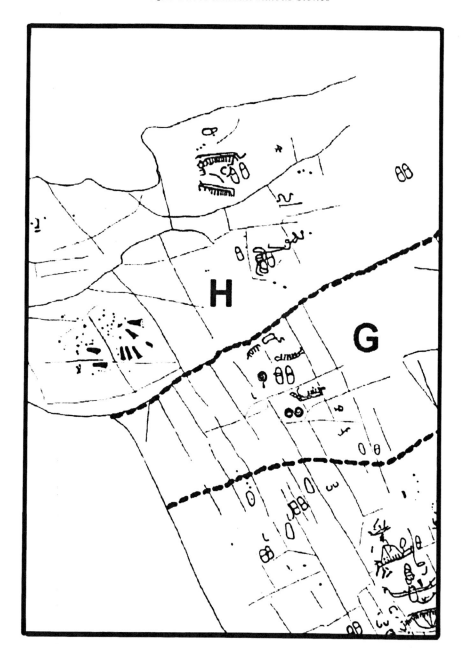

Figure 4.22 Järrestad: carving groups G and H. After Coles (1999).

four boats, three with crew and two which are 'upside down' when seen from below.

Panel H (Fig. 4.22). This contains a distinct group of feet to the left or south-west, one of which is a matched pair, the others being individual lefts or rights. These face down or across the slope. Shoe-soles, paired or individuals, occur to the right facing down the slope, apart from one at the top facing across the slope. A meandering snake-like design is also present together with a horse rider and at least three boats, the two largest of which are upside down when viewed from below. Cup marks scatter the surface but are densely concentrated by the feet.

A number of points can be made about the organization of the designs in relation to these panels:

1. The presence of unique design signatures in each apart from panel A.
2. The presence of the horse riders in panels E, G and H on the south-western side and their absence on the north-eastern side. All these riders, like the majority of the boats, move across rather than up or down the rock, both to the right and to the left, and are meant to be seen from below.
3. The increasing concentration of cup marks towards the bottom of the slope almost as if these are weighting down the rock.
4. The organization of the boat designs demands that you move across the rock to see them from above and below, occasionally from the left or the right.
5. All but a few of the shoe-soles point down the rock. Those few that do not do so point across the slope. By contrast, the feet, except in one case, on the extreme northern end of the rock, and outside the main panels of designs, all point down the rock if they are matching pairs. The majority of individual left or right feet point down the rock but some in panels B, C, D, E and F point upwards, and a few isolated examples occur which point across the rock. While the paired feet and shoe-soles appear static, the individual depictions suggest movement up and down it. Both the feet and the shoe-soles appear in the dips and the crests of the frozen waves.

Barrows in the Landscape

It has long been noted that the vast majority of Bronze Age barrows in Skåne have a striking coastal distribution (Fig. 4.23). Relatively few occur at a distance greater than 10 km from the contemporary coastline and most are within 4 km, the primary settlement zone in Skåne (Hyenstrand 1984; Olausson 1992). Finds of bronzes from non-barrow contexts are similarly concentrated (T. Larsson 1986). The barrows throughout the study region use the local topography to great visual effect, the majority being sited on ridges, knolls or the ends of spurs, indicating that they were meant to be seen. Such is the density of the barrows in some areas that this

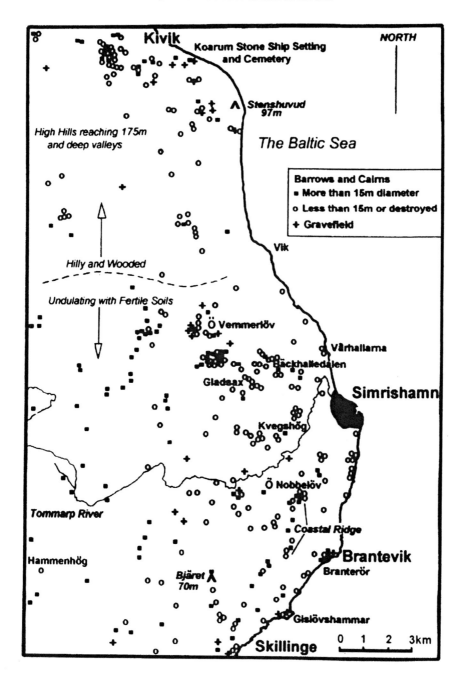

Figure 4.23 The distribution of Bronze Age barrows and cairns in the study area.

in itself indicates a relatively open landscape during the Bronze Age, as does the evidence from available pollen diagrams, with settlement areas and barrow locations being closely related (see Olausson 1992: 34).

Intervisibility is generally restricted to localized barrow groupings. Those sited directly along the coast have very restricted inland visual fields, often limited to a few hundred metres or less, but are coastal landmarks when seen from the sea. The massive cairn at Kivik is a good example of this. However, relatively few barrows are located right next to the sea and the vast majority occupy 'inland' locations in a band 2–4 km away from the coast. Large areas in the north of the study region to the south of Kivik have relatively sparse barrow densities compared with those in the south, with the exception of areas of the inland plain south, north and east of Hammenhög (Fig 4.23).

The barrows in the southern part of the study region occupy a number of distinctive landscape zones. Most of the barrows situated along the coastal strip immediately to the south of Simrishamn just above the present-day shoreline are relatively small and probably late Bronze Age in date. From these barrow sites there are extensive views out to sea but an extremely restricted visual field inland because of the rise of slope. Between Skillinge and Brantevik there occurs an intermediate coastal band of large barrows situated on the lower seaward slopes of the coastal ridge which are sometimes skylined from the barrows below on the coast but have a similarly restricted inland visual field (Figs 4.24, 4.25). All these barrows are concealed from inland barrow sites while being visible from the sea. A third belt of barrows are situated on high points in the landscape paralleling the coast. These have panoramic visual fields with extensive views both out to sea and inland.

Moving inland, the barrows form tight concentrations north of Skillinge and up to Östra Vemmerlöv in the north. In the northern and western parts of the arable plain the barrows are preferentially sited on low spurs, hills and ridges commanding extensive views in all directions (e.g. Villfarahög with its decorated stone). Many of these large barrows are skylined in relation to each other. So from inland barrows the large barrows high up on the coastal ridge to the east are skylined and other barrows are skylined in most directions. There are very few barrows on the limestone pavement areas north and west of Simrishamn except at their western margins. Within this area there are distinct viewsheds defined by areas of higher land. So, for example, the barrows which occur north of Gladsax cannot be seen from those which occur to the south of the carving area at Järrestad (Figs 4.14, 4.23). Mention has already been made of the distinctive clusters and alignments of barrows to the east of the decorated megalithic tombs of Ekenäs and Rosdala. It is notable that here the distinctive ridge to the west of the tombs does not have a barrow positioned on its summit or towards the southern or northern ridge ends, typical barrow locations found elsewhere reinforcing the notion that this landscape feature was very special, too special to be surmounted by a barrow.

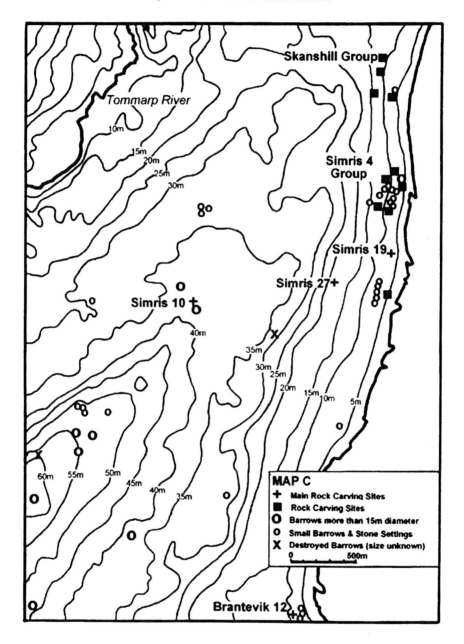

Figure 4.24 Rock carving sites and barrows south of Simrishamn (see Fig. 4.2 for location).

The visual fields of the barrows in the southern part of the study region vary significantly. There are fairly well-defined clusters, alignments or groups of barrows sharing a similar visual field. In some cases this is restricted, as in the

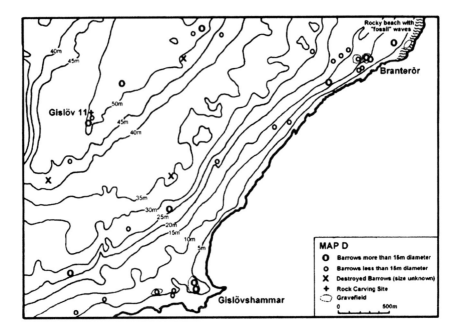

Figure 4.25 Rock carving sites and barrows in the south of the study region (see Fig. 4.2 for location).

vicinity of the Rosdala passage grave, where it extends between 0.5 and 2 km (Fig. 4.10). In other cases, as at Villfarahög, it can extend to as much as 5 km west across the agricultural plain and up to 3 km to the north and south. At Kvegshög (Figs 4.23, 4.26) the visual field from the barrow extends about 4 km to the west and up to 3 km to the north and south, and is extensive across the sea to the east. In short there are inland barrows commanding extensive views across the landscape and those which have more restricted and intimate visual fields. Those in the centre of the agricultural plain have the most extensive views, while those along the coast have the most restricted views. They are hidden in the landscape except when seen from the sea.

In the northern part of the study region individual barrows or groups of barrows and cairns invariably occur on the tops of localized hills and rises, repeating the pattern found in the south. However, the density of barrows is relatively low. Because the topography here is so hummocky and undulating, their visual fields are generally quite restricted in all or two to three cardinal directions. The barrow groups form distinctive groupings in relation to localized variations in the topo-graphy (Fig 4.27). Earlier barrows tend to occupy the most prominent topographic locations while later cemeteries with smaller barrows occupy less prominent places, perhaps representing an infilling of the landscape that Olausson (1992) has

Figure 4.26 The large Kvegshög barrow.

described for the Ystad area of southern Skåne. No large barrows occupy the coastal strip; they are invariably located on higher ground some way inland. The major exception is the Kivik cairn.

The Kivik cairn   The Kivik cairn, 75 m in diameter, is the largest in Sweden, the 'pyramid' of the north. Discovered over 250 years ago, it has been extensively discussed in the literature (see L. Larsson 1993 and Randsborg 1993 for recent accounts). It is situated a few hundred metres to the east of the coastline and was constructed of beach pebbles and erected on a low knoll, thus increasing its height. On the old ground surface there were traces of Neolithic settlement, or use: pits, scatters of flint debris, etc., indicating that this was already a significant place in the landscape which became monumentalized through cairn building in the earlier Bronze Age. This 'habitation' layer extended from the cairn several hundred metres to the west, south and north. About 50 m to the south a stream flows into the sea and beyond this a cup-marked stone is recorded. The original height of the cairn (much quarried away and now restored) must have been at least 6 m and possibly as much as 10 m. The cairn is situated 2 km north of Stenshuvud, the most dramatic coastal landmark in the area, but it is not visible because of heavy woodland cover. From the cairn there are extensive views along the coast to the north, while to the south and west the land rises up, restricting visibility. The cairn is, in effect, an artificial hill built of rounded boulders probably taken from the beach, a hill made

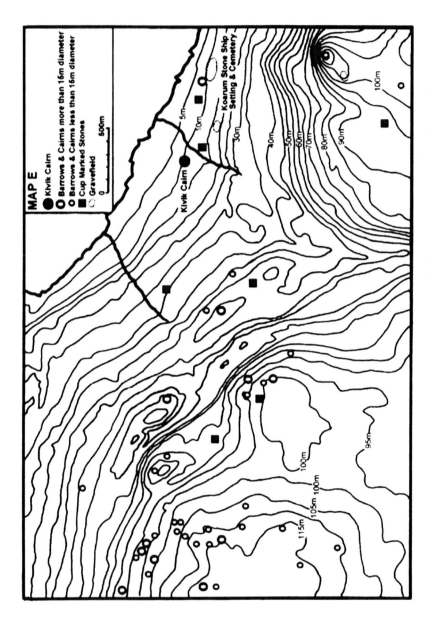

Figure 4.27 Cup-marked stones, barrows and cairns in the north of the study region (see Fig. 4.2 for location).

from stones taken from the sea shore. The cairn was never prominent from the surrounding landscape but may have been when seen out to sea. Today occasional large blocks of white Cambrian sandstone are visible on the surface of the reconstruction made after the 1931 excavations. Unfortunately we have no record of the original surface appearance of the cairn prior to its destruction for building stone, but if it had been covered with pebbles and boulders of Cambrian sandstone it would have been a very dramatic sight indeed, befitting its enormous size.

The cairn covers a stone cist orientated north–south originally about 3.6 m long × 1 m wide and about 1.2 m high. At the northern end of the cist (where the presumed head of the deceased was, looking south) most of the fragmentary artefact finds were made in the 1931 excavation: parts of an embossed bronze cauldron, fibulae, a sword with pommel or full metal hilt, and a large double button belt hook (see Randsborg 1993: 35f.). The stone slabs are of a fine-grained gneiss with a unique series of eight decorated slabs framed by borders reminiscent of textile designs (special cloths used to wrap the deceased?). These decorated slabs occur on the west and east sides of the cist, whose opening was at the southern end. The northern end slab of the cist, closest to the sea, is undecorated. The quality and degree of elaboration of the decorations on the side slabs of the cist are quite unique. There is little doubt that this was a chief's grave, and the decorated slabs would only have been visible for a brief period of time during the burial ceremonies, after which the cist was invisibly sealed, forever, into the stone cairn.

This was an inhumation burial. The style of some of the artefacts (bronzes) depicted on the slabs and the remains of metal finds in the cist indicate a dating to an early part of the Bronze Age (Period II) and the cist was probably decorated and used at the same time as rocks were being carved in the area to the south around Simrishamn. There are no other rock carvings in the entire northern part of the study area apart from occasional cup-marked stones.

Both the cairn itself, used as a quarry for building stone in the past, and the cist have been much mutilated. We accept Randsborg's (1993) detailed arguments that the surviving slabs are in their original positions. Seen from the south, the eastern or right-hand side of the cist has a series of panels with individual or paired motifs (see Fig. 4.30 below and the detailed discussion on pp. 202–5). Two slabs with definite narrative scenes occur on the western or left-hand side of the cist at its southern end or opening. These represent the culminating point of the sequence of carved slabs, which, we assume, are meant to be read from the south to the north of the cist on the eastern side and from the north to the south on the western side. Put another way, the designs are intended to be understood in terms of movement down the cist towards the sea and away from it. The eastern or right-hand side represents in a general way movement towards the sea and the left and western side movement away from it. The head of the deceased was placed at the end of the cist

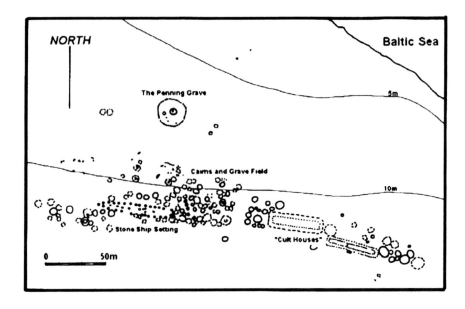

Figure 4.28 The Koarum ship setting and grave cemetery.

closest to the sea. This is an important observation because the unique location of the cairn and the way in which the cist is orientated towards the coast represents an interesting inversion of the relationship between rock carvings elsewhere in the study region, where the sea is to the east.

The Koarum ship setting and grave cemetery (Fig. 4.28) About 400 m to the south-east of the Kivik cairn there is a large grave field with 130 or so small mounds and cairns and two 'cult' house foundations, both over 40 m long, together with a large 60 m-long stone ship setting also of possible late Bronze Age date (Arne 1925; L. Larsson 1993). This grave field may originally have covered a much more extensive area to the north extending as far as the Kivik grave, which would have marked its northern end. It may have been in continuous use after the erection of the Kivik cairn, which marked its establishment in Period II of the Bronze Age right into the early Iron Age (L. Larsson 1993: 145). This is by far the largest grave field of its type known in Skåne, and its occurrence together with the cult houses in the vicinity of the massive Kivik cairn is clearly no coincidence. About 125 mounds are known in the vicinity of the cult houses and ship setting and there may originally have been 200 or more. Both the ship setting and the cult houses share the same general orientation, east to west and parallel with the coast. The ship setting occurs to the south of the Kivik cairn just as the ships on the decorated grave slabs travel south. The presence of two 'cult' houses with the southern house internally divided into two parts repeats the emphasis on pairing and symmetry found in depictions on the slabs of the Kivik cist, suggesting that this is an important structuring principle of social organization objectified in material forms. Furthermore the ship setting itself is divided into two parts laterally at its central point by internally placed stones. Most of the stones are of a rough pinky granite but quartzite stones, shiny and utterly different in character, all occur at the western end, reinforcing its symbolic division into two parts.

What effectively links and unifies the very different worlds of the northern and southern parts of the study region are the presence of barrows in the landscape. Apart from the Kivik grave, all the most massive barrows are in the south and, with the exception of the now destroyed cairn at Branterör, mainly located inland and away from the coastal strip with rock carvings.

Cairns, Barrows and Carving Sites

In contrast to many of the barrows, none of the carved rocks are highly visual landscape markers, with the exception of the capstone of the Rosdala passage grave and the large decorated granite stone at Ängshög. Few carved stones are intervisible, the exception being the rocks just mentioned and some nearby carved areas of limestone pavement north of the major carving surfaces at Simris. While the barrows are often conspicuous landscape markers, the carved rocks are not. However, the gleaming white limestone pavements with carvings from Simrishamn to Brantevik look striking when seen from the sea. On the one hand the location of the carving sites is clearly determined by the presence of outcrops of the Cambrian sandstone, the preferred carving medium. Yet, on the other hand, large areas of the pavements, perfectly suitable, were not carved. The particular locations of the carving sites in the landscape must therefore have had a specific significance.

Besides the Kivik grave, three cairns or barrows with decorated stones are known from the study region:

1. The gable end of a now destroyed cist with covering cairn is recorded a short distance to the east of the major carved rock at Järrestad. The quartzite stone depicts two manned boats, one above the other. The lower has eight crew strokes moving to the right. The top boat, with at least fourteen crew strokes, is possibly moving left. The bottom boat is double-hulled, the top boat single-hulled. They are interspersed with cup marks (absent at Kivik). A principle of dual symmetrical opposition is evident.
2. The Villafarastenen. This comes from a now badly mutilated cairn. The granite stone does not appear to have formed part of a cist but part of a (circular?) stone

setting or kerb beneath or surrounding the monument. This depicts two manned boats, one above the other, both sailing left. As at Järrestad, the upper boat has more crew stokes. Again these are associated with cup marks (c. 37) and above them there is a chariot pulled by two horses (without rider) similar in form to that on Slab 7 at Kivik and in the same position (top left-hand corner of the slab). This grave yielded a flint dagger and Period II belt hook.

3. A cairn at Brantevik, situated on the beach, now destroyed. This barrow was 30 m in diameter, surrounded by a kerb with a central 2 m-long stone cist. According to an early antiquarian depiction, this had a circle carved in the top of the middle slab of the northern long side (Randsborg 1993: 76; Strömberg 1985: 56f.). Since the cairn occurred in an area where the Cambrian sandstone outcrops, the cist is likely to have been constructed of this material.

There is an obvious contrast between the richness and degree of elaboration (and size) of the Kivik cairn compared with these other examples of barrows or cairns with decorated stones, at least two of which (the precise original location of the Branterör cairn is uncertain), unlike Kivik, are situated within 1 km of major carved rock surfaces with figurative designs.

It is apparent that there is not a particularly close relationship between the distribution of the largest and most massive barrows dating back to the early Bronze Age and the rock carving sites. Where barrows do occur in the same areas as the rock carvings, they are small and probably all late in date. The only two exceptions are Gislöv 11 and Simris 10. Otherwise, large barrows and rock carving sites on rock outcrops are not intervisible, with the exception of the site of Järrestad (see above). All the coastal rock carving sites from Simrishamn to Brantevik remain invisible from all but the locations of small barrow sites in their immediate vicinity.

Iconography, Burial and Landscape

Boat Depictions and Ship-shape Societies

There are enormous differences between the carved rock surfaces along the coast at Simris, the inland panels at Järrestad, the carved stones at Rosdala and Gislöv and the decorations found on the slabs of the Kivik grave. All these places contrast in terms of both the content of the designs and their locations in the landscape. One striking unifying feature encountered everywhere is the presence of depictions of boats. It has been noted that the boat depictions are stylistically very heterogeneous. There are no two identical boats of the 27 or so on the panels at Järrestad or the 45 representations on the rock at Simris 19. Moreover, these boat designs occur not only at Kivik but at all other known grave sites with recorded figurative designs, the destroyed site of Branterör being the only possible exception. On the carving surfaces a tendency has been noted to the pairing of boat depictions, and sometimes their depiction in groups of four or eight. Such more complex arrangements are most obvious on the rock of Simris 27, on which boats are the most common design. Boats have specific visual effects or an agency to affect an observer which is not matched by any other type of design. They encourage movement around the rock surfaces to see them 'right way up', from the bottom, the top or from one side or another.

Boat depictions are, of course, the most frequent of motifs in all Scandinavian rock art from Skåne in the south to arctic Norway, apart from cup marks, so their appearance on the rocks around Simrishamn is hardly unique. There is little doubt that the boat was a fundamental symbol within Bronze Age cosmologies but equally important may have been its significance as a metaphor for society as a whole. What we are suggesting is that society itself was conceived in terms of boats. Boats signified both social groups and the structuring principles in terms of which these groups were organized in relation to each other. In an obvious sense boats, whether real or mythological, contain boatloads of people; the fundamental social unit and the differing style and form of the boats may therefore signify differences between social units. Their arrangements in pairs and groups suggests complementary oppositions, alliances and relationships between these units.

Such 'ship-shape' societies are historically known throughout South-east Asia where people are organized into small political systems. The evidence is summarized by Manguin (1986): Boats are

> felt as among the best modes available to define and regulate relations among members of the smaller units, between the latter and higher social groups (the village community sphere, or a small political system), and between all these social units and the material world . . . They provide models for encompassing various orders of social, political, economic (and cosmological) classifications, together with their expression in myths and rituals. (*ibid.*: 190)

In these societies parts of houses may be named after parts of boats (Leacock and Brans 1975; Kana 1980), and the inhabitants of the same village may regard themselves as belonging to the same 'villageboat':

> this is the large communal boat which is jointly possessed by the whole community and is used on special occasions, when the social order needs to be signified and revalidated (marriages, alliance renewals with other communities, warfare, death etc.) . . . Ritual dances are performed in boat order . . . The village itself, as well as the whole island at times, are spatially organized as a boat and its crew. The dead are disposed of in boat burials. Myths refer to early voyages from overseas: the village spatial classification as

that of the communal boat is said to be a reflexion of the original journey. (Manguin 1986: 190)

Varied depictions of boats occur in rites of passage on shipcloth weavings, bead-work and mats. Elaborate shipcloths were used during birth, marriage and death ceremonies, and particular shipcloth designs themselves signified social rank and rights. Many aspects of ship burial rites are linked to beliefs about boats being needed for the souls to travel to another world and the ship of the dead or the 'flying' ship is loaded with cosmic symbols (*ibid.*: 196).

Boats, we suggest, in the southern Scandinavian Bronze Age, had the following meaning ranges:

1. They symbolized principles of social order. Groups of boats in pairs, groups of four, eight, etc., are expressing a social principle of complementary opposition between different social groups. This accounts for the manner in which boats are arranged and organized in relation to each other on some carving surfaces, as at Simris 27, in the individual panels at Järrestad and on the slabs of the Kivik cist.
2. They are individual signifiers of 'houses' or groups of people: the minimal social units making up society. This accounts for the great variety of the ways in which they are depicted. There are no two identical boats amongst over one hundred depictions on the rocks.
3. Differences between the boats are related to their relative rank in relation to each other, which in turn might be related to social rank, relative age and seniority between the houses or groups of people that the boats represent. This accounts for the great variation of the boats in terms of size and complexity. Some are very small and simple depictions, others are very large, complex and elaborated, and the very largest boats are usually those most deeply carved and thus emphasized. The largest and most complex boats are often centrally located on the carving surfaces.
4. Similarities between boat depictions might conversely be related to networks of social alliances and exchanges. So boats with similar styles of hull, prow heads, etc., signified relations between different houses or groups of people.
5. Some of the boats being depicted could only have been for the use of a few individuals or a family. Others are clearly collective or communal vessels used by a larger social group. So distinctions between styles of boats were related to those between boats which represented individuals and those collectivities and principles of social leadership.
6. On the level of cosmology, boats related to the cyclical movement of the sun across the sky, death and the regeneration of life, and symbolically carried the souls of the dead to the sea of the underworld (see discussion below).

Boats metaphorically signified the flow and transmission of life and the path of death. They could signify rank and leadership, alliances, social connections and social distinctions, principles of social order and cosmological ideas in the Bronze Age. On any individual rock carving surface they might be signifying any one of the individual points listed above, or a combination of all of them at the same time. Any distinction between the rock carvings as representing principles of the social order or alternatively cosmological and mythic principles is entirely artificial. Both were intimately related, forming part of each other. Similarly, the rock carvings could both simultaneously represent 'real' things (e.g. boats, axes, feet, etc.) and aspects of ceremonies and events which took place and mythic principles about the origins and ordering of the world. Their power and significance resided in this very capacity to link and relate the social and the cosmological domains, life as lived, ceremonial practices and cosmologies, principles of social order and principles of cosmic order. It is perhaps then not so surprising that they are so frequent and ordered in a seemingly bewildering variety of ways in terms of both individual depictions and the manner in which they are arranged and associated on the rock surfaces.

The Circle Cross, Solar and Boat Symbolism

The circle cross, or wheel, like the depictions of boats, occurs on all the major carving surfaces and on the Kivik grave. Such a sign undoubtably had a broad meaning range, depicting a wheel, a sun, signifying the passage of the seasons, a possible navigational device, and so on. In the centre of the great rock at Järrestad we see an ambiguous transformative relationship between this sign and conjoined shoe-soles. Referring to the famous 'chariot of the sun' found in Trundholm bog in Denmark, Kaul argues that the sun image from Trundholm must 'represent the belief that a horse pulled the sun over the heavens. The chassis and wheels on the other hand are a kind of practical device to make this belief "operational" in the ritual reality. In other words, the belief has to be put on wheels in order to represent the movement of the sun in the ritual' (Kaul 1998: 32). The depiction of wheel circles alone – all of which, like the wheels on the Trundholm chariot, have only four spokes – without the chariot or the horse, may be condensed signifiers of this belief, representing both the sun itself and the horse chariot carrying it across the sky. The circular arrangements of boat images around central sun wheels at Gislöv and Simris 27, their pairing in the Simris grave, and their central position at Järrestad are an association that must have had a particular significance. Kaul has provided an excellent account of what exactly this might be. In a detailed study of decorated Bronze Age razors he first notes that ships bearing sun images or ships above which sun images are to be seen, in some way or other . . . must be representations of, or refer to, the belief that the sun could be transported on board ship . . . Bronze Age religion in Scandinavia can be described as a cyclic religion, in which an attempt is made with the help of the iconography to explain and 'steer' the daily movements of the sun. This cyclic idea of the course of the day was presumably also transferred to the cycle of the seasons, thus also involving concepts such as life, death and rebirth, reflecting the daily 'death' and 'rebirth' of the sun. (*Ibid.*: 53)

Kaul notes that the direction of the travel of the sun in the heavens, seen from the earth, is from the east to the west, from the left to the right, where it 'dies', to appear once more in the east invisibly carried back through the night to its starting point, either underneath the land or under the sea (*ibid.*: 33–4). The ship depictions on Danish bronzes that he examined are predominantly (4/5) sailing to the right. When sun representations are associated with these ships, Kaul found that these images were always associated with ships sailing to the right (*ibid.*: 186). The ships carrying the sun discs can therefore be considered to be iconographical representations of the journey of the sun across the sky. The ships moving to the left may thus be the night ships transporting the sun back again. In Kaul's reading of the depictions on the bronzes the movement of the boats drawing the sun across the sky and back again are assisted at various points in the cycle by a horse, a fish and a snake. The horse is associated with noon, the highest point of the sun in the sky, the fish with the night. As Bradley has noted, this recalls the association between the sea and the land of the dead characteristic of northern mythologies (Bradley 1999: 662 and see the discussion in Tilley 1991: 126-41). On the various rock carving surfaces in the study region roughly equal numbers of boats move to the right and to the left on the coastal Simris sites and at Järrestad. None carry what might be interpreted as sun symbols but they consistently occur close together with circle cross or sun wheel motifs, as at Simris 19 and 27, Järrestad and Rosdala, and spin round a central circle cross at Gislöv 11. The theme appears to be one of cyclical motion and following or reversing the path of movement of the sun across the sky. At Järrestad the paths of the boats parallel the lines of the waves of a frozen dead sea. At Simris 19 they are instead strongly orientated towards or away from the breaking waves of a living sea, a theme further discussed below.

Barrow Burial and Hierarchy

Excavations of barrows in Skåne have revealed great complexity in both their structure and the form of burial practices. All the really large barrows with inhumation burials have been shown to have been constructed during the earlier part of the Bronze Age (Periods I–III) but most appear to have been used during a much longer period, containing as many as seventeen secondary graves. Some may have been in use for 1,000 years or more. Some Bronze Age barrows were built over and concealed earlier middle and late Neolithic megalithic tombs and gallery graves. Many barrows later became the focus for flat grave cemeteries during the later part of the Bronze Age, when large barrows were no longer constructed, e.g. Grosshög in the south-west of the study region (Strömberg 1985: 56). Their locations were thus related to those of earlier monuments and were in turn reused.

During the earlier Bronze Age the barrows were frequently built on, extended and further monumentalized. Up to three or four building phases have been recognized in well-excavated examples. The enormous size of the Kivik cairn needs to be emphasized. Having a diameter of 75 m, it is about three times the size of other larger cairns and barrows in the study area, which range between 15 and 25 m in diameter (more numerous smaller barrows range in size from about 2 to 10 m in diameter). The very largest of the rich early Bronze Age Danish barrows with inhumation burials only reach 40 m in diameter. This cairn is absolutely exceptional.

Excavations in Skåne have shown that earlier central burials occur in stone or oak cists while secondary graves with cremations occur in smaller cist or urn burials within and around the mounds. The Kivk cairn appears to lack secondary burials, which again makes it unusual (Randsborg 1993). Osteological analysis has shown that men, women, infants and juveniles were buried in the barrows. Since only a small proportion of the population could have received burial in a barrow, these individuals must have constituted part of a social elite. Others may have been buried at sea. As Jennbert (1993) has argued, the continual use and reuse of these monuments suggests that they had a collective rather than individual significance, i.e. that they were the resting places for the remains of individual families or clan groups and thus had a genealogical significance for the populations of the living (for recent summaries and discussion of the evidence, see Jennbert 1993 and Olausson 1993 for Skåne and Burenhult 1999 more generally for southern Scandinavia).

Thomas Larsson's examination of the metalwork recovered from early Bronze Age barrows shows a distinct wealth distinction between south-east Skåne and other coastal areas of Skåne, with a marked concentration of rich burials here in the southern part of the study region and immediately to the south and west of it (Fig. 4.29). There are very few early Bronze Age metal finds from the vicinity of the Kivik cairn. Overall there is clear evidence of social stratification in that access to and rights to use bronze in a prestige goods economy were clearly limited to a minority of the population, with a distinct 'wealth pyramid' being apparent in the numbers of bronzes deposited with the dead (T. Larsson 1986: 121f.). With the shift from inhumation to cremation and burial in flat graves as opposed to burial in barrows, deposition of metalwork with the dead decreases enormously, with few indications of major distinctions in rank or status, as evidenced in the late Bronze

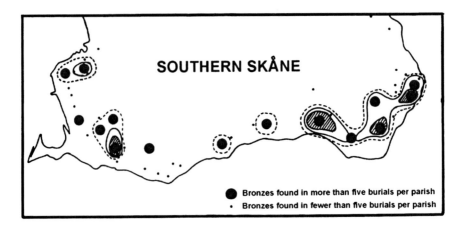

Figure 4.29 The density of metalwork found in Bronze Age barrows and cairns in southern Skåne. After T. Larsson (1986).

Age flat grave cemetery at Simris less than 2 km distant from the major carving sites of Järrestad and Simris 19 (Stjernquist 1961; T. Larsson 1986: 128). In tandem with this there are significantly greater numbers of late Bronze Age metalwork finds in the vicinity of Kivik, at a time when the cairn was ancient and had lost its original significance.

Dual Symbolism, Magic and Chieftainship

Kristiansen (1987, 1998, 1999) has interpreted the sociopolitical institutions of the early Bronze Age in southern Scandinavia as being related to the rise of a warrior aristocracy together with the institution of twin rulers, the chief of rituals and the chief of war. He points to a number of widely dispersed strands of evidence to support this proposition: the depiction of the twin male cult axe bearers on the rock at Simris 27; twin male burials, richly endowed with grave goods, from southern Jutland; and bipartite divisions of Bronze Age longhouses. The notion that there may have been twin rulers is based on references to Minoan evidence. Irrespective or not of whether we might agree with this specific interpretation is the all-pervading archaeological evidence for dualism and opposition. The notion that chiefly or 'aristocratic' powers had a magical basis and significance is borne out by a considerable body of archaeological evidence, in particular the belt purses with their startling collections of materials recovered from Danish barrows (Glob 1974; Randsborg 1993: 124; Kaul 1998: 16f.). A chief with magical or ritual powers may, of course, have been the principal expert responsible for both building and commanding communal boats, combining technical and magical powers. There is little doubt that boats played major social and economic roles in facilitating social networks and exchange relationships. The ship master was the leader of the local social group, and the ships brought the bronze, whose exchange was carefully controlled. The ship was simultaneously a metaphor for power, hierarchy and for the manner in which society was organized in terms of both rank and complementary opposition between groups. The elaborate prow heads depicted on many of the ships indicate that these vessels were designed to impress and dazzle, symbols of the power of the local community and its leader. The limited space in a boat and strict navigational rules tend to keep the paddlers or crew at the right distance in relation to each other, not too close and not too far apart, and this is precisely the manner in which the crew and crew strokes are depicted in the rock carvings. A crew are both together and apart, and thus the boat and the boat journey become perfect ways for conceptualizing principles of similarity and difference, endogamy and exogamy (Lévi-Strauss 1978: 191). In depicting boats, people were thus making fundamental statements about themselves to themselves and about the principles of social and political and cosmological order.

In the rock carvings found in the study region, dualism is apparent everywhere: the consistent pairing and opposition of the horses and other motifs on the Kivik grave, that of the ships and axes on the rock carving surfaces at Simris, the paired feet and shoe-soles at Järrestad, the paired axe bearers at Simris 27. It is also manifested in the dual cult houses at Koarum and the bipartite division of the ship setting south of the Kivik cairn and the frequently noted pairing or matching of objects in votive depositions in bogs (Oldeberg 1974; T. Larsson 1986). Beyond the pairing and oppositions of motifs and structures we also see consistent emphasis on groups of four and eight evident on the decorated Kivik cist slabs, the groupings of boats at Simris 27, the division of the Järrestad carvings into eight main panels and the grouping of axe/lurs in one of the central panels, the eight main groups of axes and boats at Simris 19, and so on.

Structuring principles of dualism and opposition are also apparent in the burial practices documented in the late Bronze Age and early Iron Age flat grave cemetery at Simris, only 2 km from the major carving sites at Järrestad and from those along the coast. Here double depositions of cremated bones have been documented from a single urn; remains of two individuals were found in cremation pits or urn cremation pits. Sometimes two urns occur together in a cist, and from examination of pyre remains it is clear that the bones of one individual were placed in an urn, others in a cremation pit in which the urn stands (Stjernquist 1961). If the social unit was the 'boatload' whose members hunt and fish and farm together, a village would consist of so many families or boatloads of people, perhaps up to eight in number. These 'boatloads', in dual symmetrical opposition, are one of the principles being represented in various ways in the rock art.

If cosmic order was organized according to a tripartite division of the world into the heavens, the middle world of humans and the sea of the dead, it appears that the middle human geographical world was also conceived in terms of a duality between coastal and inland areas and, simultaneously, opposing social groups associated with each. The utterly distinctive rock carvings along the coast at Simris compared with the inland site of Järrestad would seem to confirm a fundamental coast/inland distinction, and this, we will argue, was in turn linked with different cosmological expressions. The major coastal rock carvings at Simris 19 and 27 depict ceremonies and rituals associated with the living and the flow of life between different communities. The inland site of Järrestad, by contrast, was linked with the supracommunal cult of the dead.

The Kivik cist provides a unique opportunity to compare and contrast styles of sealed and invisible funerary art associated with a single person of chiefly status with the kinds of rock carvings occurring in the open air, and accessible to all. We begin with an iconographic analysis of the decorated slabs as a starting point to further consider the other carvings in the study area. The task before us is to imaginatively attempt to reconstruct the mythic and cosmological system and the manner in which it relates to principles of social organization on the basis of an interpretation of the iconography. Some of the interpretations given below are drawn from Randsborg's excellent and path-breaking original iconological analysis of the Kivik grave (Randsborg 1993: 107–22), others are our own. For the sake of brevity the reader is referred to Randsborg's text and the detailed arguments made there.

Iconographical Narrative: From Slab 1 to Slab 8 (Fig. 4.30)

Slab 1   At the top are two hafted crescent shaped axes with blades facing each other, symmetrically placed on either side of a conical hat, itself flanked by two ceremonial sword or spear images. These may signify the chief's ceremonial regalia. Below, a large boat without crew sails south (left), away from the sea. Perhaps this is a representation of the ancestral boat sailing across the waters of the dead carrying the chief's regalia to him.

Slab 2   This depicts two boats, one above the other, probably sailing south (left) with crew. These represent houses or groups of people (the boat is a metaphor for the social group, the crew strokes representing the individual members of that group, which, as strokes, or lines, remain undifferentiated) and the structuring principle organizing the social world: dual symmetrical social organization with groups of people organized in terms of a lower and upper moiety. The particular form of the crew strokes on this badly damaged slab suggests that they represent

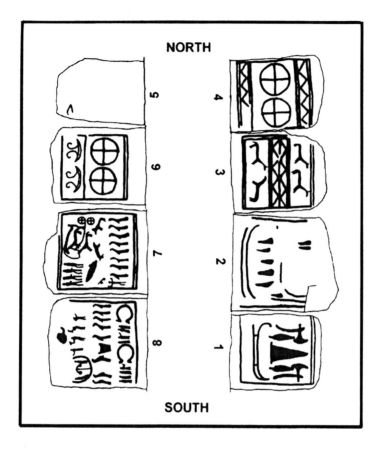

Figure 4.30 The carved slabs of the Kivik cairn.

upraised paddles like some form of greeting gesture on arrival at land. Slab 1 thus refers to an individual chiefly person, hierarchy and power; Slab 2 to a general organizing principle of society.

Slab 3 This shows four horses arranged in two panels, upper and lower. On the upper panel the horses face in the same direction: north. On the lower panel they face each other, north and south, towards and away from the sea. The horse as domestic animal has a special cosmological and social status, being closest to both humanity and the gods. The spatial arrangement of the horses refers again to the principle of dual symmetrical social organization involving relations of similarity and pairing (top) and opposition and difference (below). The depiction of the horses also relates the human world to the animal world. The horses are separated by central zig-zag bands. On the basis of the presence of waves in the Cambrian sandstone rocks in the south of the study region we suggest that these zig-zag lines might be schematic representations of waves with the horses placed above and below them. The horses appear static, their movement arrested. If horses pull boats across the sky or below the sea, this suggests the land has been reached. The journey is over.

Slab 4   The zig-zag wave bands on Slab 3 are stretched and separated to the top and bottom ends of the slab, which are occupied by two large sun wheels representing both the sun itself and the horse-drawn chariot wheels that pull the sun across the southern sky from east to west every day to die and be reborn. Slab 4 thus refers to a cosmological ordering principle.

Slab 5   Nothing appears on this slab apart from a possible line. To view the slab requires turning around to face the west, associated with the death of the sun in the sky.

Slab 6   This slab refers to the passage of day, and of night, the moon and the sun. Above are two crescent-shaped moons/axes. Below are two paired sun wheels. Day passes into night and night passes into day.

Slab 7   This slab is divided into three friezes. The lower frieze depicts a procession of eight S-shaped cowled figures with bird-like heads and single arms like seal flippers. These figures are half-human, half-animal (fish). These figures all process in the same direction, south, led by an androgynous human figure with upraised arms. Above these are four representatives of the animal world, clan totems. Two (to the left) face in the same direction (south), two face each other, thus repeating the pattern of the horses seen on Slab 3. They are distinguished from the human and bird/fish humans on this slab by being positioned diagonally rather than in rows. These are all probably animals associated with feasting and sacrifice and none are domestic. The bottom frieze represents the spirits being led from the watery land of the underworld (hence the seal flippers and strange [seabird] heads) into the land of the living (middle frieze) organized according to two moieties and four clans, each with its own sacrificial and totemic animal.

The upper frieze shows a chariot moving to the left with two horses and two sun wheels and the rider with reins. This represents the world of the heavens with the sun chariot moving across the sky. To the left are four human figures, at least two bearing swords, who also appear to be facing south: a ceremonial procession moving in the same direction as the sun chariot. These are ancestral and cosmological representatives of each of the four clans. Randsborg's overall reading of the iconography on Slab 7 of the Kivik grave is that it suggests a tripartite division of the world: above, the world of light, the sun and the heavens; in the middle, the world of the living, people and animals; below, the sea of the dead (Randsborg 1993: 119f.).

Slab 8   In the bottom frieze there are two groups of four figures each standing to the left of an open circle, with the entrance to the south: the unsealed Kivik grave cairn. Those to the left, possibly led by a sword bearer, may be facing right (north) towards the cairn opening. In the second group of four figures to the right there appear to be two groups of two individuals facing each other and both towards and away from the cairn opening: dual symmetrical opposition. The middle frieze shows the eight cowled figures from Slab 7 now arranged on either side of the Kivik grave burial cist, inside the cairn. Two large figures face each other with the cist in between, with a group of two figures to the left and four to the right. These represent the spirits of the underworld taking away the soul of the deceased from the cist (which represents a boat or ship holding the body of the deceased), a state of liminality. The upper frieze consists of four human figures to the right (north). The two figures on the right are lur blowers. To the left two human figures are depicted standing opposite each other with a staff with two suspended circular objects in the middle. The chief is probably also a shaman, a master of ceremonies, and the object in the middle of the circle could therefore represent the shaman's staff or tree linking together the three worlds of the underworld, land of the living and the cosmos or heavens. Originally the staff and human figures were probably completely enclosed in a circle – representing the now sealed Kivik grave cairn. The two figures standing in the circle represent, not the Kivik chief, who is signified by the staff, but the enduring principle (surviving his death) of dual symmetrical organization or complementary opposition between groups. At the very top of the frieze is what originally may have been a circular motif: the sun? The overall themes are of death and the regeneration of life and the enduring principle of dual symmetrical social organization. While the depictions on the Kivik cist clearly relate to the burial ceremonies of an important chief, they are also about cosmology and its linkage to social obligations, alliances and exchange.

Järrestad and the Cult of Death

While the Kivik grave was clearly linked with the symbols and death rites associated with the burial of a prominent single individual who can be conceived as a technical and ritual expert, a shipbuilder and master of ceremonies, the Järrestad rock appears to have had a communal rather than individual significance. It contrasts with all the other rock carvings in the study region in terms of its sheer size and the relative density of the depictions. The carving sites elsewhere are separated from each other in the landscape and most are not intervisible. At Järrestad the evidence for the organization of the designs in terms of panels created by large and distinctive cracks in the rock surface leads Coles to suggest that this place represents 'the combined wealth in ideologies and beliefs of several communities, jointly selecting this place above all others for their individual representations, each working its own Panel with its own imagery over the decades, obeying the constraints of the major fault lines in the rock, using the minor cracking for their own internal organisation' (Coles 1999: 184). Another major difference between this and the other carving sites, with the exception of Brantevik 85, is the presence of the fossil waves traversing the rock surface and inverting the directionality of the real waves on the sea. Themes of structural inversion whereby the world of the dead is conceived of as an upside-down version of the world of the living are commonplace in world religions and mythologies, past and present. The carvings at Järrestad were executed on and across the waves of an ancient frozen sea representing the watery underworld to which the souls of the dead returned. The single most dominant and largest image on this rock, the swimmer, is located near to the bottom of the rock under the waves. The sheer contrast in size and form of this image with all others on the same rock and elsewhere makes it as unique as the Kivik cairn itself. The swimmer must have been no ordinary person but one of chiefly status returning to the underworld. Apart from the tiny horse riders and a few even smaller representations of human figures in some of the boats at Järrestad, people are only being metonymically represented here by the naked feet, many of which cluster around the swimmer, and shoe-soles. If these representations symbolize communities or collectivities, the swimmer must symbolize individual power and rank. Coles (*ibid.*: 186) 'hazards a guess' that the swimmer (to him a dancer) might be the person buried in the distant, and visible, great barrow of Kvegshög (see Fig 4.26). However, equally large and dramatic barrows would also have been visible on the distant coastal ridge to the south (now virtually or entirely destroyed). Our suggestion is that the swimmer represents the chief buried in the great cairn at Kivik. In this respect it is interesting to note the great similarity between two of the horse riders who are depicted on this panel of the rock, with reins curving over the heads of the horses, and the one depicted in the top right-hand corner of Slab 7 of the Kivik grave, and a more general similarity in form between the S-shaped profile of the swimmer and the peculiar shrouded figures that occur on the bottom of the same slab and in the middle of Slab 8. At Järrestad the swimmer acts as a shamanistic motif representing passage down into the sea of the dead.

Why the emphasis on feet and shoe-soles at Järrestad, on pairing and representations of individual feet and shoe-soles? Coles (1999) regards these as 'static' depictions, whereas for Bradley (1999) they are moving down the rock from the graves above the Järrestad rock towards the sea and the underworld of the dead. But the graves here are probably much later in date than the carvings and may represent a reuse of this place, and both principles of stasis and motion are apparent. The left and right pairs suggest a lack of motion, individual representations of lefts and rights, a process of movement down the rock. While none of the shoe-soles move up the rock, some of the feet clearly do. The motion of the shoe-soles is down into the sea of the underworld. As Bradley has argued, these shoe-soles may thus symbolize the movement of the spirit souls of the dead into the watery underworld of the sea. In contrast, the naked feet may signify a movement of return from death: the regeneration of life or the movement of the souls of the dead from the underworld to the heavens, like the cyclical death and rebirth of the sun when it sinks into the water in the west to be reborn out of the sea in the east. Feet also suggest a naked rather than a clothed body, a body which, rather than being weighted down by shoes, can return from the water. Feet are associated with the nakedness of birth, a state to which one returns at death to be reborn. Furthermore, a distinction between feet and shoe-soles may also relate to structural principles of complementary opposition between different social groups and perhaps between summer and winter, clans ritually and ceremonially linked with the summer months and those with the winter, and a distinction between sea (coastal) and inland social groups, water and land, which might be arranged in the following array of structural oppositions:

Group A	Group B
Summer	Winter
Water	Land
Coast	Inland
Birth	Death
FEET	SHOE-SOLES

It is not necessary to choose between any of these potential meanings. Over and above them the representation of feet and shoe-soles suggest that social identity is rooted in the land and in the fixed points, rocks, that ground and make permanent these identities. If the feet and the shoe-soles relate principally to individuals and their personal relationship to the land, the boats relate to social principles of group membership. If the social unit is the 'boatload', the boat symbolism is a recognition that social identities are not just related to the land but also grounded in movement, principally by water through the boats that connect people together and facilitate exchange. Boats move both among the living and in the celestial realm, and in both domains their movement is understood as being cyclic in nature. At Järrestad the boats move not down into the frozen waves but parallel with them, horizontally rather than vertically across this frozen sea. They move in approximately equal numbers to the left and the right, some right way up and some upside down (when seen from above or below), from the perspectives of the shoe-soles moving down the rock and some feet moving up it. The boats thus connect together the different 'visual' perspectives of some of the feet and the shoe-soles. The ambiguous conjoined shoe-soles/circle-crosses in the central panel of the rock also link them with a cyclic solar symbolism connected with rebirth.

Simris and the Flow of Life

The coastal Simris rock carvings appear to be representing a different theme altogether. On Simris 19 and Simris 27 we see depictions of axe bearers in opposition to each other. They are bearing elaborate ceremonial shaft-hole axes of identical form to those found in votive depositions such as the find from Borrby, just to the south of the study region (Strömberg 1976: 53; Fig. 4.31) and those depicted in the Kivik grave. These are undoubtably real axes used in the ceremonies of the living. Although the axe blades are orientated in a variety of different ways, none face to the west, the direction of death of the sun. And here the rocks are animated by the sight, sound and the pungent smell of rotting seaweed washed up on the coast during the summer months. There are no visible fossil waves running across the rock here reminding one of an ancient sea. The beach is, of course, an important liminal zone between the sea and the land, a place where boats are drawn up and people meet and exchange, and cosmologically it is a transition point between the world of the living and the underworld of the dead.

At Järrestad, movement, as indicated by the boats, feet and shoe-soles, is either vertical or horizontal, up or down the rock, and one can see virtually all the motifs right way up by looking at them from above or below in a single visual field or movement of the eyes. At Simris 27 all the motifs cannot be seen at once. Here most boats move towards or away from the living sea and fossil waves are absent. To see all the motifs at Simris 19 requires a constant circular 'dancing' bodily motion. This suggests a dynamism and interaction with the designs on the part of an observer that is largely absent at Järrestad. This is repeated in a similar fashion at the Gislöv rock carving, at Simris 27 and through physical acts of movement at Simris 27, Simris 4 and Brantevik 85 in order to see the carvings. At all these places axes and boats are paired in various ways and, of course, axes would be required both to make boats and bespell them or perform the ceremonies associated with their construction and use. At Simris 19 we see some axe forms being depicted that could have actually been used to make the boats, as opposed to the ceremonial axes connected with their ritual empowerment. While the boats and feet/shoe-soles at Järrestad are connected with movement on the water and on the land, the ceremonial axe with its moon-shaped crescent head links the domains of water and land to a vertical plane connecting together water and land to the sky.

An inland/coastal, high/low, west/east distinction between the rock carving sites at Järrestad and Simris, with the former referring to death cults and the latter to the world of the living, is complicated by the consideration of other smaller carving locations: Gislöv 11, Simris 10, Rosdala, Ängshög and Brantevik 85. Apart from the major carved surface at Järrestad, it is only the rock carvings at Brantevik that occur on a rock exposure that, in part, has a distinctively wavy surface reminiscent of a fossil sea. Most of the carvings here were executed on flat or only slightly

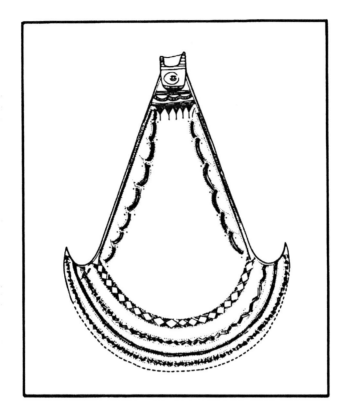

Figure 4.31 The engraved bronze axe from Borrby. Length 33 cm. After Strömberg (1976).

dipping rock surface, apart from some of the depictions on the north-west section of the rock where the waves are prominent. The large oval frame figure here has an opening and an extension in the form of a line at the northern end. An almost identical figure at Simris 19 has an opening and extended line in a westerly direction. They are effectively inversions of each other. If these are schematic representations of the Baltic Sea, then that at Simris 19, with its entrance to the west, represents the sea as lived and experienced (the opening of the Baltic into the Öresund and the North Sea is in the west), then that at Brantevik, associated with the fossil waves, represents the sea of the dead with its opening to the south.

At Gislöv 11 and Simris 10, situated, relatively speaking, high up in the land-scape and away from the coastal strip, we have seen that there is a close connection between the carvings and barrows that may have originally or partially concealed them, and therefore are likely to be connected with a death cult. Geographically, both these places are transitional between the coastal strip and the inland carvings at Järrestad and Rosdala. Both are, unusually for the figurative carvings, executed in granite, a contrast which in itself must have had considerable significance. The circular, or cyclic, motion of the boats at Gislöv around a central sun wheel, requiring constant bodily movement on the part of an observer to view the motifs 'right way up', connects them with the carvings at Simris 19. At Rosdala the carvings were executed on the capstone of a megalithic tomb, again likely to be associated with death and having generalized ancestral connotations for the Bronze Age populations, whereas the huge stone at Ängshög may have itself been taken to represent an ancestral monument.

Marking the Land: From the Neolithic to the Late Bronze Age

There is little doubt that to mark stones with cup marks was a practice going back into the Neolithic. The large numbers of cup marks found on the capstones of megalithic tombs in Skåne and elsewhere in Sweden itself suggests this (Tilley 1996; 1999b). It is also likely that cup marks were executed on boulders and rock outcrops during the same period, continuing into the Bronze Age. The corridors of cup-marked boulders leading towards rock carvings at Järrestad, and the Rosdala and Ängshög stones, may also date back to the Neolithic, and at least some of the cup marks on the rock surfaces with major collections of figurative carvings may be of similar date. It is interesting to note the occurrence of cup marks here in the heels of some of the naked feet as if they have been used as a starting point for a later depiction, just as fossil depressions were used as the starting point for the production of cup marks on the nearby rock outcrops at Järrestad 4:2. Burenhult has additionally argued, partly on the basis of drawing certain similarities with designs in Irish megalithic art, that other designs at Järrestad, principally the spiral and snake symbols and certain 'dagger' motifs, may also be of late Neolithic age or earlier (Burenhult 1980, 1981: 342f.), but design overlap here is of no help in relative dating (Coles 1999: 178).

The first permanent markings of the capstones of graves and rocks in the landscape connected them together and added significance and power to processions across and through the landscape. These peoples were marking and engraving stones already significant to them: capstones of tombs, anomalous stones on the Cambrian sandstone, significant boulders and rock exposures. The Neolithic builders of the Rosdala passage grave had selected a gleaming white Cambrian sandstone block for the capstone, in contrast to the nearby Ekenäs passage grave and elsewhere, where granite was always chosen. Such a block dramatically making the landscape and decorated on its uppermost surface with cup marks must have attracted the Bronze Age rock carvers, who further engraved figurative designs on this stone, marking a monument that for them may have represented another ancestral time. That the Cambrian sandstone was recognized to have had special qualities in the Neolithic is clearly demonstrated by finds of numerous beach pebbles of this material found during excavations outside the entrance to the Rosdala passage grave together with numerous offerings of elaborate decorated pots and flint axes of middle Neolithic date (Burenhult 1981: 325).

There is an enormous difference between the Neolithic and the Bronze Age in terms of the significance of barrows in the landscape. The Neolithic barrows never occupy the highest points, which are dominated by the Bronze Age barrows and cairns. During the Neolithic the barrows were revered as the resting places of the ancestral dead celebrated by offerings and ceremonies. The barrows presenced the dead in the landscape and mediated between the ancestors and the living. In the Bronze Age the ancestral souls of the dead depart from the barrows into the sea of the underworld. The barrow, while being used time and time again for burial, is no longer a place for ancestral veneration because the dead are now in another world. Ceremonies and offerings no longer take place outside these barrows as they did outside the entrances to the dolmens and passage graves. The barrows symbolize genealogical ties between the living and the dead but are regarded as entry points or portals for the dead to reach another world rather than permanent and fixed ancestral resting places. In other words, while the primary relationship of the barrow in the middle Neolithic was between the living and the dead, in the Bronze Age it signified relationships to and rights to land and resources among the living, the souls of the dead having departed forever, requiring, after the initial death ceremonies, no further veneration. This may account for the evidence for 'disrespectful' reuse of Neolithic barrows throughout the late Neolithic and Bronze Age, being built over, reused and remodelled in various ways. Water was in all probability conceived as a liminal medium between the living and the ancestral dead, a medium through which the souls of the dead passed on their journey to the underworld. A conceptual connection was being made between the dead, whose journey into the underworld through the waves of a frozen sea is being expressed at Järrestad, and boats. The boats on the rock carvings link both the living and the dead, the heavens and the underworld, as well as connecting together the communities of the living. While the barrows expressed the identities, genealogies and relationships of families to the land on which they lived, the boats were a symbolic expression of a network society entirely dependent on alliance patterns and exchange. They became universal polysemous symbols of life, sociality and the cosmos. They mediated and linked together the dualisms of complementary opposition in social organization with those of land and sea, coast and inland, life and death, to opposing principles of social hierarchy, inequality and asymmetry.

The carved panels at Järrestad, situated in the west and connected with the death of the sun, and those at Simris, linked with the living and the emergence of the sun from the sea at daybreak, articulate these ideas both in the visual and spatial form of the carvings and the rock surfaces on which they are engraved. This is reinforced by the experience of these places in relation to the sea: at Järrestad an inert glassy glimpse on the horizon; at Simris, the smell of rotting seaweed, the sound of the waves and the taste of salt. The living sea is mobile, volatile, viscous, animated and buoyant. The sea of the dead, by contrast, is forever cold, icy, dead and static, with its waves in suspended motion. Such a sea does not sustain life. There are no fish and one cannot move across it to reach, exchange with or influence other persons. This is an icy underworld of the dead in which normal life becomes totally arrested and transformed.

The carved motifs at Järrestad and those at Simris perform active work in relation to an observer in very different ways. At Järrestad there are obvious figure/ground reversals according to which boats, shoe-soles and feet occur right way up or not in relation to each other, eliciting a change in perspective of the viewer, but this remains fairly static compared with the circular motion demanded at Simris 19. In both cases an image of transformation is being formed by the transformation of an image, but at Simris 19 in a more violent and unregulated way which is also mediated by the experiential presence of the living sea.

The dominant visual presence of Bronze Age barrows within the agrarian landscape of the southern part of the study region was necessary precisely because they related to a living landscape of ongoing social relations rather than representing a relationship between the living and the ancestral dead. Constructed, extended, used and reused for burials, they were monuments of and for the living and channelling points through which the dead could reach another world and leave forever the world of the living. Separation from the remains of the dead was made permanent in these barrows, contrasting with the access made possible to ancestral bones in the stone chambers of the Neolithic dolmens and passage graves. Burial in a barrow therefore served to disconnect the living from the dead but acted to cement ties, rights and affiliations among those carrying out the death rites. Thus individual family groups sited new barrows in particular relationships to other barrows in the landscape. The patterning of groups of barrows in the landscape came to represent, through time, relationships between families, founding families and persons who were buried later, and in this way traditions and continuity between social groups was maintained through the relational placement of barrows in the landscape. The barrows thus expressed particular social ties among the living rather than symbolizing links to ancestral forces and powers contained within them. The ancestors could no longer be reached and communicated with in a fixed place at the burial mound. Rather, the barrows created on the ground a genealogical map of kin relations between local social groups. Gradually all the higher points in the landscape became filled up with these barrows, and then around the middle of the Bronze Age new mortuary practices involving cremation and burial in flat graves begin to dominate. The physical remains of the dead now become removed from the landscape altogether and their remains are consumed by fire. Family genealogies are no longer being marked out and monumentalized in the landscape. If, during the earlier Bronze Age, water was the medium through which the souls of the dead passed to another world, fire may now instead have become the transformative medium.

Apart from at Gislöv 11 and Simris 10, large, and presumably fairly early, Bronze age barrows do not occur in the vicinity of the rock carvings, and indeed most carving sites and barrows are not intervisible. Small barrows do, however, occur directly above the carved panels at Järrestad. Excavation has shown them to be late Bronze Age date cremation burials in urns (Althin 1945: 81f.). Small barrows, probably also of similarly late date, also occur in the immediate vicinity of the rock carvings at Simris 4 by the coast. The majority of the rock carvings that can be stylistically dated appear to have been created during a relatively brief period (Periods II–III) of the early Bronze Age. When these small burial mounds were built at Järrestad, the rock carvings may have already lost their original significance and now, being very old, were simply regarded as generalized ancestral work or signatures. They became reconceptualized as ancestral signed places in the vicinity of which it was now appropriate to raise small barrows with cremation burials. The rock carvings became for the first time linked to an abstract notion of an ancestral world rather than to the day-to-day communal ceremonies of the living concerned with the flows of life and the passages of death. During the later Bronze Age the old barrow mounds and the carving sites therefore may have had more or less equivalent roles in relation to the living, which is why both could equally well serve as a focus for small barrow cemeteries and flat graves. During the earlier Bronze Age the carving sites were expressions of cosmologies related to life and death ceremonies. These were linked with structuring principles of social organization. By contrast, the barrows related to genealogical ties among the families of the living and were physically separated from the rock carvings in the landscape. In the later Bronze age such a distinction became lost.

Randsborg (1993) has commented on the relative marginality and peripheral location of the great Kivik cairn in the landscape. We might surely expect such a massive cairn to be located in the far richer agrarian landscape of the southern part of the study region and in closer association to the major rock carving locations. Or perhaps somewhere else altogether in southern Sweden. Why just here in the south-east of Skåne? And why is it that there is such a massive concentration of bronze documented in precisely the same area as the rock carvings occur? A possible explanation for both may reside in the powers of place and the powers of stone. A 'marginal' burial location might be entirely suited for a chief with magical transformative or shamanic powers. Controlling access to bronze used in ceremonies for the living and the dead would require a strategic mind but not necessarily a central location. And what ultimately attracted the bronze to this corner of Sweden may have been intimately related to the peculiar and unique qualities of the frozen sea of the Cambrian sandstone and the particular manner in which the mythological relationship between it and the sea of the living carrying life, sustenance and wealth was conceived. The outer surface of the Kivik cairn itself might have been covered with this rock. It is located in the most northerly area in Skåne where the bedrock is composed of this stone, which does not outcrop here, as in the south, in the form of exposed pavements but is exposed and visible along the coastline. Eight km to the south of Kivik and approximately equidistant between it and the coastal Simris carving sites, the water-filled 'Parson's bathtub' is exposed in the Cambrian sandstone on the foreshore (see Fig. 4.3). Might this have been understood as the burial place of a mythological founding ancestor and the portal for his or her entry into the sea of the dead? Might the similarly coastally located Kivik grave built some way away at a respectful distance be replicating this (only to us) geological structure? This would certainly provide an explanation of the absence of any large cairns or barrows located along the coastal strip apart from that at Kivik, to the south, except far away and beyond the Simris rock carving localities in the vicinity of Brantevik where Branterör, with its decorated cist, once stood.

The qualities of the Cambrian sandstone rocks may have themselves been understood in the earlier Bronze Age as having a magnetic power that could attract and mesmerize boats, and persons, transporting the bronze from continental Europe. The mere sight of these gleaming white rocks would make them stop and come ashore bearing bronzes. It was thus the very agency of the rocks that attracted the bronze and they became the ultimate source of chiefly power. We have suggested that the swimmer at Järrestad represents the Kivik chief in shamanic form passing through the sea of the dead. The chief's 'signature' is also present at Simris 19 in the form of the omega design at the bottom of the rock closest to the sea. Ceremonial axes, with axe bearers, of the same type depicted on the Kivik cist occur on the Simris 19 and Simris 27 carving sites. As noted above, three of the horse riders depicted at Järrestad holding reins extending over the heads of the horses are identical in form to the horse rider on the top of the seventh slab of the Kivik grave. All the principal carving surfaces are thus directly linked with the decorated slabs of the great cairn in various ways. Carving and animating the rocks, and thus making a claim to them, was simultaneously a way of making a claim to and ensuring the supply of bronze, necessary for social reproduction and the maintenance of social hierarchy.

Conclusions

We have argued that the significance of the rock carvings lies in the ways in which they combine an experience of the surrounding landscape and qualities of the rock itself with a capacity to think and feel in images requiring movement and having definite bodily effects on an observer. They condensed realms of ideas about society, place and landscape and allowed complex relationships, connections and associations to be perceived and grasped. The images and the stone on which they were carved, and its landscape context, had the power of eliciting, or causing to perceive, meanings according to how they were seen, when, in what sequence and where. Knowledge in the Bronze Age was acquired through visiting these places, just as we acquire knowledge of them through visiting them today. Such images must have been conceived as being animate, about the life process, about death, and the cosmological link between the two. We have attempted to understand something more about these images through relating them to the experiential qualities of the rocks on which they appear and through considering their relationship to barrows.

Meaning did not just reside in the image but also in relation to the stone in which it was carved and the way in which both were related to an experience of landscape, a homeland for all thought. Remembering that the rock carvings were used in the context of performances, the sensual experience of carving and using them would have been a means of access to knowledges and supernatural powers. Different carving places were meant to be experienced and encountered in different ways, and what was seen and touched was inseparable from how this took place, from where this took place, and the kind of activity that was been engaged in.

-5-

Conclusions
The Past as Dreamwork

Persons make things and things make persons. This book has attempted to explore the multiple ways in which prehistoric social identities were created or sustained, reproduced or transformed through the agency of stones. The argument in a nutshell is that social relations are simultaneously relations between material forms. Since the meanings and significance of artefacts and places, landscapes and representations are intimately linked, separations between them are inevitably of an artificial character. As Bradley (2000) has cogently expressed it, artefacts can be places and places may be artefacts, monuments can be landscapes and landscapes may be monuments.

Social identity is always experienced and enacted in specific contexts. Having a processual character, it always requires specific concrete material points of reference in the form of landscapes, places, artefacts and other persons. It is therefore constituted through various forms of subject-to-subject and subject-to-object relations, giving it a transactional and performative character. The contexts in which identities are experienced, reproduced or transformed may be conventional and familiar, in which persons know how to act and carry on, habitual and routinized, or less familiar, requiring a much greater degree of discursive reflection with regard to what having a particular identity might entail. Material forms may thus act as key sensuous metaphors of identity, instruments with which to think through and create connections around which people actively construct their identities and their worlds.

One of the primary problems that we have always had in understanding the significance of material forms and being able to theorize them adequately in relation to persons stems from the binary dualisms that govern our own thought, in which mind becomes separated from body, nature from culture, subject from object, the literal from the metaphorical. We have inherited one dominant Anglo-American ethnophilosophical analytical tradition which is about three hundred years old, originating in the reflections of Descartes. In the famous *Cogito* argument, 'I think, therefore I am', the mind and cognition become split from the body, which becomes an object form. As a concomitant, culture as a set of ideas about the world becomes separated from brute nature. Either nature is held to dominate and human cultures must adapt themselves to its exigencies or, alternatively, it becomes a kind of blank slate on which people arbitrarily impose their own cognitive versions of reality, doing more or less as they please, sometimes in Marxist positions theorized within the constraints of a 'last instance' of economic and environmental determination. As opposed to active thinking subjects, material culture becomes regarded as passive and inert dead matter. From such a perspective, material culture cannot really matter. In a relatively trivial fashion it simply reflects and reifies social relations and intentional minds.

Our other ethnophilosophical tradition is sometimes labelled as 'continental philosophy' and includes various attempts to transcend and mediate the dualisms which have pervaded Western thought since the Enlightenment. In the process we need to consider things *seriously*. This includes the dialectical thought of Hegel and Marx, and various hermeneutic and phenomenological positions. From Marx's inversion of Hegelian thought, we have the central notion of objectification: that there is an intimate connection between persons and things; through making things, persons make themselves. Objects are generative of thought and action: both constituted and constituting. Our social identities are simultaneously embodied in our persons and objectified in our things through a dialectic of externalization and internalization in which persons actively appropriate things and create meaning. We experience objects and places socially in the same manner that we experience people. It follows that the meanings people give to things are part and parcel of the same meanings that they give to their lives.

An approach stressing objectification processes remains central to any understanding of material culture. We can perhaps readily agree that material forms objectify culture and persons in various ways, but there are, of course, a myriad of ways in which this can take place which cannot be predicted in advance. Objectification approaches tend to collapse a concept of mind into a concept of culture, thus ignoring or replacing the latter with the former. They also have relatively little to say about the body and processes of embodiment. These shortcomings are precisely those which are addressed in the phenomenology of Merleau-Ponty, whose work provides a fundamental conceptual ground for this book.

Ancient stones in landscapes, the subject matter of this book, cannot be known or understood simply from publications, from maps, diagrams, photographs and descriptions, because these are only representations. As representations they necessarily fail in conveying a bodily understanding of prehistoric remains. Statistical analysis, Geographical Information Systems and simulations are, if anything, far worse. There can be no substitute for the human experience of place – of being there – and it is only after this that the various technologies of representation come into play. This is a difference between a first-order knowledge and a second or surreptitious order of knowing. In this sense all attempts to represent the past or the present, including the present book, are necessarily failures or at best diminish the impact and significance of what we are trying to understand. This is a basic dilemma of all research.

All the descriptive observations made in this book can be checked in the field, validated, refuted or modified. It is an irony that this is impossible in relation to archaeological excavation, sometimes claimed to be generative of an objective knowledge of the past, because it can never be experienced by others. Having destroyed that which it uncovers, its results, to a large extent, always remain unverifiable. Unless you are a seasoned excavator, from a diagram you cannot imagine a trench. This is a privileged and professional experience which cannot be revisited. You certainly cannot see the textures, colours and characteristics of a section. You cannot feel or smell the soil. There is no bodily experience of space or place.

A strong gut reaction by some to a phenomenological approach is that one must be able to verify experience in some way. Otherwise might it not just be a product of personal whim? Our work here is open – radically open – to new interpretations in a way that excavations can never be since anyone can visit these stones and experience these places themselves, make new observations and check old ones. By contrast, archaeological excavation results in an absolute closure of the past and the reports only provide limited possibilities for further understandings and reinterpretations because all that is left is a representation of that which has been disturbed, at best, or destroyed.

The three studies in this book are intended to be empirical without being empiricist and we believe that care and attention to detail is a key to understanding. The empirical facts naturally constrain how we interpret, but also, by their very nature, provide a springboard for multiple understandings. We obviously interpret the stones through a contemporary cultural frame, and a theoretical perspective that we share with others. In this sense there are no personal or 'individual' under-standings whatsoever in this book since all 'individual' experiences are necessarily social and can never be absolutely unique. Nor are there any purely 'subjective' understandings of place and landscape because both experience and interpretation derive from and relate to the objectivity of the material presence of forms that we perceive. The material experience of stones *in place* is fundamental. The stones exert their muted agency in relation to us. They make an impact. We cannot describe them in any way that we like.

Experiencing stones in place links an understanding of them to memory. It is memory that serves to connect knowledges of one place to another, without which experience remains shallow and non-contextual. In the course of fieldwork, one visits initially an unfamiliar series of places that are often confusing and bewilder-ing in their complexity of form. After a while, through revisiting these places, through a process of 'dwelling' in them, one hopefully achieves a feeling and sensibility for place, of repetitive elements and individual and unique features, which permits one to compare and contrast and deepen an interpretative understanding of the significance of these places for prehistoric populations. This understanding derives from the attempt to provide a thick description of place: how one encounters, feels, sees and senses that place, informed by an understanding of places that have previously been encountered. Necessarily, this process involves continuous re-evaluation and changing perspectives until a final account is written which momentarily arrests and fixes these experiences and can, it is hoped, provide a starting point for re-evaluation by others, something to react against, alter or modify. Consequently, this style of research is both fragile and democratic in that it is open to all, at least in principle, to re-evaluate. The aim is not to control or fix knowledge but rather, through our practice, to open up perspectives and create opportunities for further understanding. We enter a landscape and create a subjective but culturally bound perception of it. We also interact with the materiality of place and the place interacts with us and affects the manner in which we perceive. Our vision of place, or sense of place, may change as the dynamic world is always changing. An objective bodily experience of place does not understand a place as a fixed and definite thing but rather as something fluid and flowing. Our approach thus transcends the 'subjective' and the 'objective' as these terms are normally understood.

It also transcends a distinction between 'nature' and 'culture'. Since its inception, modern archaeology has been, above all, about artifice: identifying, classifying and recording cultural work and distinguishing between material culture and those forms and materials which are not a product of human agency. Thunderbolts became recognized as axes, long mounds and cairns were recorded as cultural work, separate, divorced and opposed to natural features of the landscape. It can easily be claimed that recognizing and recording culture, as opposed to nature, provides the conceptual basis for all field archaeology. From such a perspective, nature only becomes a worry: might this mound be an unaltered feature of the landscape? What we understand to be natural tends to be ignored precisely because it is not culture and is therefore considered to be relatively unimportant in interpretation. The argument throughout this book has been that in thinking about, describing and interpreting cultural landscapes, we need to spend as much time and effort considering 'natural' form as 'cultural' form. Nature provides a fundamental resource through which to think through culture. Meaning is created through a dialectic between the two. Nature and culture are two sides of a coin which cannot be separated, part of a complex system of signification.

We do not live in a physical or social environment. Such a position immediately posits our separation. Rather, we have an environment and we are part of it and it is part of us. The world is not what I think, but rather what I live through. We are immersed in it as fish are immersed in the sea. Through our senses the body extends into the world. The boundary of the body does not end at the skin.

Experience of the world is embodied and flows from the body. The body mediates our experience and such experience is always synaesthetic, involving all the senses. The phenomenal field is thus not an inner world, a mental fact, but the structure of lived material experience. Perceiving an artefact, a place or a landscape is thus not just a visual practice but involves the whole living body: experiencing hot and cold, sounds, smells, textures and surfaces. There is a very real sense in which we cannot know beforehand, prior to experience, what a place or a stone actually *is*. We certainly did not envisage the Breton menhirs as being 'complex' monuments prior to a detailed investigation of their morphologies, surfaces and landscape locations.

At the heart of this work is a dialogic description and understanding of stones and landscapes in place. We enter into them, they in turn enter into us; we form them, they form us. We have attempted to describe what we see, feel and understand through our senses, and with our bodies. So this is work produced from the human scale. Our attempt at thick descriptions of place contrast with the standard mode of thin technicist archaeological description which effectively dehumanizes the past and makes it remote and sterile because such technical descriptions are based on abstracted Cartesian conceptions of space and time.

Experiencing places in the landscape involves taking as much account of the landscape in which the place is embedded, its relationship with its physical and topographical context, as of the place itself. Throughout, we assume that what makes the place significant is its relationship with other 'natural' and 'cultural' places. We are thus concerned with the dialectics of place and surroundings. Methodologically, this requires sensing place from without and from within from a variety of vantage points and pathways. No adequate understanding of the social and cultural geography of a place can be achieved without considering its relationship with others and experiencing its situation in the landscape at a human scale requiring moving and walking through and exploring its surroundings.

The concept of embodiment provides a fundamental starting point to discuss, phenomenologically, the significance of stones for people. The most general argument that is being made is that the immediacy of our embodied experiences of the world has a profound effect on the way in which we relate to both things and persons. The body is both interpretational constraint and enabling condition for the construction of meaning. Every perceived object is situated within a spatial horizon or a background from which it is distinguished. Figure can always become ground or vice versa, depending on how and what we perceive. But the context of a stone is not simply its spatial background or horizon. It always involves time as well. The backgrounds of a thing are constituted out of a whole network of past experiences and future expectations which are not, in any empirical sense, part of our immediate sensory fields. Thus the invisible aspects of a stone are as essential to its meaning and significance as those that are visible. The diachronic aspect of context constantly affects the way in which we perceive figures and grounds. Thus stones have culturally emergent properties. So stones always have meanings and relationships extending beyond themselves. They are not replete unto themselves. They are always more than themselves: in a process of *becoming* rather than a static state of being.

Things and places are active agents of identity rather than pale reflections of preexisting ideas and sociopolitical relations. Having real material and ideological effects on persons and social relations, things and places can then be regarded as much subjects as objects of identity. In this book an attempt has been made to explore the significance of the agency of landscapes and places at both a macro- and a micro-scale of analysis. So in Chapter 2 a large-scale regional analysis was presented of a particular class of monuments, Breton menhirs, through a micro-analysis of the forms and surfaces of the stones. Chapters 3 and 4 are concerned with much smaller regions, more or less equivalent in size, and incorporate micro-relational analyses of individual places and stones. In all these studies we have been concerned not only with landscape settings and dynamics but equally with the material qualities of what one encounters and how this feels. We have described textures, colours, tactile contrasts, sounds, sometimes smells, and how they connect together to create a physical dynamic in relation to which the body reacts and responds. For example, in Chapter 4 we were concerned with why certain rocks within specific landscape settings were chosen by prehistoric rock artists and others were ignored. What was special about them? We specifically attempted to address the following seven sets of general questions:

1. Was it the shape, surface texture, colour, intrinsic characteristics such as cracks or fissure lines of the rock that were of significance?
2. Was it the particular relationship of the rock to others in the surrounding landscape that made it important? Was a carved rock significant, not in isolation, but only in relation to others with their own specific forms and characteristics in the immediate area surrounding it?
3. Was the landscape setting of a carved rock, or series of rocks, intimately related to the fact that it was carved? How might it relate to prominent local topographic features
4. How does one's experience of the carved rocks change and alter as one approaches them from other carved rocks and different kinds of places, following different paths of movement? Are there specific groupings of designs in relation to different visual fields on a decorated rock or can one see them all at once? Can one see from one carved rock to another? How easy is it to approach a carved rock? What other kinds of rocks (carved or uncarved) does one have to pass, or clamber over, to reach it?

5. Going beyond vision, what do the rocks and the carvings feel like? Might changes in tactile sensations be important? What about the relationship between carved rocks and auditory dimensions of experience that can still be recorded in the surrounding landscape, such as the sound of the near or distant sea?

6. How do points 1–5 relate, if at all, to the specific characteristics of the rock art: the form, size, position, orientation and arrangements of designs on specific rocks?

7. Going beyond the decorated rocks themselves, how do these relate to the locations of other known cultural features of the landscape, either contemporary with the rock art, or those which are earlier or later such as cairns and barrows, monuments and settlements, votive deposits, distributions of local or exotic artefacts, etc.?

Similar types of questions inform the other landscape studies in the book, and in Chapter 3 in particular we have also directly addressed issues of bodily posture, with standing upright, stooping or crawling, and with the kinaesthetics of movement in the exploration of place and with light and darkness and the changing qualities of experience that these create within the contexts of the interior spaces of the Maltese temples. In Chapter 4 we were concerned to consider the manner in which the rock carvings might be viewed, and the effects of this on bodily position and movement. Such an approach likewise informed an understanding of the appearance of the Breton menhirs discussed in Chapter 2.

Understanding place is a gradual process of familiarization in which description is ultimately the last act. Sensing, perceiving and understanding are conjoined in a fundamental way. Understanding and experiencing a place is a process of learning how to understand and how to feel. It involves a gradual act of familiarization equivalent to getting to know a person, in which first impressions can, as often as not, be misleading. It takes time and cannot be hurried. The first encounter with any place is likely to be disorientating because one brings to that place an entire intellectual baggage which needs to be unravelled and thought through again in order to move towards an understanding of it. One needs to explore first before recording anything. Writing is essential to the task at a later stage because it produces a vision and feeling for place. Taking photographs or making video recordings of places are, by comparison (unless well scripted in advance), relatively passive acts which do not produce knowledge in the same way. For us these acts of the visual appropriation of place only take on essential importance following its description. We then know how to look and what to see.

Writing is so essential because it slows thought and perception down. This change of speed is quite critical because writing arises in the interaction of self and place and provides the medium through which a knowledge of place is achieved. Writing in effect forces one to perceive actively, to make connections, to articulate thoughts and feelings which would otherwise remain at a prereflective or practical level of consciousness. Writing is thus the primary (academic) medium of inter-action between self and place and it constantly surprises how much understanding comes through the forced act of translation of experience into the written word, even if much is also lost or can never be appropriated in this way. This has import-ant methodological implications. At least half of this book has not been written on a desk but in the context of the places described and discussed while sitting and walking, while perceiving and sensing the stones in Brittany, Malta and Sweden.

Experiences of places are inevitably contingent and fragmentary, and this is precisely why it is essential that they be recorded in place and in the time of our study. It would be impossible to write up these experiences two or three years later for they are fragile and inevitably dulled with the passage of time. There is a fraility to this process which is challenging. Physical conditions are occasionally – inevitably – difficult. This means that a sustained engagement is necessary in exactly the same way that good anthropological research demands participant observation. What comes before is library and archival research, recovering and revisiting previously recorded information. What comes afterwards is the articula-tion of these field observations and descriptions with a re-analysis and critical evaluation of the preexisting literature, narrative construction and the hermeneutics of interpretation through the use of metaphor and metonymy. The first phase of research informs an initial understanding; the fieldwork phase leads to an experi-ential reevaluation and new understandings. The third and final phase recontextual-izes the first two to produce something that is different again. Our understandings in the field are changing all the time in relation to our successive encounters with places and landscapes, and these, in turn, change in terms of the final re-analysis. The accounts thus produced are themselves entirely provisional. Where they end is intended to facilitate another beginning.

A 'pure' phenomenological approach on its own remains inadequate. It has to be linked to an awareness of the hermeneutics of interpretation that goes beyond a descriptive exercise (Ricoeur 1981) and involves the exploitation of metaphoric and metonymic linkages between things (Tilley 1999a). What is required is a constant attempt at an articulation between our bodily experiences and the produc-tion of reinterpretations using inspiration from existing texts which may inform us, be they archaeological, anthropological, geographical or geological or works in cultural and critical theory.

Studying material culture both demands and requires a multidisciplinary per-spective and various types of empirical work and data collection. As regards the latter, trying to make sense of the Maltese temples and their landscapes involved using existing archaeological texts and excavation reports, general guidebooks, visiting museum exhibitions, visiting and encountering the sites, being guided through the hypogeum as part of a tourist group, using maps and diagrams of varying scales, walking in the landscapes surrounding the sites, driving through the wider landscape, visiting the coastlines, speaking to local informants, buying locally available postcards and representations, experiencing the weather, experiencing the monuments, touching the stones, looking at the stones on ancient and modern buildings, moving through the temple spaces, reading geographical and geological and anthropological accounts, and so on. This is a synthetic process bringing together what may seem at first totally unrelated elements. Such research is not reducible to a set of rule-book procedures which might guarantee 'useful' knowledge.

This work might be termed an exercise in a philosophical anthropology in that it attempts to draw together past and present, the previous work of archaeologists, without which we acknowledge our work would be impossible, and our own bodily experiences. We inevitably mediate between our present circumstances and the past. In doing so we produce a present past, a narrative which is neither the way the past really was, nor a simple reflection of present-day values and interests.

Writing the past in the present is always a creative act, a conceptual dreamwork. This book is an act of dreaming in the sense that it is a work of the intellectual imagination conjoined with contemporary bodily acts of sensing place. It is informed by particular creative responses to the past in the present which are anthropologically informed. The significance of an anthropological interpretation of the stones cannot be over-emphasized. Human beings, and their responses to the world around them, are infinitely flexible, and the power of the human imagination in response to place has few limits. Inevitably, our creative response to the remains that we have studied is a metaphorical work of 'art' for which we make no apology. This is to stress the contemporaneity of archaeological discourse and practice as always something produced in the present and for the present, and ultimately for our own edification. Writing the landscapes of the past is an ordering of a disorded reality. It gives them a place in the future and thus makes them relevant to our lives.

References

Abram, D. (1996) *The Spell of the Sensuous*, New York: Vintage.

Almgren, B. (1960) 'Hällristningar och bronsåldersdräkt', *Tor* 6: 19–50.

Althin, C.-A. (1945) *Studien zu den Bronzeitlichen Felszeichnungen von Skåne*, Lund: Gleerup.

Arne, T. (1925) 'Hus från bronsåldern i Sverige, *Rig*: 1–2.

Bender, B. (1986) *The Archaeology of Brittany, Normandy and the Channel Islands*, London: Faber and Faber.

Bender, B. (ed.) (1993) *Landscape: Politics and Perspectives*, Oxford: Berg.

Bender, B. (1998) *Stonehenge: Making Space*, Oxford: Berg.

Bird-David, N. (1999) '"Animism" revisited: personhood, environment and relational epistemology', *Current Anthropology* 40: 67–79.

Bonnano, A. (1996) 'Temple megalithism vs funerary megalithism: the case of the Maltese islands', *Colloquia* 9: 103–7.

Bonnano, A., Gouder, T., Malone, C. and Stoddart, S. (1990) 'Monuments in an island society: the Maltese context', *World Archaeology* 22: 190–205.

Bourdieu, P. (1977) *Outline of a Theory of Practice*, Cambridge: Cambridge University Press.

Bradley, R. (1999) 'Dead soles' in A. Gustafsson and H. Karlsson (eds) *Glyfer och arkeologisk rum – en vänbok till Jarl Nordbladh*, Gothenburg: Gotarc Series A, Vol. 3.

Bradley, R. (2000) *An Archaeology of Natural Places*, London: Routledge.

Briard, J. (1990) *Dolmens et menhirs*, Lucon: Jean-Paul Gisserot.

Briard, J., Gautier, J.-M. and Leroux, G. (1995) *Les mégalithes et les tumulus de Saint Just, Ille-et-Vilaine*, Paris: Comité des Travaux Historiques et Scientifiques.

Broodbank, C. (2000) *An Island Archaeology of the Early Cyclades*, Cambridge: Cambridge University Press.

Broström, S.-G. and Ihrestam, K. (1996) 'Skåne: 1996 års inventering av hällristningar på Österlen', unpublished manuscript.

Broström, S.-G. and Ihrestam, K. (1998) 'Hällristningar dokumenterade 1996 från Skåne och Bohuslän', *Adoranten* 1998: 72–5.

Burenhult, G. (1973) *The Rock Carvings of Götaland, Part II: Illustrations*, Lund: Gleerup.

Burenhult, G. (1980) *Götalands Hällristningar. Del I*, Stockholm: Gleerup.

Burenhult, G. (1981) *Stenåldersbilder. Hällristningar och stenåldersekonomi*, Stockholm: Sureförlaget.

Burenhult, G. (ed.) (1999) *Arkeologi i Norden* (2 vols), Stockholm: Natur och Kultur.

Burl, A. (1985) *Megalithic Brittany*, London: Thames and Hudson.

Burl, A. (1993) *From Carnac to Callanish*, New Haven: Yale University Press.

Capelle, T. (1991) 'Bronzezeitlich hausbilder' in K. Jennbert, L. Larsson, R. Petré and B. Wyszomriska-Webart (eds.) *Regions and Reflections: Essays in Honour of Märta Strömberg*, Lund: Gleerup.

Carserud, L. (1992) *Geologiska Sevärdheter i Skåne*, Lund: Sveriges Geologiska Undersökning.

Casey, E. (1993) *Getting Back into Place*, Bloomington: Indiana University Press.

Casey, E. (1997) *The Fate of Place: A Philosophical History*, Berkeley: University of California Press.

Cauchi, A. (1982) *Dwejra: Its History and Natural Beauty*, Ghajnsilem: Gozo Press.

Classen, C. (1983) *Worlds of Sense: Exploring the Senses in History and Across Cultures*, London: Routledge.

Coles, J. 1999. 'The dancer on the rock: record and analysis at Järrestad, Sweden', *Proceedings of the Prehistoric Society* 65: 167–87.

Cosgrove, D. (1984) *Social Formation and Symbolic Landscape*, London: Croom Helm.

Cosgrove, D. and Daniels, S. (eds) (1988) *The Iconography of Landscape*, Cambridge: Cambridge University Press.

Csordas, T. (1994) 'Introduction: the body as representation and being in the world' in T. Csordas (ed.) *Embodiment and Experience*, Cambridge: Cambridge University Press.

Cutajar, N. (2000) 'The archaeological dimension of the Hal Saflieni conservation project: excavations in the hypogeum upper level 1990–1992' in A. Pace (ed.) *The Hal Saflieni Hypogeum 4000 BC–2000 AD*, Malta: Museums Department.

Dann, K. (1998) *Bright Colors Falsely Seen*, New Haven: Yale University Press.

Descola, P. (1996) 'Constructing natures: symbolic ecology and social practice' in P. Descola and G. Pálsson (eds) *Nature and Society: Anthropological Perspectives*, London: Routledge.

Dillon, M. (1998) *Merleau-Ponty's Ontology*, Evanston, IL: Northwestern University Press.

Douglas, M. (1970) *Natural Symbols*, Harmondsworth: Penguin.

Edmonds, M. (1999) *Ancestral Geographies of the Neolithic: Landscape, Monuments and Memory*, London: Routledge.

Evans, J. (1959) *Malta*, London: Thames and Hudson.

Evans, J. (1971) *Prehistoric Antiquities of the Maltese Islands*, London: Athlone.

Evans, J. (1996) 'What went on in a Maltese megalithic "temple"?' in A. Pace (ed.) *Maltese Prehistoric Art 5000–2500 BC*, Malta: Progress Press.

Faron, L. (1962) 'Symbolic values and the integration of society among the Maouche of Chile', *American Anthropologist* 64: 1151–64.

Feld, S. (1996) 'Waterfalls of song: an acoustemology of place resounding in Bosavi, Papua New Guinea' in S. Feld and K. Basso (eds) *Senses of Place*, Santa Fe: School of American Research Press.

Feld, S. and Basso, K. (eds.) (1996) *Senses of Place*, Santa Fe: School of American Research Press.

Fodera, S., Hoskin, M. and Ventura, F. (1992) 'The orientations of the temples of Malta', *Journal for the History of Astronomy* 23: 107–19.

Gaffin, D. (1996) *In Place: Spatial and Social Order in a Faeroe Islands Community*, Prospect Heights: Waveland Press.

Gell, A. (1995) 'The language of the forest: landscape and phonological iconism in Umeda' in E. Hirsch and M. O'Hanlon (eds) *The Anthropology of Landscape*, Oxford: Oxford University Press.

Gell, A. (1998) *Art and Agency*, Oxford: Clarendon Press.

Gibbs, R. (1994) *The Poetics of Mind*, Cambridge: Cambridge University Press.

Gibson, J. (1986) *The Ecological Approach to Visual Perception*, Hillsdale, NJ: Lawrence Erlbaum Associates.

Gill, J. (1991) *Merleau-Ponty and Metaphor*, London: The Humanities Press.

Giot, P.-R. (1988) 'Stones in the landscape of Brittany' in C. Ruggles (ed.) *Records in Stone: Papers in Memory of Alexander Thom*, Cambridge: Cambridge University Press.

Giot, P.-R. (1995) *Bretagne des mégalithes*, Rennes: Ouest France.

Giot, P.-R., L'Helgouach, J. and Monnier, J.-L. (1979) *Prehistoire de la Bretagne*, Rennes: Ouest France.

Glob, P. (1974) *The Mound People*, London: Faber and Faber.

Gooch, P. (1998) 'Being-in-the-world: the phenomenology of indigenousness' in A. Hornborg and M. Kurkiala (eds) *Voices of the Land: Identity and Ecology in the Margins*, Lund: Lund University Press.

Gouletquar, P., Kayser, M., Le Goffic, M., Leopold, G., Marchand, G. and Moullec, J.-M. (1996) 'Ou sont passés les mésolithiques côtiers bretons? Bilan 1985–1995 de prospections de surface dans les Finistère', *Revue Archéologique de Ouest* 13: 5–30.

Griaule, M. (1965) *Conversations with Ogotemmeli*, Oxford: Oxford University Press.

Grima, R. (2001) 'An iconography of insularity: a cosmological interpretation of some images and spaces in the late neolithic temples of Malta', *Papers from the Institute of Archaeology* 12: 48–65.

Hamberg, L. (1990) 'Tidevands – og stormdominerade afleringsmiljöer i den nedre Kambriske Hardebega formation i Skåne og på Bornholm', *Dansk Geologisk Forenings Årskrift for 1978–79*: 15–20.

Hammond, M., Howarth, K. and Keat, R. (1991) *Understanding Phenomenology*, Oxford: Blackwell.

Haslam, S. and Borg, J. (1998) *The River Valleys of the Maltese Islands*, Malta, Formatek: Malta.

Helms, M. (1998) *Ulysees' Sail: An Ethnographic Odyssey of Power, Knowledge and Geographical Distance*, Princeton: Princeton University Press.

Hertz, R. (1960) *Death and the Right Hand*, New York: Free Press.

Hibbs, J. (1983) 'The Neolithic of Brittany and Normandy' in C. Scarre (ed.) *Ancient France*, Edinburgh: Edinburgh University Press.

Hirsch, E. and O'Hanlon, M. (eds) (1995) *The Anthropology of Landscape*, Oxford: Oxford University Press.

Hoskins, J. (1998) *Biographical Objects*, London: Routledge.

Howes, D. (ed.) (1991) *The Varieties of Sensory Experience*, Toronto: University of Toronto Press.

Hyde, H. (1955) *The Geology of the Maltese Islands*, Malta.

Hyenstrand, Å. (1984) *Fasta Fornlämningar och Arkeologiska Regioner*, Stockholm: Riksantikvarieämbetet Rapport 1984: 7.

Ingold, T. (1996) 'Hunting and gathering as ways of perceiving the environment' in R. Ellen and K. Fukui (eds) *Redefining Nature*, Oxford: Berg.

Ingold, T. (2000) *The Perception of the Environment*, London: Routledge.

Jennbert, K. (1993) 'Släkters hågkomst: om bruket av bronsåldershögar' in L. Larsson (ed.) *Bronsålderns Gravhögar*, Lund: Institute of Archaeology Report Series 48.

Kana, N. (1980) 'The order and significance of the Sauvunese house' in J. Fox (ed.) *The Flow of Life: Essays on Eastern Indonesia*, Cambridge, MA: Harvard University Press.

Kaul, F. (1998) *Ships on Bronzes: A Study in Bronze Age Religion and Iconography*, Copenhagen: National Museum (2 vols).

Kirk, T. (1993) 'Space, subjectivity, power and hegemony: megaliths and long mounds in earlier Neolithic Brittany' in C. Tilley (ed.) *Interpretative Archaeology*, Oxford: Berg.

Kristiansen, K. (1987) 'From stone to bronze: the evolution of social complexity in northern Europe 2300–1200 BC' in E. Brumfield and T. Earle (eds) *Specialization, Exchange and Complex Societies*, Cambridge: Cambridge University Press.

Kristiansen, K. (1998) *Europe before History*, Cambridge: Cambridge University Press.

Kristiansen, K. (1999) 'Symbolic structures and social institutions: the twin rulers in Bronze Age Europe' in A. Gustafsson and H. Karlsson (eds) *Glyfer och Arkeologiska Rum: En Vän bok till Jarl Nordbladh*, Gothenburg: Gotarc Series A, Vol. 3.

Lakoff, G. and Johnson, M. (1980) *Metaphors We Live By*, Chicago: University of Chicago Press.

Larsson, L. (1993) 'Relationer till ett röse – några aspekter på Kiviksgraven' in L. Larsson (ed.) *Bronsålders Gravhögar*, Lund: Institute of Archaeology Report Series 38.

Larsson, T. (1986) *The Bronze Age Metalwork in Southern Sweden: Aspects of Social and Spatial Organization*, Umeå: Archaeology and Environment 6.

Leach, E. (1979) 'Taste and smell' in M. Csaky (ed.) *How Does it Feel? Exploring the World of Your Senses*, London: Thames and Hudson.

Leacock, R. and Brans, G. (1975) 'The boat as architectural symbol' in P. Oliver (ed.) *Shelter, Sign and Symbol*, London: Barrie and Jenkins.

Lecerf, Y. (1999) *Les Pierres Droites: Réflexions autour des menhirs*, Rennes: Document Archéologique de l'Ouest, Asociation pour la Diffusion des Recherches archéologiques dans l'Ouest de la France.

Le Pontois, B. (1929) Le Finistère préhistorique, Paris: Émile Nourry.

Le Roux, C.-T. (1985) 'New excavations at Gavrinis', *Antiquity* 59: 183–7.

Le Roux, C.-T. (1999) *L'outillage de pierre polie en métadolérite type A: Les ateliers de Plussulien (Côtes-d'amor): Production et diffusion au Néolithique dans la France de l'ouest et au-delà*, Rennes: Travaux du Laboratoire Anthropologie, Préhistoire et Quaternaire Armoricaines.

Le Rouzic, Z. (1913) *Carnac – menhirs – statues avec signes figuratifs et amulettes ou idoles des dolmens du Morhiban*, Nantes: A. Dugas.

Lévi-Strauss, C. (1966) *The Savage Mind*, London: Weidenfeld and Nicolson.

Lévi-Strauss, C. (1973) *From Honey to Ashes*, London: Jonathan Cape.

Lévi-Strauss, C. (1978) *The Origin of Table Manners*, Chicago: University of Chicago Press.

Lévy-Bruhl ([1910] 1926) *How Natives Think*, New York: Knopf.

L'Helgouach, J. (1965) *Les sépultures mégalithiques en Amorique*, Rennes: Laboratorie d'Anthropologie Préhistorique

Lindström, M. (1967) 'Funnel grabens and early Palaeozoic tectonism in south Sweden', *Geological Society of America Bulletin*: 1137–54.

Lovell, N. (ed.) (1998) *Locality and Belonging*, London: Routledge.

Low, D. (2000) *Merleau-Ponty's Last Vision*, Evanston, IL: Northwestern University Press.

Madison, G. (1981) *The Phenomenology of Merleau-Ponty*, Athens, GA: Ohio University Press.

Malmer, M. (1981) *A Chorological Study of North European Rock Art*, Stockholm: Almquist and Wiksell.

Malone, C., Stoddart, S. and Trump, D. (1988) 'A house for the temple builders: recent investigations on Gozo, Malta', *Antiquity*: 62: 297–301.

Malone, C., Bonnano. A., Gouder, T., Stoddart, S. and Trump, D. (1993) 'The death cults of prehistoric Malta', *Scientific American* 269: 110–17.

Malone, C., Stoddart, S., Bonanno, A., Gouder, T. and Trump, D. (1995) 'Mortuary ritual of 4th millennium BC Malta: the Zebbug period chambered tomb from the Brochtorff Circle at Xaghra (Gozo)', *Proceedings of the Prehistoric Society* 61: 303–45.

Manguin, P.-Y. (1986) 'Shipshape societies: boat symbolism and political systems in insular southeast Asia' in D. Marr and A. Milner (eds) *Southeast Asia in the 9th to 14th centuries*, Singapore: Institute of Southeast Asian Studies.

Maniscalco, L. (1989) 'Ochre containers and trade in the central Mediterranean copper age', *American Journal of Archaeology* 93: 537–41.

Marguerie, D. (1992) *Evolution de la végétation sous l'impact human en Armorique du Néolithique aux périodes historiques*, Rennes: Travaux du Laboratoire d'Anthropolgie Préhistorie.

McLuhan, M. (1962) *The Gutenburg Galaxy: The Making of Typographic Man*, Toronto: University of Toronto Press.

Merleau-Ponty, M. (1962) *Phenomenology of Perception*, London: Routledge.

Merleau-Ponty (1964a) 'Eye and mind' in M. Merleau-Ponty *The Primacy of Perception*, Evanston, IL: Northwestern University Press.

Merleau-Ponty (1964b) *Signs*, Evanston, IL: Northwestern University Press.

Merleau-Ponty, M. (1968) *The Visible and the Invisible*, Evanston, IL: Northwestern University Press.

Mifsud, A. and Mifsud, S. (1999) 'The subterranean sanctuary at Hal Saflieni' in A. Mifsud and C. Ventura (eds) *Facets of Maltese Prehistory*, Malta: Prehistoric Society of Malta.

Mornand, J. (1998) *Préhistoire et protohistoire en Presque'île de Crozon – Tome 1: Crozon Lanveoc – Inventaire des mégalithes*, Crozon: Association Être Daou Vor.

Morzadec-Kerfourn, M.-T. (1985) 'Variations du niveau marin à l'Holocène en Bretagne (France)', *Eiszeitalter und Gegenwart* 35: 15–22.

Munn, N. (1986) *The Fame of Gawa*, Cambridge: Cambridge University Press.

Needham, R. (ed.) (1973) *Right and Left: Essays on Dual Symbolic Classification*, Chicago: University of Chicago Press.

Olausson, D. (1992) 'The archaeology of the Bronze Age cultural landscape – research goals, methods and results' in L. Larsson, J. Callmer and B. Stjernquist (eds) *The Archaeology of the Cultural Landscape: Field Work and Reseach in a South Swedish Rural Region*, Stockholm: Almquist and Wiksell.

Olausson, D. (1993) 'The Bronze Age barrow as a symbol' in L. Larsson (ed.) *Bronsålderns Gravhögar*, Lund: Institute of Archaeology Report Series 48.

Oldeberg, A. (1974) *Die Ältere Metallzeit in Schweden*, Stockholm: Kungliga Vitterhets Historie och Antikvitets Akadamien.

Ong, W. (1982) *Orality and Literacy: The Technologizing of the Word*, London: Methuen.

Pace, A. (ed.) (1996) *Maltese Prehistoric Art 5000–2500 BC*, Malta: Progress Press.

Pace, A. (2000) 'The prehistoric hypogeum at Hal Saflieni' in A. Pace (ed.) *The Hal Saflieni Hypogeum 4000 BC–2000 AD*, Malta: Museums Department.

Patton, M. (1993) *Statements in Stone: Monuments and Society in Neolithic Brittany*, London: Routledge.

Patton, M. (1996) *Islands in Time*, London: Routledge.

Pedley, H., House, R. and Waugh, B. (1976) 'The geology of Malta and Gozo', *Proceedings of the Geologists Association* 87(3): 325–41.

Pinney, C. (1995) 'Moral topophilia: the significance of landscape in Indian oleographs' in E. Hirsch and M. O'Hanlon (eds) *The Anthropology of Landscape*, Oxford: Oxford University Press.

Priest, S. (1998) *Merleau-Ponty*, London: Routledge.

Prigent, D., Visett, L., Morzadec-Kerfourn, M.-T. and Lautrido, J. (1983) 'Human occupation of the submerged coast of the Massif Amoricain and postglacial sea level changes' in P. Masters and N. Flemming (eds) *Quaternary Coastlines and Marine Archaeology*, New York: Academic Press.

Randsborg, K. (1993) 'Kivik: archaeology and iconography', *Acta Archaeologica* 64(1): 1–147.

Renfrew, C. (1973) *Before Civilization*, Harmondsworth: Penguin.

Ricoeur, P. (1981) *Hermeneutics and the Social Sciences*, Cambridge: Cambridge University Press.

Ridley, M. (1976) *The Megalithic Art of the Maltese Islands*, Poole: Dolphin Press.

Robb, J. (2001) 'Island identities: ritual, travel and the creation of difference in Neolithic Malta', *European Journal of Archaeology* 4(2): 175–202.

Rubin E. ([1915] 1958) 'Figure and ground' in David C. Beardslee and Michael Wertheimer (eds) *Readings in Perception*, Princeton, NJ: Van Nostrand, Inc.

Scarre, C. (2001) 'Modelling prehistoric populations: the case of Neolithic Brittany', *Journal of Anthropological Archaeology* 20: 285–313.

Schama, S. (1996) *Landscape and Memory*, New York: Knopf.

Shee Twohig, E. (1981) *The Megalithic Art of Western Europe*, Oxford: Clarendon.

Shore, B. (1996) *Culture in Mind*, Oxford: Oxford University Press.

Stoddart, S. (1999) 'Mortuary customs in prehistoric Malta' in A. Mifsud and C. Ventura (eds) *Facets of Maltese Prehistory*, Malta: Prehistoric Society of Malta.

Stoddart, S., Bonnano, A., Gouder, T., Malone, C. and Trump, D. (1993) 'Cult in an island society: prehistoric Malta in the Tarxien period', *Cambridge Archaeological Journal* 3: 3–19.

Stoller, P. (1989) *The Taste of Ethnographic Things: The Senses in Anthropology*, Philadelphia: University of Pennsylvania Press.

Stjernquist, B. (1961) *Simris II: Bronze Age Problems in the Light of the Simris Excavations*, Lund: Acta Archaeologica Lundensia.

Strömberg, M. (1976) *Forntid i Sydostskåne*, Lund: Föreningen för Fornminnes – och Hembygdsvård i Sydöstra Skåne

Strömberg, M. (1985) *Jägare, Flintsmed, Bonde, Järnsmed i Gislöv*, Simrishamn: Gislöfs Smidesmuseum.

Thomas, J. (1993) 'The hermeneutics of megalithic space' in C. Tilley (ed.) *Interpretative Archaeology*, Oxford: Berg.

Thomas, J. and Tilley, C. (1993) 'The axe and the torso: symbolic structures in the Neolithic of Brittany' in C. Tilley (ed.) *Interpretative Archaeology*, Oxford, Berg.

Tilley, C. (1991) *Material Culture and Text: The Art of Ambiguity*, London: Routledge.

Tilley, C. (1994) *A Phenomenology of Landscape*, Oxford: Berg.

Tilley, C. (1996) *An Ethnography of the Neolithic: Early Prehistoric Societies in Southern Scandinavia*, Cambridge: Cambridge University Press.

Tilley, C. (1999a) *Metaphor and Material Culture*, Oxford: Blackwell.

Tilley, C. (1999b). *The Dolmens and Passage Graves of Sweden: An Introduction and Guide*, London: Archetype Books.

Trump, D. (1966) *Skorba*, London: Society of Antiquaries Research Report 22.

Trump, D. (1976) 'The collapse of the Maltese temples' in G. Sieveking, I. Longworth and K. Wilson (eds) *Problems in Economic and Social Archaeology*, London: Duckworth.

Trump, D. (1981) 'Megalithic architecture in Malta' in J. Evans, B. Cunliffe and C. Renfrew (eds) *Antiquity and Man*, London: Thames and Hudson.

Trump, D. (2000) *Malta: An Archaeological Guide*, Malta: Progress Press (second revised edition).

Van Der Kroef, J. (1954) 'Dualism and symbolic antithesis in Indonesian society', *American Anthropologist* 56: 847–62.

Vassallo, M. (1999) 'Sun worship and Malta's megalithic temples I', Malta, *Sunday Times*, 23 January: 40–1.

Vassallo, M. (2000) 'Sun worship and Malta's megalithic temples II & III', Malta, *Sunday Times*, 30 January: 44–5; 6 February: 36–7.

Ventura, F. and Tanti, T. (1990) 'Orientations of Malta's megalithic temples', Malta, *Sunday Times* 5 August: 16–19.

References

Welinder, S. (1974) 'A study on the Scanian rock carvings by quantitative methods', *Meddelanden från Lunds Universitets Historiska Museum* 1973–74: 244–75.

Zammit, T. (1930) *Prehistoric Malta: The Tarxien Temples*, Oxford: Clarendon Press.

Zammit, T. (1994) *Malta: The Prehistoric Temples of Hagar Qim and Mnajdra*, Malta: Interprint.

Zammit Maemphel (1977) *An Outline of Maltese Geology*, Malta.

Index

Abram, D., 26–7
Althin, C.-A., 151, 152, 154
Amboyna (of Indonesia), 8–9
analogic logic, 8, 21, 23
ancestral connotations
  Maltese temples, 136, 137, 144
  menhirs, 51, 57, 75, 85, 86
  Swedish rock-carving sites, 202, 210, 211,
    213, 214
animals
  depicted in rock-carvings, 153, 159, 204
  Maltese temple rituals, 132–3, 137, 139,
    141–3
animism, 17, 19–22, 30
anthropology, 27, 28, 225
anthropomorphism, 17, 19–22
  shapes of menhirs, 34, 54, 57, 66, 69, 78, 85
archaeologists, access to Maltese temples, 145
archaeology
  and culture, 220
  excavation, 219
architecture
  Maltese temples, 87, 88–9, 98–9
  menhirs, 34, 35
Aristotle, 6
art see decorative art; representation
artefacts
  embodied experience, 9
  evidence for use of Maltese temples, 93
  from rock-carving sites, 191, 194
axes
  motifs in Swedish rock-carvings, 153, 158,
    160, 161–4, 168, 177, 178, 201, 202, 204,
    208, 214
  symbolism of menhirs, 34, 37, 47–8, 85,
    85–6

Baltic Sea, 147, 156, 163, 209
barrows (south-east Sweden), 168, 168–70,
  171, 172

burial and hierarchy, 198–200
  decorated stones, 193–4
  differences in Neolithic and Bronze Ages,
    211–13
  in the landscape, 152, 166, 184–93, 194, 206
Bas Léon (Brittany), menhirs, 36, 37, 39–49,
  54, 57, 80, 82, 83, 85, 85–6
Bird-David, N., 21
birds, depicted in Maltese temples, 135, 137
boats
  depicted in rock-carvings, 136–7, 153,
    158–64 passim, 168, 171, 177, 178, 180,
    184, 193–8 passim, 202–3, 208, 210
  symbolism in Bronze Age Scandinavia,
    195–6, 201, 211
  see also ships
body
  dyads in embodied experience, 4–10, 29
  effects of Maltese temple spaces, 99, 118,
    130, 131–3, 223
  and experience, 2–4, 220–1
  experience of entering rock-cut tombs, 98
  metaphors, 22
  and perception, 10, 11, 12, 26, 30
  relationship with places and landscapes,
    25–6, 31, 220, 224
  synaesthesia, 15, 16
  see also carnality
Bonanno, A., 99
Bornholm (Danish island), 147
Bourdieu, P., 31
Bradley, R., 198, 206, 207, 217
Brantevik, Sweden, 148, 150, 156, 158, 164–5,
  172, 194, 208–9, 214
Brittany see menhirs (Finistère, Brittany)
Brochtorff Circle, Gozo, 92–3, 98, 109, 131,
  134, 138
bronze, 199, 201, 213–14
Bronze Age
  artefacts depicted on Kivik cairn, 191

Printed in the United Kingdom by
Lightning Source UK Ltd., Milton Keynes
136715UK00002BA/2/P